second edition

Housing Policy in Korea

Woo Hyun, Cho
Man-Hee, Han

서울시립대학교출판부
UNIVERSITY OF SEOUL PUBLISHING

Contents

PART Ⅲ.
Future Direction of Housing Policy in Korea

Preface to the Second Edition

The housing market in Korea looks like a living creature. It is changing continuously. A small problem occurring in a part of the market spreads out to the whole market and makes all the participants recognize the trouble. Ups and downs in the housing market are hardly predictable especially in Korea. When we compare the market situation in 2015 with that in 2020, it's no exaggeration to say that a sea change has happened in the Korean housing market. The sharp contrast between the market situation in the first half of 2010s and that in the second half vividly illustrates the volatility of the Korean housing market and the magnitude of the difficulty facing the Korean government to resolve this problem.

The initial reason why we decided to publish first edition was to expound the housing problems that Korea had experienced for a long period and policy responses that the Korean government had adopted to cope with these problems and to provide implications for foreign government officials who were going through similar problems in stabilizing their housing markets. In our view, the initial goal has been reached to some extent.

However, the housing problems that Korea has been experiencing in the latter half of 2010s are requesting another kind of policy initiatives that are significantly different from those introduced in previous years. It also is thought that similar problems are or soon will be occurring in other countries at any time. Therefore, in preparing this revised edition, we tried to analyze and explain those problems in more detail.

The housing market and housing problems vary from country to country and thus a kind of universal solution applicable to any country cannot be found. However, we are convinced that the experience of a country can provide an implication for other countries seeking for relevant policy alternatives and, in that aspect, we hope that this book will be helpful for policy makers and experts in those countries suffering form severe housing problems.

January 2022

Woo Hyun Cho and Man-Hee Han

Preface to the First Edition

Korea has come to follow a unique path to achieve national development that has not been seen in many other countries. Within 60 years, the country has formed a different structure of economy and society that is rather different from those in the 1950s and 1960s. Indeed, Korea has exhibited a rapid change and profound transformation of the national system in a short time.

Housing also is one of the many fields which has shown a drastic change during the period. Due to the significance that housing can meet the basic needs of humans, the Korean government has taken the housing issue into a central position in economic policy for several decades. In particular, many housing policies have been developed and available national resources to assist the policy measures have been effectively put into use.

While there remain various issues that need continuous attention and effort from the government, the effect of housing policy has been rather substantive in Korean society. More specifically, Korea has succeeded in raising the housing supply ratio over 100% and providing various housing welfare support to lower-income people.

In particular, researchers and policy makers in many developing countries currently facing severe housing problems have shown a strong interest in the detailed contents of the housing policy in Korea. However, published materials on the Korean housing policy written in English have been relatively limited and incomprehensive. Recently, Cho (2012) was published to overview the development of the housing policy which contributed to delivering the historical development and main contents of Korean housing policy to many foreign researchers and policy makers. However, newly developed and introduced policies in this dynamic housing sector highlight the necessity of updating the emerging key issues continuously. Therefore we decided to revise the previous edition by adding newly introduced policy measures and elaborating the background and theoretical bases of main policy initiatives to provide a better understanding.

This book consists of four parts. The first part is the introduction chapter which portrays the overall context of housing policy and the main issues surrounding the housing demand and supply in Korea. The second part explains the historical development of Korean housing policy and the contents of introduced systems mainly before 2010. The third part concentrates on the housing problems that occurred and countermeasures introduced mainly in the 2010s. The structural change of the Korean housing market in recent years can be grasped in this part. Since the housing policy measures introduced and implemented for a prolonged period are unable to be divided by specific periods, it seems inevitable that certain cases are mentioned multiple times. The final part is on the future direction of housing policy in Korea for further development.

The main purpose of this book is to aid foreign researchers and policy makers to understand the background and contents of Korean housing policy and to deliver them a possible implication for the development of housing policy in their own countries. As such, the theoretical explanation of the housing market and policy has been reduced to a minimal level. It will be a great pleasure for us if this book can be of help for those who want to understand and utilize the experience and know-how of the Korean government and people.

May 2017

Woo Hyun Cho and Man-Hee Han

Tables

Figures

Abbreviations

ABS	asset-backed security
AMC	asset management company
BCR	building coverage ratio
CGT	capital gains tax
CHSS	comprehensive housing subscription savings
CPT	comprehensive property tax
DTI	debt-to-income
FAR	floor area ratio
GB	green belt
HH	household; Happiness Housing
HOR	home ownership ratio
HSR	housing supply ratio
HUD	Department of Housing and Urban Development
HUG	National Housing and Urban Guarantee Corp.
KHFC	Korea Housing Finance Corporation
LH	Korea Land and Housing Corporation at present (LH
LIHTC	low-income housing tax credit
LTCHP	Long-Team Comprehensive Housing Plan
LTPA	Land transaction permission area
LTV	loan-to-value
MBS	mortgage-backed security
MIUDCA	Act on the Maintenance and Improvement of Urban Areas and Dwelling Conditions for Residents
MLTM	Ministry of Land, Transport and Marine Affairs
MOLIT	Ministry of Land, infrastructure and Transport

MRCR ● monthly rent conversion rate(MRCR

MRS ● minimum residential standard

MRVD ● monthly rental with a variant deposit

NHF ● National Housing Fund

NHUF ● National Housing and Urban Fund

NTIT ● new town in town

PIR ● price-to-income ratio

POP ● privately-owned projects

PRFS ● public housing for sale

PRH ● public rental housing

PS-RH ● public-support private rental housing

REFS ● real estate finance system

REI ● residential environment improvement project

REITs ● real estate investment trusts

RIR ● rent-to-income ratio

SAPSUR ● Special Act on promotion of and Support for Urban Regeneration

SMR ● Seoul metropolitan region

URSP ● Urban Regeneration Strategic Plan

URND ● Urban Regeneration New Deal projects

Chapter 1

Introduction

1.1. Housing Problem and Policy: Overview

1.1.1. The importance of Housing

Housing has been an important matter of concern across many countries. This is partly because the housing issue is directly related to the stabilization of people's livelihood. Accordingly, several theories and policies have been developed and suggested to meet the demand for housing and provide appropriate services. However, it has been seen that many countries have experienced difficulties in achieving residential stability over time.

Over the past decades, the existing theories have focused on factors related to housing demand and supply to explain the volume and price of housing transactions in the market. The main forces of supply and demand and the equilibrium made by the movement of supply and demand in the housing market have been the major topic for this. In addition, the role of each player such as a seller, buyer, developer, financial institution, etc. in the market and the government intervention in this process such as taxation, fiscal expenditure, financial support, etc. have been investigated.

However, since the housing market is heavily influenced by geographical location and time, problems and policy measures often differ by region and period. This means that housing policy should be developed based on their spatial and temporal conditions. In other words, there is no single policy that can solve all the problems of segregated housing markets. We need to examine housing problems carefully each time, taking into account their regional and periodical context. Only after exerting such efforts can the appropriate policy measures to solve an imminent housing problem be found.

1.1.2. The meaning of housing for human life

Before entering into the housing problem and policy, it seems worthwhile to discuss the meaning of housing for human life. The meaning of housing seems to vary according to the viewpoint of the presenter. In particular, 'housing' has varying meanings for individuals, families, communities, and countries.

For individuals, housing is the basis of living and a source of wealth. In the house, each person can manage his or her daily life in the forms of sleeping, eating, loving, playing with children, protecting oneself from intrusion, etc. In other words, housing is very essential for human life in that, without housing, everyday life cannot be maintained. For families, housing is a place where a family can be formed and live together and each member of a family can feel the sense of belonging and the comforts of a home.

For communities, housing is a source of various social services and a relationship between neighbors to make the residents enjoy social status or prestige. For countries as a whole, housing is a source and index of the welfare of its people and the growth of a national economy.

1.1.3. Housing Market Stability

We can understand the structure and function of a housing market by interpreting the movement and interaction of housing demand and supply. The movements of housing demand and housing supply lead to a market equilibrium, which decides the price and quantities of housing supplied or consumed in the housing market.

Factors determining housing demand and supply are diverse. If a certain factor influences excessively housing demand or supply, then the housing market will fluctuate and the market equilibrium will be shaken. This will result in continuous instability within the housing market.

The stability of the housing market is important from an economic, social, and political standpoint. Unstable housing markets can cause enormous problems such as economic downturns, social unrest as well as national political conflicts.

1.1.4. Housing Policy Goals and Measures

Housing policy has various goals including the balance between housing supply and demand and the improvement of residential life of those in substandard housing. To achieve these goals, diversified policy measures have been introduced, such as:

- Sufficient construction and supply of housing;
- Meeting and controlling the demand for various kinds of housing;
- Management and maintenance of existing housing;
- Rebuilding or demolition of shoddy houses or new construction.

The housing market situation varies from country to country, and thus the way to fulfill housing demand for a country is different from each other. Issues such as population size and distribution, land availability, financial constraints, etc. that each country faces are diverse, and these obstacles make it difficult to strike a balance between housing demand and supply. Accordingly, the solution to housing market problems depends on the circumstances each country or each region faces.

It is worth noting that a housing market is the aggregation of regionally segmented sub-markets. A region's housing market is significantly different from those of other regions even in the same country. For example, in Korea, the housing market in Seoul metropolitan region (SMR) shifted from a depression to a recovery stage while those of other metropolitan cities changed from a booming market to a more stabilized market since the mid-2010s.

Certainly, many governments around the world introduce and implement tailored housing policies to supplement deficiencies and correct problems to reach a balance in the housing market. For this purpose, a variety of policy measures encompassing economic and non-economic tools are mobilized. Without such types of policy measures, it is usually impossible to reach a socially acceptable equilibrium automatically and smoothly.

Another important goal of housing policy is to assist low-income households to find suitable dwellings. Since low-income people tend to fall victim to competition in the housing market, governments are making efforts to support these people. The improvement of the quality of houses and eventually the living standard of people is another important objective to be achieved. Even for advanced countries that have a housing supply ratio of well over 100% how to improve the quality of existing housing is an important issue of policy concern.

1.2. Housing Policy in Korea: Overview

1.2.1. Housing Situation in Korea

(1) Housing Supply Ratio

The housing situation of a country can be conjectured through the examination of the housing supply ratio (HSR). This ratio is acquired by dividing the number of housing units (A) by the number of households (B). In short, (A) divided by (B) is the housing supply ratio.

Table 1 ● Housing supply ratio by year

	1970	1980	1990	2000	2010	2015	2016	2017	2018	2019	2020
No. of Housing Units (000s) (A)	4,360	5,319	7,357	11,472	14,677	19,559	19,877	20,313	20,818	21,319	21,674
No. of Households (000s) (B)	5,576	7,470	10,167	11,928	12,995	19,119	19,368	19,674	19,979	20,343	20,927
Housings/ Households Ratio (%)(A/B)	78.2	71.2	72.4	96.2	112.9	102.3	102.6	103.3	104.2	104.8	103.6

(Source: Ministry of Land, Infrastructure and Transport [MOLIT])

The housing supply ratio in Korea was 78.2% in 1970, 71.2% in 1980, and 72.4% in 1990. This change in the ratio from 1970 to 1990 demonstrates the aggravating housing situation in Korea. During the period, the number of housings increased from 4,360 thousand to 7,357 thousand units, a 68.7% increase. In the same period, however, the number of households increased more rapidly from 5,576 thousand to 10,167 thousand households, up 82.3%. This difference resulted in the decline of HSR from 78.2% to 72.4%.

However, with the successful implementation of the 'two million housing units construction plan' the housing supply ratio rose to 96.2% in 2000, and surpassed 100% in 2005. This can be assessed as a remarkable achievement of housing policy. In 2010 the number of housing units was 14,677 thousand and the number of households was 12,995 thousand, hence HSR reached 112.9%. With the change in the housing market situation with the increase of one or two-member households and the emergence of various housing types, the Korean government inevitably introduced a new counting system concerning households and housing units. Thus, the HSR has been lowered to 102.3% in 2015 and rose again to 103.6% in 2020. The decrease in the housing supply ratio in 2020 was caused mainly by a rapid growth of the number of one or two member households. All sizes of households and all types of housing units were included in these statistics.

1) Population and Households

During the period, there were also significant demographical changes. First, the population growth rate has lowered consistently. It was 1.82% in 1970, 0.99% in 1990, 0.46% in 2010 and 0.23% in 2020. It is found that the population, population growth, and the number of households in 2020 were 51.8 million, 0.23%, and 21.5 million respectively.

Table 2 ● Changes in the total population, population growth, and number of households

	1970	1980	1990	2000	2005	2010	2015	2016	2017	2018	2019	2020
Total Population (000s)	32,241	38,124	42,869	47,008	48,138	49,410	51,069	51,270	51423	51,607	51,709	51,829
Population Growth Rate (%)	1.82	1.37	0.99	0.84	0.21	0.46	0.4	0.39	0.28	0.23	0.20	0.23
Number of Households (000s)	5,576	7,969	11,354	11,928	12,491	12,995	19,119	19,368	19,674	19,979	20,343	21,485

(Source: MOLIT, Statistics Korea)

The younger generation in Korea hesitates in regards to marriage and having children. Considering the prolonged life span of the Korean population which has increased by the aged people, the net birth rate of married couples can be said to have turned to a minus.

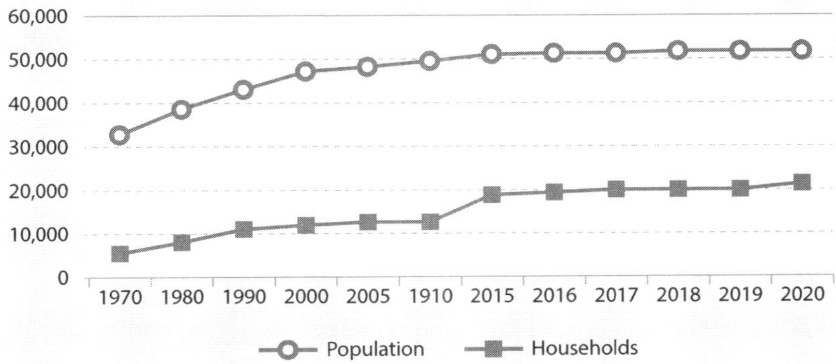

Figure 1 ● Changes in the total population and households
(Source: Korean Statistical Information Service (KOSIS))

By contrast, the number of households has increased faster than that of the population. From 1970 to 2020, the total population increased by 60.8%, while households increased by 285.3%. This means that there have been changes in the form of households specifically an increase of one or two-member households.

According to the Population Census conducted by Statistics Korea, mini-households with one or two members in the whole nation have accounted for 53.3 percent of the population, i.e. 27.2% of single-member households and 26.1% of two-member households in 2015. The number of mini-households increased further and reached 59.8% in 2020. These demographic changes have aggravated the problem of housing imbalance even further.

1.2.2. Overview of Housing Policy by Period

(1) The Socio-economic and Housing Policies by Policy Regimes

In 1988, Seoul Olympic Games were held. Until then the utmost priority of the Korean government was on economic development and, thus, housing was not able to take top priority. It was common for Korean people to hear that construction plans had not been fully implemented and housing welfare did not draw much interest. Housing supply was made mainly for middle-income households.

With the successful completion of the Olympic Games, the Korean economy began to boom and this trend continued until the beginning of the 1990s. Household incomes increased and house prices grew rapidly. Furthermore, Korean people became more outspoken with a democratization movement throughout the country, the so-called empowerment of citizens. These changes in the economic and social climate required a new approach toward housing problems and housing policies. In particular, a drastic change in the housing supply system was imperative.

Table 3 ● The socio-economic and housing policies by period - 1

	Before 1988	1988~1992	1993~1997
President	Presidents Park, Chung-hee (1962~79) Choi, Kyu-ha(1979~80) Chun, Doo-hwan(1980~)	President Roh, Tae-woo	President Kim, Young-sam

	Before 1988	1988~1992	1993~1997
Socio-Economic and Political Settings	• 1st priority on economic development • Low priority on housing	• Household income increased • Rapid housing price increase • Empowerment of citizens	• Stabilized housing price • Market-oriented policy and deregulation
General Housing Policy	• Non-achieved construction plans • Housing supply for the middle-income households	• 2 million housing construction plan ('88~'92) • New town development • Introducing different housing strategies for different income households	• Retreat of government roles in the housing market • Promotion of private rental housing supply
Housing Welfare Approach	• Not much interest	• Recognizing the need for housing welfare	• Political interest in housing welfare decreased
Notable Programs	• Squatter redevelopment • Construction plans	• Construction of permanent public rental housing	• 5-yr rental housing • 50-yr rental housing

As a result, President Roh, Tae-woo introduced various policy initiatives. During his term (1988~1992), a series of policies had been implemented such as a two million housing construction plan, new town development plans including Bundang and Ilsan, and the introduction of different housing supports for different income households.

Also, people and the government began to recognize the necessity of housing welfare. It is worth noting that the public's opinion was taken into account when the housing welfare programs were proposed. The government decided to construct 「Permanent Public Rental Housing」. It was the starting point of the real housing welfare system in Korea.

The next period, from 1993 to 1997, was the term of President Kim, Young-Sam (YS) government. This period can be labeled as a period of 'status quo' in housing policy. Stabilized housing prices and a market-oriented policy led by deregulation represented the housing market and policy in this period. Being surprised by the inflation and heavy government expenditure caused by the construction of two million housing units the YS government retreated on its role in the housing market and promoted private rental housing supply. Furthermore, political interest in housing welfare withered. Instead, the YS government increased the supply of 5-year and 50-year public rental housing (PRH).

Table 4 ● The socio-economic and housing policies by period – 2

	1998~2002	2003~2007	2008~2012
President	President Kim, Dae-jung	President Roh, Moo-hyun	President Lee, Myoung-bak
Socio-Economic & Political Settings	· Foreign exchange crisis · Recession of housing and real estate market	· Rapid increase of the housing price · Emphasis on the social safety net	· Economic recession and high unemployment rate · Housing market recession
General Housing Policy	· Relaxation of housing regulation · Establish long-term public rental housing supply plan ('Kukmin' public rental housing)	· Fight housing speculation · Strengthen regulation on the housing market · Heavy tax on real estate	· Development of GB areas for the low- and low-middle income households ('Bogeumjari' housing site) · Gradual deregulation
Housing Welfare Approach	· Expanded housing Welfare · Substantial increases in government budget	· Expand housing welfare - even more than before	· More government spending for housing welfare · More support for homeownership as well as tenants
Notable Programs	· Introduction of 'Kukmin' PRH supply Scheme	· Increased the Kukmin PRH supply · More public money	· 'Bogeumjari site housing'

President Kim, Dae-Jung (DJ) came into power in 1998. At that time, the Korean economy encountered a foreign exchange crisis sweeping the Asian region. Naturally, this economic crisis resulted in a recession in the housing and real estate market. To overcome this unprecedented crisis, the government relaxed housing regulations and introduced a 「Long-term Public Rental Housing Supply Plan」 with the name of 'Kukmin' (meaning 'national') public rental housing.

This Kukmin rental housing required a huge amount of government expenditure because 30~40% of the total expenditure for the construction of this type of housing was planned to be funded by the public coffers, which led to the expansion of housing welfare expenditure during the term of DJ. In short, the introduction of the 'Kukmin' public rental housing supply scheme was the most important housing policy for the DJ government.

In 2003, the Roh, Moo-hyun (RMH) administration was launched. Back then, Korea experienced a rapid rise in house prices. To cope with this housing price hike, especially to fight against housing speculation, the RMH administration introduced a series of strong policy measures including the tightening of regulations on the housing market and heavy taxation on real estate. On the other hand, the government expenditure on the housing supply and welfare began to swell enormously because the Kukmin PRH which had been planned in the DJ administration began to be constructed on a full scale. The fact that people began to move into the Kukmin PRH had a significant implication in terms of housing welfare.

President Lee, Myoung-bak, who was nicknamed "MB", came into power in 2008. As soon as the MB administration started, the economic crisis originating from the US mortgage market hit the world including Korea. Therefore, Korea, like other countries, suffered from economic recession, high unemployment rates, and a depressed housing market. During his term, the 'Bogeumjari[1] Housing' policy for low-income and low-middle income households was initiated. For this policy, it was allowed to develop land in green belt (GB) areas that have been designated in the areas surrounding the major metropolitan cities to strictly restrict development activities since the beginning of the 1970s. Also during this period, the deregulation in the housing market continued steadily.

The 'Bogeumjari Site Housing' introduced by the MB government as a signature housing policy is a public housing scheme consisting of rental housings and small housings for sale. Combined with the construction of permanent rental housing resumed by the MB administration as a part of the Bogeumjari housing scheme, the government spending for housing welfare increased markedly. And by supplying Bogeumjari housing, the MB administration was able to achieve its goal of promoting homeownership as well as supporting the

1 The 'Bogeumjari' means a nest.

residential life of tenants.

President Park, Geun-Hye administration was inaugurated in 2013. This government has made various efforts to overcome the housing market depression, and from the latter half of 2014, the government's endeavors began to achieve a result with an increase in housing transactions and a slight rise in house prices. Within the framework of Bogeumjari housing, or public housing, the Park, Geun-Hye government emphasized the specific policies to increase public rental housing for young employees (Happiness Housing) and private rental housing, especially for middle-income households (New Stay).

President Moon, Jae-in government has faced polarization of economy between industries and regions and over-heating of Seoul housing market, especially Gangnam. Confronting these problems Moon Jae-in government introduced strong regulations on housing speculation in Seoul and higher taxation on multi-homeowners. Regarding housing welfare, an expansion of public rental housing, i.e. 170 thousand units/year, and an increase of housing supply for newly-weds, youths, and low-income households were emphasized. Housing supply through urban regeneration and strengthened house price control are also emphasized in this administration. Notable programs are urban regeneration and government-support private rental housing.

Table 5 ● The socio-economic and housing policies by period - 3

	2013~2017	2017~2022
President	President Park, Geun-Hye	President Moon, Jae-in
Socio-Economic &Political Settings	• Economic recession and high unemployment rate • Housing market recession * Recovery from late 2014	• Polarization of Economy between Industries and Regions • Over-heating of Seoul Housing Market (esp. Gangnam)
General Housing Policy	• Development of vacant public land for newly-weds, young employees, university students, etc. ('Happiness' Housing) • Deregulation	• Strong regulation on housing speculation in Seoul • Higher taxation on multi-homeowners
Housing Welfare Approach	• More diversified financial support for the purchase of housing in middle- and lower-income households • Housing Voucher for lower-income tenants • Promotion of private rental industry (New Stay, etc.)	• Increase of public rental housing (170 thousand units/year) • Increase of housing supply for newly-weds, youths, low-income households • Housing supply through urban regeneration • Strengthened house price control
Notable Programs	• 'Happiness Housing' • 'New Stay'	• Urban regeneration • Government-support private rental housing

2) Factors affecting housing supply and demand and price determination

The housing market has been influenced by various factors including the population concentration in the Seoul metropolitan region (SMR) and other metropolitan cities, income growth, shortage of supply, the domestic and global economic condition as well as the general over-supply of housing. However, looking back on the housing demand and house prices in the market during the last 30 years, we can find that there have been differences between periods in main factors affecting demand and price. The following table shows the market situation of each period and the main factors causing such a situation.

Until the 1980s, housing demand was very strong and prices rose sharply mainly due to the population concentration in SMR and other metropolitan cities, income growth, and a shortage of supply. In addition, speculative demand anticipating capital gain aggravated the housing market situation. In the 1990s before the outbreak of the Asian financial crisis in 1997, the housing market maintained stability for the most part because of a massive supply of housing in new towns and semi-agricultural areas offsetting the increase of demand.

The outbreak of the financial crisis at the end of 1997 resulted in the collapse of housing demand and price and consequently the housing market. This situation continued until the beginning of 2002. The recovery of the housing market began from mid-2002 with a return of strong demand and speculative investors showing another round of price hikes in the mid-2000s. However, the world economic crisis which started in the US housing market at the end of 2007 and over-supply of housing once again brought about a steep decline of housing demand and prices and, ultimately, stagnating the housing market until 2014.

The Korean government introduced various policy measures to restore the housing market including financial and tax incentives as well as deregulation. Aided by government efforts and the growth of actual housing demand the Korean housing market began to show signs of recovery by late 2014.

Table 6 ● Market situation and main factors

Period	Market situation	Main factors
~ 1980s	D⇈ P⇈	Population concentration in SMR and metropolitan cities, income growth, shortage of supply, speculative demand
~ 1997 Financial crisis	D↑ P→	Massive supply of housing offsetting the increase of demand (New towns, semi-agricultural land)
~ 2002	D⇊ P⇊	Financial crisis
~ 2008 World economic crisis	D⇈ P⇈	Increased demand, speculative demand
~ 2014	D↓ P↓	Over-supply, World economic crisis
~ Present	D↑ P↑	Growth of actual demand(residential stabilization), deregulation, and incentives Intrusion of speculation

3) Total Government Welfare Spending and Housing Welfare Spending

It is necessary to consider the amount of government spending for housing welfare. The graph below shows the growth of government expenditure for housing welfare has been sluggish compared to the total government expenditure and welfare budget. This can be interpreted in such a way that, with the housing supply ratio exceeding 100% and the necessity of building public rental housing being decreased, the government expenditure on housing welfare has been stagnating compared to other expenditures. However, to stabilize or improve the residential life of low-income households, this expenditure needs to be increased consistently.

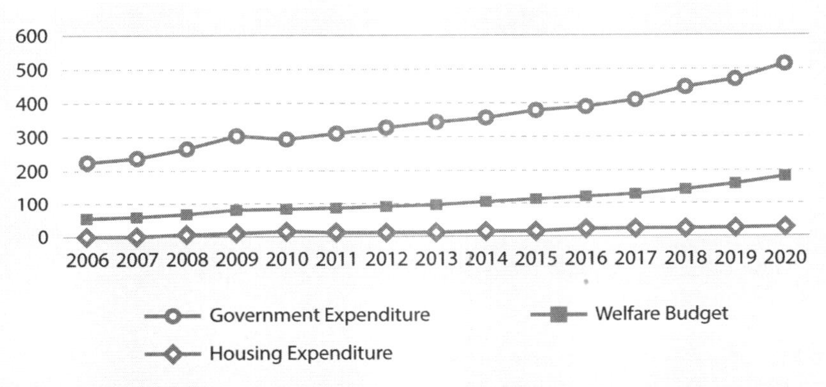

Figure 2 ● Total government welfare spending and housing expenditure

1.2.3 Legal System of the Housing in Korea

(1) Overview

Housing Act (1972) and Rental Housing Act (1984) had played a central role in constructing, maintaining, financing, purchasing, and using housings in Korea until the 2000s. These two laws contained various clauses to deal with all kinds of issues related to housing. However, during the period, there have been changes in circumstances surrounding housing such as housing supply ratio exceeding 100%, demand for quality housing, the growing importance of housing finance and housing welfare, etc. Since the mid-2000s, diverse housing laws regulating specific fields have been enacted to meet the changing circumstances, e.g. Housing Benefit (or Subsidy) Act, Special Act on Private Rental Housing, etc. However, Laws necessary for the supply of housing land are still effective without any significant change during the last 30 years.

(2) Main Housing Laws in Korea

The table below lists the main housing laws in operation.

Table 7 ● Main housing laws in Korea

Laws	Enactment Date (Promulgation)	Contents
Framework Act on Residence (Housing Security)	Dec. 23, 2015 (June 22, 2015)	- Setting up of Basic Principle of Dwelling policy - Making of Comprehensive Dwelling Plan - Housing welfare delivery system
Housing Act (Former Housing Construction Promotion Act)	Jan. 15, 1973 (Dec. 30, 1972)	- Construction and Supply of Housing - Management of Housing market by way of Housing Price Control, etc.
Housing and Urban Fund Act	Jul. 1, 2015 (Jan. 6, 2015)	- Establishment and management of NHUF - National Housing and Urban Guarantee Corp.
Housing Benefits Act	Jan. 1, 2015 (Jan. 24, 2014)	- Eligibility of Housing Subsidy recipients - Payment standard of Housing Subsidy
Special Act on Private Rental Housing (Former Rental Housing Act)	Mar.27,2018 (Dec.27, 2017)	- Supply and management of Private Rental Housings - Registration of Private rental business and operator
Multi-family Housing Management Act	Aug. 12, 2016 (Aug. 11, 2015)	Systems, support and dispute conciliation, etc. for the management of Multi-dwelling houses.

Laws	Enactment Date (Promulgation)	Contents
Special Act on Public Housing (Former Rental Housing Act)	Jul. 1, 2004 (Dec. 31, 2003)	- Setting up of Public Housing Supply and Management Plan - Construction, operation and management of Public Housing

* **Separately enacted laws**
- Act on the Support for Improving the Quality of Lives of Tenants in Long-Term Public Rental Housing (Jan.1, 2010/ Mar.25, 2009)
- Act on Support of the Disabled, the Aged, and Other Housing-Disadvantaged People (Aug.22, 2012/ Feb.22, 2012)

The Framework Act on Residence (or Housing Security) enacted in 2015 is the fundamental law providing the legal basis for housing in Korea. This law stipulates the setting up of the Basic Principle of Dwelling Policy, making of the Comprehensive Dwelling Plan, a housing welfare delivering system, etc. The Housing Act was renamed from formerly the Housing Construction Promotion Act and regulates the housing issues such as construction and supply of housing, management of housing market through housing price control, etc. The Housing and Urban Fund Act was separated from the Housing Act in 2015 to stipulate in detail the establishment and management of the National Housing and Urban Fund(NHUF) and the National Housing and Urban Guarantee Corp.

The Housing Benefits Act was also enacted in 2015 to stipulate the eligibility and payment standard of housing subsidy recipients, etc. with the introduction of the housing voucher system.

The Special Act on Private Rental Housing, formerly the Rental Housing Act became effective on March 27, 2018. This law regulates supply and management of private rental housings, registration of private rental business and operator, etc. The Multi-Family Housing Management Act enacted in August 2015 stipulates systems, support and dispute conciliation, etc. for the management of multi-dwelling houses.

The Special Act on Public Housing separated from the former Rental Housing Act in 2004 is to regulate the issues related to public housings including the setting up of the Public Housing Supply and Management Plan and the construction, operation, and management of public housing. In addition, the Act on the Support for Improving the Quality of Lives of Tenants in Long-Term Public Rental Housing and the Act on Support of the Disabled, the Aged, and Other Housing-Disadvantaged People became effective on Jan.1, 2010, and Aug.22, 2012, respectively to support low income and weak people in the housing market.

1.3. Housing, housing problems, and housing policy

1.3.1. Housing

1) Common Definitions

A house can be defined as a dwelling that serves as living quarters for one or more families. A house is a structure or building which has the feature of a physical object. The dwelling has the meaning of putting someone in a safe place. It is usually felt that a dwelling is much safer than a shelter. The shelter has the meaning of a temporarily provided place to escape from disaster or accident.[2]

On the other hand, housing means the 'structure intended for residential use'[3] or collectively the structures in which people are housed. Usually, the word 'housing' is used for indicating ① stocks of houses, apartments, and other types of dwellings[4] and ② a process converting houses into homes by adding human factors, e.g. housing the low-income families in newly-built public rental housing.

2 According to Oxford American Dictionary, house is a 'building made for people (usually one family) to live in' while housing is 'accommodations'. Accommodations are defined as 'living premises' and dwelling is 'a house, etc. to live in'. Shelter is 'a structure built to keep rain, etc. off people'

3 Barron's Dictionary

4 In this way, housing is used as a useful residence for individual or household.

A household is "one or more people inhabiting a housing unit as their principal residence"[5]. Usually, not always, a household is a person or people who are related by blood.

The pictures below show various types of housings in Korea. There are some structures other than dwellings. Basically, these structures are not produced to function as housing, but used for the purpose mainly for the lower-income people or the people with special occupations.

① Traditional Korean house

(Source:https://cdn.pixabay.com/photo/2015/09/23/08/10/haemieupseong-953103_960_720.jpg)

② Fusion style single house

(Source:https://commons.wikimedia.org/wiki/File:Bigger_single-family_home.jpg)

③ Apartment houses

(Source: LH)

④ Residential-commercial multi-purpose building

(Source:https://cdn.pixabay.com/photo/2015/11/06/11/48/office-building-1026495_960_720.jpg)

Figure 3 ● Various types of housing in Korea

5 Ibid.

The housing types used in Korea include traditional Korean houses; fusion-style single houses, apartment houses, official[6], residential-commercial multi-purpose buildings, accommodation for job applicants (a private dormitory), container houses, vinyl houses, etc. All these houses and facilities are used as either permanent or temporary dwellings for Koreans these days. The numbers of housings by dwelling types in Korea are listed in the following table. Apartment houses take up 62.9% followed by single houses and multi-family houses.

Table 8 ● Numbers of housings by dwelling types in Korea (as of 2020) (000units)

Total	Single Houses	Apartment Houses	Row(Town) Houses	Multi-family Dwelling	Buildings or Structures other than dwellings	Vacant Houses
18,526	3,898 (21.0%)	11,662 (62.9%)	522 (2.8%)	2,231 (12.0%)	214 (1.2%)	1,511

(Source: Statistics Korea, 2020 Housing Census)

2) Characteristics of Housing

Housing has various features. The first and most important feature of housing is fixity and immobility. This means that once a house is built, its location is fixed. Having a location by being built on a designated land is the most important factor determining the features and values of

6 An 'officetel' is a portmanteau of 'office' and 'hotel'. This is a multi-purpose building used for both residential and commercial purposes, and has the feature of studio apartment or studio flat. (Wikipedia)

the house. Due to immobility, housing is affected by externality. There are two kinds of externality:

- Positive externality. This is the beneficial influence coming from outside the occupants of a house. For example, a fire-proofed house improves the fire safety of neighbors.
- Negative externality. In contrast, a negative externality is a harmful influence from outside affecting the occupants. For example, abandoned houses can cause a neighbor's house price to fall.

The second feature of housing is durability. Unlike consumption goods, a house lasts long at least 20 or 30 years, sometimes hundreds of years. With the characteristics of durability, houses become durable consumption goods and concurrently profitable assets which generate both cash flow and capital gain.

Thirdly, housing has a characteristic of inhomogeneity or heterogeneity in location, design, size, etc. As a result, housing differs from each other in every aspect by physical attributes (size, number of rooms, facilities), by public service (safety, environment, sanitation), and by accessibility, etc. This means that even the houses built by a house builder using the same design are different from each other and, consequently, differ in their values.

Fourthly, housing has a feature of a long production period. Housing production takes a long period, e.g. at least 6 months to build a single detached house and even 7~8 years for apartment houses. Therefore, the amount of newly built housing supplied is small compared to the existing housing stock and supply in the housing market. As a result, proper maintenance of existing housing stock and smooth and seamless transactions among house owners and tenants in the housing market are of vital importance for the stabilization of the housing market.

Fifthly, housing necessitates complex transaction procedures and costs in securing property rights. Transaction of a house requires complicated procedures including the search for the property, making a contract, registration, moving, etc. These procedures naturally incur lots of expenses to parties involved in the transaction. The expenses include transfer tax consisting of acquisition tax and registration tax, commission for realtors and lawyers, moving expenses, etc. Tax is an important factor for people in deciding to acquire and hold housing. In Korea, the transfer tax rate is relatively high (1.1~3.3% of housing price per transaction) compared with the property tax rate (0.1~0.4% of declared housing price which is about 70~80% of market price per year). This is different from many advanced countries where the property tax rate tends to be higher than the transfer tax rate.

Sixthly, another feature of housing is the external influence of the environment or circumstances surrounding local, regional and national markets. Housing and housing markets tend to be influenced by external factors or conditions such as business cycles, government regulations, population mobility, etc.

And finally, unlike other fields, government intervention in the forms of price control, public housing supply, and regulation applies substantially to the housing field in every country. Since housing is important for individuals, households, and the national economy, governments tend to intervene proactively in the market with various housing policy measures to lead the housing market towards a targeted direction. This is even more so in Korea

3) Key Values of Housing

The value of housing can be figured out from various viewpoints:

Firstly, physical values (physical facility). Housing has value as a space of living or shelter. A physical structure to live in is the most important feature of housing. Without housing, people cannot take a rest, be protected from invasion, and manage a household. This feature is inevitably related to spatial location, which is a salient factor for real estate. In addition, physical values are closely related to the accessibility to certain facilities. The accessibility to favorable or unfavorable areas and facilities leads to positive or negative externality. Among others, the accessibility to good schools is critical for ordinary families in Korea.

Secondly, economic values (durable consumer goods) are another important feature. Housing is a durable consumer good and is the biggest investment target for most individuals. It is also used as a means to write off tax and to accumulate equity with mortgage payments or through house price appreciation. House owners can enjoy the right to use, right to exclude, and right to transfer, whereas various responsibilities including the payment of property tax and management costs accompany.

Thirdly, housing has social and communal values such as diversified services, relationships with neighbors, etc. Living in a house gives privacy and is a starting point of a social relationship. Various types of communal relationships and activities are made among neighbors. Often quality housing in a good location with a higher value can provide a sentiment of social status and privilege to the dwellers living in the house. For example, an individual living in Gangnam district, especially Daechi-dong is often regarded as the upper or middle class in Korea.

Finally, there are national values. Housing is a source of tax revenue for central and local governments. The housing industry is significant for the national and regional economy with its multiplier effect on job creation and production. Economic cycles of the housing market, with its huge housing stock, have an enormous influence on the national economy. Indices of real estate such as housing supply ratio and home ownership ratio are interpreted as a social welfare level.

Clothing, food, and shelter are regarded as the three necessities of human life for Koreans. Among these, clothing and food problems have largely been solved along with the increase of income, whereas housing issues remain.

4) Importance of urban housing

In urban planning, residential areas take up a large part of the urban sprawl. In Seoul, residential area (201 km^2) makes up the largest portion (35%) in the total area (605 km^2), and forest (140 km^2, 24%), road, rice paddy, farm land follow in order of size. Housing takes 66.5% of the total number of buildings in Korea and 76.5% in Seoul. This difference implies that the population density in Seoul is much higher than in other cities, and to contain this large population, more housing units are necessary, hence the high percentage of housings out of the total number of buildings in Seoul.

Housing tends to take the largest share of an individual's assets. Koreans invest more than 70% of their asset in real estate, especially in housing. By contrast, Americans possess less than 40% of their assets in real estate, and the rest in financial assets. Housing has a special meaning in the national economy with both its huge number (18.5 million units in 2020)[7] and colossal cumulative values (average price of transactions 0.31 million USD in 2020). All of these figures show the importance of housing in the national wealth and the national economy.

However, to build and manage a city to make it a livable one, we have to consider how to provide the city with various kinds of functions that are necessary for the everyday life of people in a harmonious way.

---

7 This number is the one announced before the change in housing counting method applied in the 2019 Population and Housing Census.

Just building an enormous volume of housing densely in a city is not desirable.

5) Major Indicators of housing

(1) Housing Supply Ratio (HSR)

As explained above (1.2) the housing supply ratio is the number of housing stocks divided by the number of households. In Korea, the housing stock is calculated by adding the total of the housing stock of last year and newly-built houses from this year and then subtracting this year's demolished houses, while the number of households is computed by multiplying the number of households of last year by the sum of one plus average increase rate of households.

Recently, the increase of households has been accelerated mainly due to the growth of one or two-member households. The index of 'housing stocks per 1000 people' together with the housing supply ratio is being announced to make it possible to compare the housing condition of Korea with those of other countries. This index stood at 411.6 in 2019 and 418.2 in 2020 showing a substantial increase from 356.8 in 2010 and 383.0 in 2015.

(2) Home Ownership Ratio (HOR)

This is the percentage ratio of owner-occupied dwelling units in the total occupied dwelling units in an area. Korea's HOR is smaller than the US, Britain, and even Japan. Specifically, the HOR of Korea was

56.8% (2015) and 57.9% (2020), whereas that of the USA was 65.1% (2019), Britain 63.5% (2015), and Japan 61.7% (2018). In the case of the USA, the HOR had been on the decline since it reached a peak in 2005. This was caused by pessimistic consumer sentiment based on high unemployment rates of college graduates, low savings ratio of the elderly, etc. In short, this declining HOR indirectly indicates that the USA housing market was not fully recovered from the global financial crisis that started in 2007, although the US economy has strengthened since then.

The housing supply ratio in Korea surpasses 100%, but HOR is just 57.9%. Furthermore, this indicator was on a continuous decline until 2014. Low HOR in Korea implies that many Koreans put their own houses to lease and are living in rental houses elsewhere mainly due to education and the workplace.

(3) Minimum Residential Standard (MRS)

This is the minimum criterion of housing that enables residents to live a pleasant and decent life as human beings. This criterion was stipulated in the Housing Act 2004. MRS includes the number of rooms by usage, minimum standard of indispensable facilities including kitchen, bathroom with or separated from flush toilet, etc., and minimum dwelling size by household.

Table 9 ● Minimum Residential Standard

Member(s) of household	Standard household structure	Type*	Dwelling size(m^2)
1	single-person household	1 K	14
2	couple	1 DK	26
3	couple + 1 child	2 DK	36
4	couple + 2 children	3 DK	43
5	couple + 3 children	3 DK	46
6	parents + couple + 2 children	DK	55

* Note: K is the kitchen, DK is kitchen-cum-dining room, the figure is the number of bedrooms
(Source: MOLIT)

In 2020, 0.99 million households (4.6% in total households) were living in houses below MRS. This is a big improvement from 2.68 million households (16.6%) in 2006 and 1.84million (10.6%) in '10. However, the number of households living in houses below MRS was slightly increased from 0.98 million in 2014.

Table 10 ● Changes in the number of households below MRS

Year	2006	2010	2012	2014	2016	2017	2018	2019	2020
Number of households below MRS (million)	2.68	1.84	1.28	0.98	1.03	1.14	1.11`	1.06	0.99
Percentage of total households (%)	16.6	10.6	7.2	5.3	5.3	5.9	5.7	5.2	4.6

(Source: MOLIT)

MRS can be used as a yardstick to evaluate the effects of housing welfare policy such as, for example, the reduction of households living in substandard housings. MRS is also useful for deciding the target for public housing policy including the volume of rental housing to be constructed and its regional allocation and the number of funds necessary to support the repairing of substandard housing.

(4) Price to Income Ratio (PIR)

This indicator also is used often in understanding the housing state in a country or a region. PIR is a period necessary for households to purchase their own houses with their annual income. PIR is the housing price divided by the annual household income. In advanced countries, this ratio falls around 4 or 5, except in very large cities. In general, Korean households buy their own houses 10 years after their marriage. Of course, it differs year by year with the changes in housing prices and income. The PIR of the whole nation stood at 5.5 in 2020. In the case of Seoul, PIR recorded 8~10, similar to those of Tokyo, New York, and Hong Kong.

1.3.2. Housing Problems

1) Definition

Housing is important individually, socially, and economically. Housing can be a source of either dissatisfaction and conflicts or satisfaction and harmony. Is the reasonable distribution and use of housing possible if all people behave according to market principles? Indeed there are various reasons which cause unfair and unreasonable distribution and use. In other words, problems may occur in all kinds of activities including construction, supply, use, transaction, and so on concerning housing.

The main reason for housing problems is 'market failure'. Then why do market failures and housing problems occur? A house is an indispensable good for people to live in and requires expensive land, materials, and labor to build. With the prominent features of housing including high prices for ordinary households, the influence of location and environment, etc. housing is prone to induce price instability. In addition, the growth and movement of population in certain regions or cities and the change in domestic and global economic climate cause fluctuations in housing demand and supply, and consequently price. All in all, housing problems are likely to increase with subtle changes in and around the housing market.

Housing problems have appeared and intensified due to rapid industrialization and urbanization. Specifically, industrial development concentrated mainly in specific areas has caused shortages in the labor force, causing people from rural backgrounds to move to industrialized areas to find work, i.e. urbanization. With rapid urbanization, housing problems have appeared and aggravated to a higher extent in cities. In Korea, the housing problem has been serious compared to other countries due to rapid urbanization and the over-concentration of population and industry in the Seoul Metropolitan Region (SMR).

2) Nature of Housing Problems

Housing problems are twofold, quantitative problems and qualitative problems:

Quantitative problems mainly refer to the shortage of housing stock and the rise of housing prices caused by this deficiency. Qualitative problems are related to the problems in the quality of housing services and affordability of decent housing.

In general, housing problems that occur across many countries can be classified into the following four types:

① Imbalance of housing demand and supply which gives rise to a disparity between regions and between income levels;

② Rapid increase or sudden drop of housing prices and the lack of affordability;

③ Existence of the housing disadvantages among low-income people and limited assistance from the government including public housing and subsidy;

④ Dilapidated housing and abandoned residential areas, in other words, worsening housing quality.

These are the most common housing problems each government faces. In reality, most countries are facing at least one or two problems and striving to solve these problems.

3) Housing Problems in Korea

(1) Main Contributing Factors

The main factors causing housing problems in Korea are as follows:

① The rapid urbanization and the concentration of population and industry in big cities especially in SMR

This has been the most decisive factor. The urbanization rate represented by the proportion of the population living in urban areas compared to the total population was 81.9% in 1990, 90.1% in 2005, 90.9% in 2010, and 91.8% since 2015. In addition, while the size of SMR is just 11.8% of the Korean territory, its population is estimated to account for 50.2% of the total in 2020.

Table 11 ● The trend of urbanization rate in Korea

Year	1990	2000	2005	2010	2012	2015	2016	2017	2018	2019	2020
Urbanization Rate	81.9%	88.3%	90.1%	90.9%	91.0%	91.8%	91.8%	91.8%	91.8%	91.8%	91.8%

(Source: MOLIT)

② The trend toward the nuclear family

With the trend of the nuclear family, the growth rate of households began to accelerate and exceed the growth rate of population in many countries including Korea. In addition, the number of single or two-person households is growing especially in metropolitan cities with a strong tendency towards independent living among the younger generation. In 2020, the proportion of one or two member households reached 59.8% in aggregate in total households.

③ The pursuit of capital gain

This has brought about speculation and instability leading to the distortion and fluctuation of the housing market. Rapid economic growth and urbanization in Korea have resulted in a continuous housing price hike during most of the 1980s and 1990s. In this period, the price of properties centering on housing rose significantly and the owners reaped a substantial amount of capital gain through these housing transactions.

Consequently, people began to purchase housing not for living but for gaining more property value. This led to a housing market full of speculative investments. Recently the possibility of a price hike in the market has substantially reduced. However, some newly-built housing sites or redevelopment areas with favorable locations have attracted enormous would-be customers pursuing capital gain. This tendency has distorted the housing market and has caused more fluctuations in the business cycle.

④ Widening income disparity from housing investment

While the wealthy expect better living conditions and more capital gain, lower-income people cannot even afford to maintain a decent standard of housing. Certainly, we can see a mismatch of new luxurious housing and old abandoned housing existing together in our cities.

(2) Types of housing problems in Korea

① Imbalance between housing demand and supply

Korea has suffered from a severe housing shortage since the outbreak of the Korean War in 1950. Therefore the goal of housing policy for several decades has been supplying sufficient houses to mitigate the shortage of housing units. Under the continued efforts of the government and industry, the housing supply ratio in Korea as a whole reached 100% in 2005. However, housing shortage problems remain at a regional or local level mainly due to the imbalance between supply and demand.

② Sharp rise in housing prices or rents, and housing speculation

Housing demand can be said to be the sum of predictable actual demand and volatile and unpredictable speculative demand. Increasing house prices and the slow growth of income made PIR (median housing market price divided by median household income) levels high by international standards and led to a stagnated housing affordability. The PIR of the whole nation was 5.5, while that of SMR reached 8.0 in 2020. International comparison between metropolitan cities shows that the PIR in Seoul is higher than London, NY, and Tokyo but lower than Hong Kong in 2018.

Table 12 ● International comparison of PIR between metropolitan cities

City	Hong Kong	Seoul	London	NY	Singapore	Tokyo	LA
PIR (2018)	20.9	9.9	8.3	5.5	4.6	9.1	9.2

(Source: The Housing Agency, Bloomberg City Lab, Kookmin Bank)

On the other hand, the rise of rent brought about a higher rent-to-income ratio (RIR). RIR in the whole nation was 19.8% in 2012 and 20.3% in 2014 showing a consistent increase from 18.7% in 2006. This rate began to decline since then and fell to 16.6% in 2020. RIR below 30% represents that the burden of housing expenses is not excessive. However, the continuous upward growth of this rate needs to be assessed with caution as it may affect the residential stability of people on lower incomes.

③ Deteriorating housing condition for low-income households

According to the Housing Surveys, 1.8 million households (10.6% of total households) were living under MRS in 2010. This figure fell to 0.98million in 2014, but it slightly rebounded to 1.03 million in 2016 and again to 1.06 million in 2019. In 2020, the number declined again to 0.99 million. High population densities in congested urban areas can deteriorate the living conditions of low-income households who have to live near city centers for job opportunities. Various types of substandard housings are listed in the following box.

Various types of Substandard housing

- Slum is a district of a city marked by poverty and inferior living conditions.
- Blighted area is a section of a city in which a majority of the structures are dilapidated.
- Squatter is the illegal use of the property belonging to others, especially public land, for temporary dwellings (e.g. Kooryong village in Gangnam District in Seoul).
- Ghetto is a substandard residential area where specific ethnic groups occupy the majority of the area.
- Harlem is a substandard living area in New York City where African Americans comprise the majority of residents.

④ Increased number of households living in rental housing

The number of households living in rental housing has increased and the main rental type has shifted from Chonsei to monthly rent. This is a result of people's disinclination to purchase housing due to stabilized housing prices. The problem with this is that the residential situation of households living in rental accommodation has been aggravated due to the decrease of Chonsei rents and, consequently, the increase of Chonsei prices.[8] This procedure can be summarized as the following: house price drop → increase of demand for Chonsei → rise of Chonsei price, house owners prefer monthly rental → Chonsei price hike and decline of monthly rent.

8 Strictly speaking, the amount of Chonsei deposit has been increased.

Various types of Substandard housing

Chonsei is a unique rental system in Korea characterized by an up-front deposit, with no monthly rent, and it has been beneficial both for house owners and tenants for a long time. In this system, owners can purchase bigger and more expensive houses by utilizing a tenants' lump sum deposit which accounts for about 40%~60% of the housing price. After the purchase, with the steady house appreciation, the owners can enjoy an increased equity. And if the owners put the Chonsei deposit into a bank account, they can earn a substantial amount of interest.
Tenants are also content because they can live without monthly rent due dates or tax payments. However, with falling house prices and interest rates, Chonsei is not beneficial for owners any more hence there is a big shift from Chonsei to monthly rental.

The introduction of rent control and contract right renewal system with the amendment of the Housing Lease Protection Act in 2020 brought financial and emotional burdens to landlords to provide Chonsei and thus ignited the massive switch of Chonsei to monthly rental housings since then. This has become another reason for the aggravated residential stability of lower-income tenants.

4) Changes in Housing Problems in Korea

Koreans have experienced different types of housing problems during the last decade. For several years after the global economic crisis, the depressed housing market and increased Chonsei prices caused new situations and problems. To confront this new market situation, it became imperative for the Korean government to analyze new housing problems in detail and find proper policy measures.

However, the housing market began to recover and changed to another booming market with abundant liquidity and housing speculations in the latter half of the 2010s. The shortage of housings being supplied inside of cities has worsened the housing problems in Seoul and major metropolitan cities.

1.3.3. Housing Policy

1) Necessities

Housing policy is necessary either solve existing housing problems including market failure or to prevent housing problems in advance. The ultimate goal of housing policy is the stabilization and improvement of the residential life of people. Governments integrate various policy measures to solve housing problems. The main policy measures frequently used are tax incentives including the alleviation of capital gains tax, financial support, easing of regulations, etc.

For example, the Park, Geun-Hye government announced a policy package in April 2013 to alleviate the pressure of an economic slump. The adjustment of supply, exemption of capital gains tax for house owners, acquisition tax exemption for first home buyers, relief for loan-to-value (LTV), and debt-to-income (DTI) regulation were included in the policy package.[9]

2) Main Objectives

The main objectives of housing policy can be classified into the following two:

① Housing market stabilization which can be achieved by solving housing shortage problems and by adjusting housing demand;

② Supporting low-income households to stabilize their residential life through various ways including public rental housing and vouchers.

Through these policy objectives, the government pursues the residential welfare of people.

9 See chapter 6 (6.5)

PART I

History and Main Structure of Housing Policy in Korea (~ 2010)

Chapter 2

Historical Development of Housing Policy in Korea

2.1. Housing Policy before the 1980s

2.1.1. Background

Urban housing became a key issue due to the influx of migrants into the city with the restoration of independence in 1945 and the Korean War in 1950. The government implemented the first and second Five-Year Economic Development Plans during the 1960s. These plans facilitated industrialization and urbanization rapidly which led to the increase in population on one hand. However, these economic strategies were available in specific urban areas which caused a shortage of housing and a lack of space for developing houses.

As a result, unauthorized dwellings or illegal settlements were built in large quantities. Demand for housing rose again significantly with the third and fourth Five-Year Economic Development Plans in the 1970s due to the rapid increase of population and households.

2.1.2. Major Programs

Systematic housing policy did not exist prior to the 1960s. However, housing policy was incorporated into the Economic Development Plan during the 1960s including policies of housing investment and housing construction.

A number of policy measures were initiated and related laws were enacted aiming to achieve the several goals of housing policy in the Economic Development Plan:

- In 1962, the Building Code was introduced covering various matters on housing construction.
- In 1967, the Korea Housing Finance (renamed as the Korea Housing Bank in 1969) was established to provide financial housing support.
- To provide public housing, the Korea National Housing Corporation was established by the Korea National Housing Corporation Act in 1962. In 1963 the enactment of the Public Housing Act facilitated the development of public housing.

- In 1967, the Rural Roof Reform Promotion Act was enacted to support houses for roof reform in rural areas by setting up the funds[1]. During the 1970s, the Korean government introduced the third and the fourth Five-Year Economic Development Plans and 10-Year Housing Construction Plan (1972~1981) to provide more houses.

Supporting legislation and regulations were set out to support the goals in the 10 -Year Housing Construction Plan:

- In 1972, the Housing Construction Promotion Act was enacted to increase the housing supply which specified the scope of public housing, project approval system, registration system for housing developers, National Housing Fund, and housing supply system.
- In 1977, the price control for new houses was introduced in order to stabilize house prices which rose sharply mainly due to speculation.
- In 1978, the central government introduced various measures including housing supply regulations to regulate sales of newly-built housing directly, application requirement to purchase (or rent) new house, and time of sale (or rent), and procedures of sale

1 The Korean government strived to improve residential circumstances in rural areas by supporting house owners to renovate their houses. At the time the change of thatched roof into zinc roof was the main part of housing renovation.

(or rent) for national and private housing[2].

2.1.3. Results

1) Foundations of Housing Policy

Housing policy developed from the Economic Development Plan during the 1960s and 1970s laid the foundations of current housing policy. Various governmental organizations were established including Korea National Housing Corporation, Korea Land Corporation[3] , and Korea Housing Bank, and the Housing Construction Promotion Act and housing supply regulations were enacted to construct more housings. Several measures, such as a long-term housing construction plan, formed a basis for addressing housing issues and contributed to a substantial increase in housing construction.

2 National Housing: In principle, National Housing is a house which is smaller than 85 m^2 in net size and financially supported by the National Housing Fund. It includes the housings constructed by the public sector (government and government corporations) and constructed by private companies.

3 The Korea Land and Housing Corporation at present (LH in this text afterward): Korea Land Corporation and Korea National Housing Corporation were merged on Oct. 1, 2009.

2) The Effort to Expand Housing Provision to Meet Housing Shortage

In order to meet a chronic housing shortage due to industrialization and the influx of population into the large cities, 2.7 million units of houses were built over 4 phases of the 5-Year Economic Development Plan.

Despite the increase in the housing supply, it is important to stress that the rise of new but smaller households and the loss of existing houses caused more housing demand, resulting in serious housing shortages.

Table 13 ● Performance of housing supply before the 1980s (Unit: House, %)

Economic Development Plan	Year	Plan			Performance			Achievement ratio	Private contribution
		Sum	Public Sector	Private Sector	Sum	Public Sector	Private Sector		
First	'62-'66	475,000	60,000	415,000	325,935	39,915	286,020	68.6	87.8
Second	'67-71	500,000	30,000	470,000	540,338	69,613	470,725	108.1	87.1
Third	'72-76	833,000	250,400	582,600	760,591	228,766	531,825	91.3	69.9
Fourth	'77-81	1,260,000	477,000	783,000	1,116,074	495,378	620,696	88.6	55.6
Total		3,068,000	817,400	2,250,600	2,742,938	833,672	1,909,266	89.4	69.6

(Source: Ministry of Construction, Housing Construction Performance (Year on Year), Korea National Housing Co. (2000), Handbook of Housing Statistics)

3) Prevention of Housing Speculation and Stabilizing House Prices

After the late 1970s, house prices rose rapidly due to a housing shortage and a new propensity in investing property to gain capital. However, the reinforcement of capital gain taxes and regulations of housing supply prevented the speculation and helped to stabilize house prices in turn to some extent.

2.2. Housing Policy in the 1980s

2.2.1. Background

While the 5-Year Economic Development Plans in the 1960s and 1970s attempted to meet the problems of the housing market in various ways, housing shortage was one of the main issues in Korea. Furthermore, from the mid-1980s, the international trade balance turned to a surplus. With these changes, open market liquidity rapidly increased and these funds flowed into the stock and real estate markets, resulting in the sudden rise in real estate prices.

Although an average of 200,000 units of new houses was provided per year at the beginning of the 1980s, the housing supply ratio steadily decreased (from 70.5 % in 1981 to 69.2 % in 1987) due to the increase in population and continuously growing new households.

Property prices rapidly increased and particularly the prices of apartments in the capital region sharply rose (e.g. in the case of the Gang Nam area in Seoul, there was a 23% rise between January and April 1989). Due to a price hike, housing expenses between 'the haves' and 'the-have-nots' became widened and caused social conflicts. To mitigate housing problems, the central government made several strategies to increase the housing supply. For example, the government announced the Two Million Housing Units Construction Plan in 1988 which became a significant turning point.

2.2.2. Major Programs

In order to alleviate the overheated housing demand, a national housing bonds purchase system in private housing was introduced in 1983.[4] In this system, those who buy second-grade national housing bonds are eligible for purchasing a right to buy a new house under the conditions and procedure in the Housing Construction Promotion Act. The rental house nurturing program for low-income people was also

---

4 National housing bonds purchase system:
- First grade: Those who want to register real estate purchased or get the permission from authorities related to real estate should buy first-grade national housing bond.
- Second grade: In the designated speculation districts, a person who wants to buy new house should buy second-grade national housing bond. The buyer who purchases the bond most is eligible for buying new house.

introduced in 1982 and the Rental Housing Construction Promotion Act was enacted in support of this initiative.

2.2.3. Two Million Housing Units Construction

Two Million Housing Units Construction Plan was designed to construct two million houses comprising 850,000 national housings, 670,000 private housings with aid of the national housing fund, and 480,000 private housings without the aid of the national housing fund between 1988 and 1992. From this program, the government aimed to provide affordable housing, particularly for the lower-income group. Thus, a number of permanent and long-term rental housing, as well as small size housing for sale, were built with extra assistance from the government. The private sector also supplied private housing without the aid of the national housing fund for the middle-income group and sometimes national housing with the aid of the national housing fund.

The total funds for Two Million Housing Construction were 25 trillion won (21.7 billion USD). Out of the 25 trillion won, the government provided 4.2 trillion won (3.65 billion USD) for permanent rental housing construction and residential environment improvement projects for substandard housing in large cities. The National Housing Fund provided 9.8 trillion won (8.5 billion USD) for small-size housing for sale and for construction of long-term rental housing. The Korea Housing Bank supported 10.9 trillion won (9.5 billion USD) for the private housing fund.

To proceed with this project, developing land was a key issue. The government made an annual land development and supply plan. To construct two million housing units, 224 million square meters of land was provided according to guidelines of land development and supply. Of the 224 million square meters, the public sector supplied 156 million square meters while the private sector provided 68 million square meters. Within the public sector, the Korea Land Corporation undertook 73.5 million square meters, while local governments and the Korea National Housing Corporation undertook 60 million and 22 million square meters respectively.

2.2.4. Construction of Five New Towns in the Capital Region

A total of 900,000 housing units out of the two million were allocated in the Seoul Metropolitan Region (SMR). However, in large cities developable land was insufficient and high prices of land made the development more difficult. Consequently, 400,000 housing units were built in the residential area of Seoul, while 500,000 housing units were built in the suburban area of Seoul which led to the development of five satellite towns; Bundang, Ilsan, Jungdong, Pyungchon, and Sanbon.

This new satellite town construction plan was set up with 48.84 million square meters of land in total: 18.78 million square meters for Bundang,

15.58 million square meters for Ilsan, 5.38 million square meters for Jungdong, 4.92 million square meters for Pyungchon, and 3.78 million square meters for Sanbon. The estimate of the total housing supply was 293,000 units for an estimated total population of 1,176,000.

The condition of the housing market became stable to some extent with newly constructed houses in the new satellite towns of Seoul as follows:

- In order to provide affordable housing, the price of newly built housing in the new satellite towns was set based on the land and construction cost in order to prevent housing speculation.
- In order to provide the house in time, the reimbursement-by-housing bond system was introduced. Through the reimbursement-by-housing bond system, the project owner (LH) was allowed to sell bonds to future home-buyers in order to raise construction funds and invest in future developable land.
- The first-time buyers and people who hold housing saving account had priority to purchase new housing at affordable price.
- In order to decrease the price gap between the price of houses in new towns and those in adjacent areas and prevent speculation, the Bond bidding system[5] became more rigidly enforced.

5 Purchasing system for new housing, the same as housing bond purchase system: Housing Supply Regulation

2.2.5. Achievements

With such effort, providing Two Million Housing Units became a recognized achievement of housing policy in the 1980s and it results in several outcomes as follows:

① Imbalance between supply and demand of housing was relieved. The housing supply ratio continuously declined from the 1960s, hitting the lowest point at 69.02% in 1987. From 1988 onwards, the housing supply ratio started to increase gradually and in 1992, it rose significantly to 76.0%.

② Unaffordable housing issue was a constant problem with the chronic shortage of housing supply until 1990. However, the price of houses started to fall in the 1990s after two million newly-built housing units were supplied.

③ Demand-focused approach was started to show the positive impact. First-time home buyers were prioritized in purchasing a (small-size) house and the government encouraged non-home owners to subscribe to a housing saving scheme. In contrast, the government made it more difficult to purchase second house for those who already have a house and prohibited resale or sublease the house for new home purchases.

④ The groundwork for housing supporting the low-income class was established. The housing supply system based on income groups was set up in the Two Million Housing Construction Plan.

The public sector played an important role in constructing and supplying public rental housing for low-income families and re-developing old and deteriorated residential areas.

⑤ The capability of housing provision was enhanced. Cooperation between public and private housing sectors and the growth of the private housing industry were crucial in achieving the goal of increasing the housing supply. The capability of housing provision was improved significantly through the provision of developable land and funds, and administrative supports.

2.3. Housing Policy in the 1990s

2.3.1. Background

During the 1990s, the newly introduced 5-Year Economic Plan between 1993 and 1997 provided a significant impact on the housing policy. The aim of the policy was focused on the expansion of housing supply particularly through the private housing sector support, stabilization of house prices, establishing a foundation for the residential stability of low-income families, and improving the quality of housing inventory. Through this, 3,120,000 units of housing were built while the central government initially aimed to construct 2,850,000 housing units. Among these, 1,160,000 units of housing belonged to the public sector while 1,960,000 units were to the private sector.

Also, the new 5-Year Economic Plan (which intended to increase private sector support) streamlined several administrative processes including the approval process, deregulation of redevelopment and reconstruction, and the promotion of specialized rental businesses by the private sector. Mortgage bonds securitization system[6] was introduced to raise housing funds. However, in the late 1990s, the interest rate on mortgage loans rose sharply and demand shrank due to the 1997 Asian Financial Crisis, resulting in a significant drop in house prices. In order to stimulate the housing market, the government undertook measures for housing market revitalization and deregulation.

2.3.2. Major Programs

In 1998, a series of policy measures were undertaken by the government to tackle the problems of the Asian Financial Crisis:

① A total of 8,990 billion won (7.8billion USD) was funded to provide intermediate payment to sell new housing, a fund for unsold housing, and a fund for repayment of lease deposits

6 Mortgage bond securitization system: See Chapter 3, 3.3.3 Korea Housing Finance Corporation

(Chonsei)[7]. The fund was used to boost a domestic market and create new jobs through the revitalization of the housing market.

② In order to boost housing supply, tax incentives were given, including capital gains tax exemption, the tax deduction for repayment of interest for housing purchase, and mitigation of mandatory national housing bond purchase.

③ The government undertook measures to promote the housing market such as intermediate payment support, private house price control (price control on new apartments)[8], purchase of unsold apartments, private participation in developing land, stimulation of reconstruction and redevelopment of old worn-out houses, simplification of the development process in semi-agricultural area[9] and expansion of developable areas.

In 1999, housing market revitalization policy was implemented to ease unemployment, and stimulate economic recovery as well as encouraging housing stability through:

① Providing financial supports for house purchases and annual rent

7 Chonsei: The unique housing rental system in Korea. When leasing a house, the tenant deposits a lump sum to the owner to lease a home for a contracted period. The deposit is paid back to the tenant after the lease ends.

8 Private house price control: See Chapter 3, 3.4.2 Price Control on New Apartments

9 Semi–agricultural area: A big tract of agricultural land designated by the National Land Utilization and Planning Law, to be developed to urban use (e.g. residential or industrial use) in the future.

for low-income workers.

② Providing housing construction funds for the building of 100 thousand units to create employment opportunities.

③ Changes in eligibility requirements for private housing from a head of household to any adult over the age of 20.

④ Reduction or exemption of capital gains tax for 5 years and a reduction of 50% of mandatory national housing bonds purchase amount when purchasing a new home.

In 2000, measures for housing market revitalization and housing price stabilization were undertaken to recover the housing market after a long period of stagnation. Specifically,

① In order to increase housing construction and promote home ownership, housing loans were given to non-home owners who run small businesses (with less than 5 employees), with the total amount of 1,170 billion won (1,060 million USD) from the National Housing Fund.

② To support housing construction, the following measures were taken:

a. Extending the period of the lower interest rate for loans from the housing construction fund,

b. Supporting the expenses of local government's public rental housing construction up to 50%,

c. Funding support for a private rental business to purchase housing for letting,

d. Increasing land supply ratio for rental housing in publicly-developed land from 10% to 20%,

e. Long-term lease of national and public land and unsold lands owned by public institutions and local governments for building rental housing.

2.3.3. Deregulations

① From 1977, there was a price ceiling for new housing, and from 1989, a cost-based restriction on housing sale prices. In 1999, with the deregulation in the housing sector as an effort to overcome the economic difficulty derived from the 1997 Asia Financial Crisis the developer was able to determine every housing sale price except small size housings less than 60 m^2 with aid from the national housing fund.

② Regulations were drastically eased, including the temporary reduction or abolishment of restrictions on purchasing multiple new housing[10], relaxation or abolishment of resale restrictions, and permission of early sales for rental housing.

10 Restriction on purchase in multiple new housing: One who purchased a new housing is prohibited to buy another new one in certain period (e.g. for 5 years or 10 years)

2.3.4. Achievements

Housing policy in the 1990s took a structural break around the Asian Financial Crisis from 1997. During the New Five-Year Economic Plan in the mid-1990s, housing policy was focused on housing supply and expansion. As a result, 3.12 million housing units were constructed, exceeding the number of houses built during the 2-million-unit plan. However, deregulating the land use plan to build more houses in the 1990s resulted in an imprudent development of land all across the country that caused a huge amount of money and time to recover.

During the Asian financial crisis, the housing market became stagnant due to an unprecedented drop in housing prices, instability of the housing market, and chain bankruptcies of housing companies. To resolve this, the government announced to provide stimulation packages. These are the financial support for housing purchase and rental payment to increase housing demand and promoting the stability of the housing market for the low- and middle-income class and the revitalization of transactions to promote housing supply. Deregulation of house price control was implemented and regulations of housing supply (i.e. housing distribution criteria under excess demand) were also eased.

As a result, the supply-oriented market formed by excessive demand turned into a demand-oriented market. As the housing supply ratio reached 96.2% in 2000, the central government was faced with a serious challenge of changing policy directions from the previous supply-oriented policy to demand-focused policy to improve the quality and environment of housing and to secure a self-controlled market as much as possible.

2.4. Housing Policy in the 2000s

2.4.1. Background

In the early 2000s, most housing regulations were relaxed to overcome the financial crisis that occurred in the late 1990s by virtue of consolidated efforts of the government and the housing industry. Consequently, housing demand which had declined due to the crisis began to rise.

Since late 2002, the housing market started to show signs of insecurity and became highly unstable with the start of the Roh, Moo-hyun administration in 2003. In response, the new government prepared the 'October 29 measures' (a package of policy interventions announced on October 29, 2003), encompassing the early introduction of the comprehensive real estate (property) tax[11], reinforcement of capital gains tax to owners with more than three houses, the introduction of

11 Comprehensive real estate holding tax, imposed on one's all property added up.

transactions registration[12], and expansion of housing supply through a new town development. As a result, house prices began to move downward and remained relatively stable in 2004. However, the housing market instability was reignited in 2005 due to a price hike in housing reconstruction areas and significantly increased selling price in the Pangyo area (one of the satellite towns near Seoul).

To stabilize the housing market, the government announced several anti-real estate speculation measures on August 31, 2005, which covered various programs and tools, such as enhancement of transaction transparency (e.g. real estate registry with actual acquisition price), strengthening of the comprehensive real estate tax, reinforcement of capital gains tax on a household with two homes, development profits redemption[13], and increase of housing supply.

Nevertheless, housing prices rose again in late 2006, due to the continued low-interest rate and expansion of credit. The government tried to manage housing finance and expand the housing supply through the 'November 15th measures' in 2006 and 'January 11th measures' in 2007 (a package of policy interventions announced on January 11, 2007). As a result, the housing market became stable until the world economic crisis in 2008,

12 When register real estate, real price must be registered simultaneously.

13 Government collects a part of profit when a property owner gains profit from development.

2.4.2. Major Programs

The Korean government implemented measures to prevent housing speculations. In April 2003, the registration of housing trade became mandatory for an apartment which is larger than 59 m^2 of net floor area or a semi-detached house that is larger than 148 m^2 of net floor area in the district where the price of houses rose over 1.5% in one month or 3% in three months. Houses, apartments, and semi-detached houses in redevelopment or reconstruction districts are also included.

On May 28th, 2003, the government announced a housing welfare road map. According to the road map, 500,000 public rental houses named 'Kookmin rental housing' were to be built over five years, which was revised upward in October 2003 for the construction of 1 million public rental houses over a period of ten years. In addition, the residential environment improvement projects were made available when those were needed.

In 2005, a series of policy measures were announced:

① The bonds bidding system was implemented again for those selling land to build apartments larger than 85 m^2 of net floor area in the publicly developed housing sites;

② The government worked out the details of the standard construction cost for developable land for the small and medium-size apartments smaller than 85 m^2 and introduced a cost-related price control system by which the sale price of housing is determined by adding up land cost and building expenses;

③ House sales prices were allowed to be used as a tax imposition standard;

④ The government introduced the publicly notified house price by determining a house price calculated against the market price.

From 2006, developers were allowed to construct housing for letting in reconstruction areas up to a certain percentage and in such cases, the floor area ratio[14] or volume ratio[15] was allowed to be adjusted upward as much as the increased quantity of rental housing. In order to ensure transparency in housing prices, the government banned the use of dual contracts (original and modified)[16] when purchasing the house. Actual market prices were to be reported to the respective local government.

The comprehensive real estate tax was imposed per household and tax bases were adjusted upward. The ceiling on property tax was abolished and the effective tax rate of the property was adjusted upward. Capital gains tax was calculated and imposed based on market price and the tax rate was increased for those owners with more than 2 houses per household. The debt-to-income ratio (DTIs) was applied to the owners of a house worth over 600 million won (USD 0.54 million) in

---

14 Floor area ratio means ratio of building area to land lot.

15 Volume ratio means ratio of total building area to land lot.

16 Dual contracts (original and modified): Making a different contract that does not show actual house price

order to regulate mortgage loans within 40% of the house price and in November 2006, DTI was applied to overheated speculation zones.

In 2007, the 'January 13th measures' introduced the 'rental support voucher system'[17] with a plan to increase the provision of public rental housing in a longer-term and to secure rental housing in reserve. In 2008 and 2009, in order to reduce the unsold houses outside the capital region, a series of tax reductions, shortening of resale restriction periods, and re-purchase restriction periods were introduced. In May 2008, the government announced the plan to construct 1.5 million units of Bogeumjari housing[18] with the low sale price in downtown or development-restricted areas (Green Belt Zone) for low-income households who do not own a house.

In 2009, in order to meet diverse demands for single families and newlyweds, building urban-lifestyle housing, such as complex type housing and studio type housing, was encouraged. The government provided financial supports and relaxing the construction standards for those housings. From 2010 to March 2011, several measures were undertaken by the government to stabilize Chonsei deposit, including loans for Chonsei and the promotion of rental housing construction.

17 Rental support voucher system: A form of housing allowance.

18 Bogeumjari housing: Houses for sale or rental houses supplied by the LH in support of the budget and National Housing Fund in order to solve the housing problem for the low income class in large cities like Seoul. (Bogeumjari means nest or home in Korean)

2.4.3. Achievements

From 2003 to 2006, the central government implemented comprehensive measures covering taxation, financing, and supplying houses. These measures were the transparent trade system, the introduction of the comprehensive real estate tax, the raise of property tax, the registration of real estate trade, the regulations on real estate secured loans, and the expansion of rental and sale housing supply.

The introduction of transparent transactions and registering real estate trade made the actual real estate transactions clearer and the parity of tax imposition. Moreover, the construction of 100,000 public rental housing every year in this period contributed to the improvement of the residential environment. The government also purchased multi-family houses in the existing urban areas and utilized these houses as public rental houses. Such an approach particularly contributed to provide housing security for low-income families. The introduction of comprehensive real estate taxes reinforced tenure taxes for high-priced houses and helped to improve parity in taxation along with the change in the capital gains tax based on the actual market housing value.

Since 2006, house-secured loan regulations were restrictedly enforced and as a result, house prices began to become stable and the market continued to remain relatively calm thereafter. Due to the measures taken against unsold housing in provincial areas in 2008 and 2009, the number of unsold houses also began to decrease. Boguemjari housings for non-homeowners were constructed which helped to provide housing for low- and middle-income households.

Chapter 3

Major Programs of Housing Policy in Korea

3.1. Administrative Procedure for Construction

3.1.1. Project Approval

1) Significance

The project approval system aims to systematically install the necessary public facilities required based on the housing construction and also looks to streamline various housing business approval processes in order to promote housing supply.

2) Major Contents

It is mandatory for a developer to obtain prior approval for a project plan that consists of construction of more than 20 apartment units or 20 houses (30 units or houses from 2014)[1] or for developing a site of more than 10,000 square meters. The project must include a site plan consisting of a main and subsidiary facilities installation plan as well as a housing construction plan. Housing construction projects of more than 100 houses or site development projects above 16,500 square meters must have installation plans for roads, facilities for water supply, drainage, electricity, gas supply, telecommunication facilities, and district heating.

In the site planning, a housing site deployment plan and a site facilities layout plan should be included. The subsidiary facilities should include site access roads, parking lots, and welfare facilities (including medical facilities, neighborhood facilities, kindergarten, and senior citizens' centers).

The project approval process starts when the developer submits the application form for the project to the local government. On receiving an application, the head of the local government such as the head of a city/ county/ local autonomous district/ mayor/ governor consults with

1 In 2014, a revision was made to raise the number of housing units from 20 to 30 units for the mandatory seeking of project approval. The approval of LH projects also was delegated to local government later.

the related agencies within 30 days of the receipt of the application and decides whether the project will be approved within 60 days of consultation. While generally, the provincial governor approves most of the projects, the Minister of Land, Transport and Maritime Affairs (currently the Minister of Land, Infrastructure and Transport) approves only those projects which are planned to be developed by the Korea Land and Housing Corporation (LH).

3) Effects of Project Approval

Project approval will bring various permits stipulated in 44 Articles in 24 related Acts into effect. These include permits regarding development, enforcement plans, and property transactions under the National Land Planning and Utilization Act, occupancy permits under the Road Act and River Act, permits under the Building Code and the Forest Law, and approval of implementation plans under the Urban Development Law. Moreover, defunct public facilities in the project sites are exchangeable with newly installed public facilities.

The developer needs re-approval of the project if he or she makes any change in the project implementation plan which is already approved. After the announcement of a subscription for a house sale, the developer is prohibited from making any changes to the contents of a project with regards to potential increases in housing prices or to changes over 2% of the size of each unit or the entire site. The developer must complete a site development based on the approved project plan within two years from the approval date.

4) Major Achievements

(1) Contribution to Large-Scale Housing Construction

The public sector has played a critical role in large-scale housing construction and the quantity of housing construction has rapidly grown.

a. Revitalization of construction through the exceptional granting of sanctions from other statutes (streamline all administrative processes) (1975)

b. The introduction of the designated house builders system which expanded the quantity of construction at an early stage through the preferential sale of public land to large house builders with substantial construction expertise (1977)

c. Operation of pre-decision making system to streamline administrative processes, which contributed to the revitalization of housing construction (1994)

(2) Providing Convenience in Residential Areas with the Installation of Public Facilities

When embarking on a project, it is mandatory for the developer to set up public facilities. Housing development sites are planned and built with convenience facilities installed for better residential environments.

(3) Contribution of Major Facilities Installations

The private housing developer is asked to build major public infrastructure as a pre-condition for approval of its project plan. If the project owner constructs public infrastructure on his own account, the expenses could be compensated by the agencies concerned. The housing developer examines the feasibility of the project with the installation of infrastructure.[2]

3.1.2. Housing Construction Project Supervision

1) Background

In the past, the project manager of a private housing construction project could choose its own supervisor under the Building Act and the Architect Act. The supervisor was prone to misuse his or her position and deviate from the actual objective with arbitrary and unreasonable supervision. This was one of the main reasons for faulty construction

2 Facilities that can be installed on a housing complex include:
- Infrastructure: road, water supply and drainage, electricity, gas, communication and district heating
- Subsidiary facilities: parking lot, control office, fence, gate, guardhouse, and septic tank
- Welfare facilities: playground, neighborhood facility, medical facility, sports facility

practices. The two million housing units were built with such experiences, and inevitably, those were completed short of materials and with a lack of proper skills.

To prevent this kind of faulty housing construction, the Housing Construction Project Supervision System was implemented on January 7th, 1994. Housing construction projects were examined at a development site to determine whether the construction work was properly carried out based on the contracted design, drawing, and specifications.

2) Major Contents

The supervision system which is regulated by different laws consists of supervision of private projects, responsible supervision of public projects, and installation supervision of electricity and fire facilities.[3] Out of these, the supervision of private projects is divided into supervision of general buildings and supervision of public housing.

Either a mayor, county governor, or head of a borough is entitled to appoint a supervisor and to approve projects. The supervisor has the authority to take measures against builders' offenses or to stop construction. It's a requirement for the Project Approver to be reported on a supervisors' allocation plan, supervision plan, and documentation

3 Supervision regarding the electricity and network system work is additionally conducted.

at the start and completion of each project construction., They are also entitled to be reported on supervisory affairs on a quarterly basis. Strong actions like cancellation of registration, suspension of the project, cancellation of license, etc. are taken against fraudulent and substandard supervisors as measures of punishment.

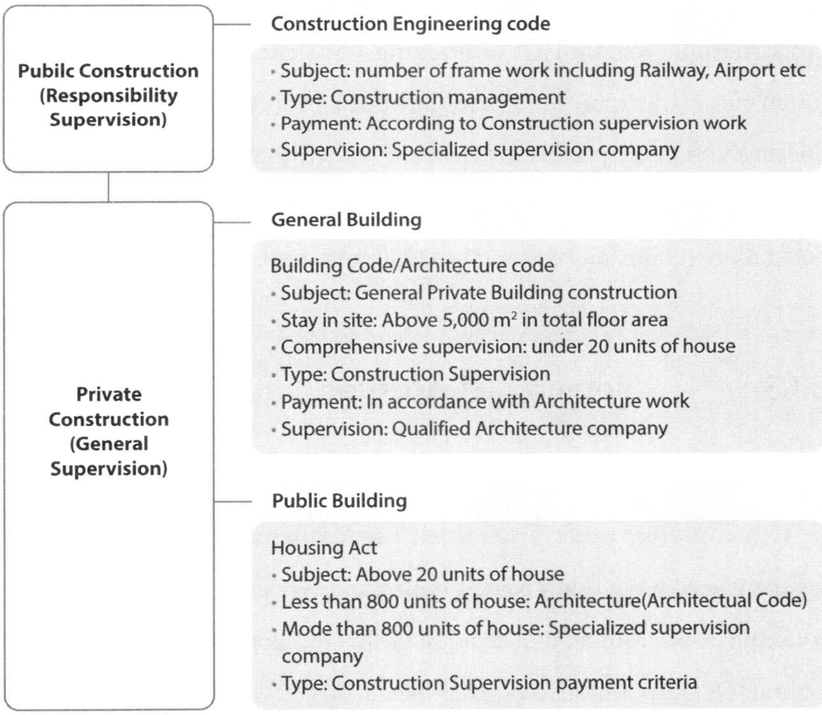

Figure 4 ● Comparison of supervision system with related codes

3) Significant Effects

The introduction of the supervision system has gained consumers' trust. As most houses were sold even before they were fully constructed, it was necessary to take measures for the protection of consumers. First, even though there was doubt and fear of faulty constructions in view of past sale experiences, the supervision system which was incorporated into the Housing Construction Promotion Act (currently Housing Act) provided consumers with a higher level of trust in the housing construction. Secondly, the housing construction process became much more transparent. There had been problems in the quality of construction in the past due to a lack of an adequate supervisory system. The implementation of a supervision system brought down the levels of corruption in housing construction to almost zero.

3.1.3. Housing Guarantee

1) Background

If a housing developer goes bankrupt before completing a residential construction project, both the buyers and tenants suffer the consequences. With an aim to address this problem, the Korea Housing Guarantee Corporation was established in 1993 for the operation and management of the housing guarantee system.

2) Major Contents

The types of housing guarantees include housing sale guarantees, housing lease guarantees, warranty guarantees, construction supervision fee guarantees, permit guarantees, and house purchase finance guarantees. The contents are shown in the following table.

Table 14 ● The types of housing guarantee

Type of Guarantee	Contents	Legal basis
Housing Sale guarantee	Guarantee that the project manager will fulfill a sale of housing or return the deposit for sale according to the terms of housing sale guarantee when it cannot fulfill the housing sale contract for reasons such as bankruptcy	Housing Act Article 76~78
Housing rental Guarantee	Guarantee that the project manager will fulfill the lease of housing or return the security deposit according to the terms of housing lease guarantee when it cannot fulfill the housing lease contract for reasons such as bankruptcy	
Guarantee for repair	Guarantee of defect repair during the obligatory period of defect repair.	
Supervision deposit Guarantee	Guarantee of construction supervision fee for the supervisor	
Permit guarantee	Guarantee of the fulfillment of the conditions promised when obtaining house construction permits from the local or central government such as installation of facilities or restorations	
House purchase Finance guarantee	Guarantee of house purchase funds loaned from the financial institution to the house buyer under a housing sale contract or to the business entities under the housing sale guarantee by the project manager	

3) Significant Effects

The sale guarantee plays a big role in protecting consumers' interests. It prevents the developer from halting housing construction and provides the consumer with either the house or a return of the sale price paid. The sale guarantee amount between 1993 and 2007 reached a total of 399,633 billion won and 3,230 thousand households were guaranteed under the scheme. Three major aspects of the housing sale guarantee were:

First, it dealt with a defect in housing construction. In other words, consumers are expected to receive necessary services for repair after a housing purchase and are entitled to be more satisfied with the purchase of their housing unit. The implementation of this system provided benefits to 2,180 thousand households amounting to 4,593 billion won from 1993 to 2007.

Second, the housing sale guarantee helped to earn consumer's trust in the government's housing policy. It provided strong consumer protection through government intervention.

And third, the housing sale guarantee led to a reliable construction of housing by construction companies. After the system was introduced in 1993, the construction companies carried out nearly four times more warranty services in 1994 as compared to those in 1993. Warranty services have continued to increase every year.

3.2. Land Development

3.2.1. Land Supply System

1) Background

Until the 1970s, Korea's land developed through a land readjustment process[4] of land substitution. In the 1980s, the public residential land development process[5], a whole purchasing method, was introduced while the land readjustment process began to wither mainly due to its long development time and inefficiency. The public residential land development process was preferred over the land readjustment process because it was highly efficient in securing land in areas of high population density and overcoming the serious housing shortages in cities caused by industrialization since the 1970s.

Since the land readjustment process allowed land to be developed through land substitution, the land was divided into smaller sections. This resulted in the inefficiency of land uses due to the difficulty in developing densely populated areas. As developed land was to be distributed to landowners, they tended to prevent building construction

4 Land readjustment process: Process of land substitution in the development site

5 Public land development process: Method of land development by Land Development Promotion Act. Public Agency (i.e. the government, LH, etc.) can develop, utilize and provide the land after appropriating the planed land (whole land purchase)

in developed lands. This was in order to monopolize the profits of the development resulting in excessive capital gains. As landowners took possession of the developed land, the housing developers had to buy land individually from the landowners, which hindered the development of multi-family housing complexes, i.e. large-scale sites of apartments.

In 1980, the Housing Land Development Promotion Act was enacted in order to address problems with the land readjustment process and to supply housings massively in order to fulfill the demand for housing ownership by urban residents. Moreover, in 2000, the Urban Development Law was enacted along with a group of land improvement processes including Land Readjustment Process, Land Development, Urban Area Construction, and Land Character Alterations (changes in the form and quality of land) were merged into a single Urban Development Process.[6] Nevertheless, most of the large-scale housing units were developed in accordance with the Residential Land Development Promotion Act and not with the Urban Development Law.

2) Major Contents

The land development process under the Residential Land Development Promotion Act takes the following several steps:

6 Urban areas used to be controlled by the Urban Planning Law and other areas by the National Land Use and Management Law. In 2000, these two were merged as the National Land Plan and Utilization Law.

- The project developer is designated by the Minister of Land, Transport and Maritime Affairs (currently the Minister of Land, Infrastructure and Transport) among the central government, local government, the Korea Land & Housing Corporation, local public enterprises constituted under the Local Public Enterprises Act and private-public joint corporate bodies;
- When the project developer proposes a site, the Minister of Land, Transport and Maritime Affairs consults with the related central administrative agencies and invites comments from local governments about the site;
- Then, the housing policy review committee headed by the Minister of Land, Transport, and Maritime Affairs reviews the proposal and designates the site for residential land development.
- After the site is designated, the developer has to undergo several processes up until completion of the housing project including preparation of development and implementation plans, compensation (paying land value), land supply, and so on.
- The Minister of Land, Transport, and Maritime Affairs has the authority to designate areas more than 200,000 m^2 in size and to approve development plans for areas larger than 3,300,000 m^2. On the other hand, local governments have the authority to approve the rest of the cases including development plans, land

supply, and so on[7].

The government took urgent action to solve serious housing problems in the capital region. The land development under the Residential Land Development Promotion Act has the following characteristics:

First, after designation and notification of the site, the developer is entitled to the right of eminent domain and this leads to a time reduction of land development.

Second, once the implementation plan is approved, decisions on zones can be automatically changed. Without any special alteration process by the National Land Plan and Utilization Law, the green area can be changed to residential or commercial zones.

Finally, the central government or local governments, or the Korea Land & Housing Corporation can be eligible for land development. Although the private sector is excluded from participating in large-scale land development, it is allowed to take part in some exceptional cases.

3) Achievements

The land development system contributed to the housing supply in

7 This regulation was changed in 2011 to delegate the designation power to the mayors of Seoul and metropolitan cities and the governors of provinces unless the size of designating land exceeds the total size of land pre-determined in the housing land supply and demand plan.

several ways.

First, the supply of a large quantity of housing land in a short period of time contributed to massive housing construction. The public land development process shortened the development period through the purchase of bulk plots of raw land, whereas the previous land readjustment process took a long time to develop sites.

Second, it played a critical role in providing housing for low-income households. Land developed for rental housing and national housing was supplied (sold) cheaper than the development cost, which, as a result, lowered house prices.

And third, it contributed to the installation of public and subsidiary facilities more effectively and easily than before.

3.2.2. New Town Development in the Capital Region

1) Background

From the early 1980s, the government acknowledged that the serious housing shortage problems in urban areas needed to be addressed. On account of this, in December 1980, the Residential Land Development Promotion Act was enacted and the government began to deal with the rising housing demand through the supply of land in large quantities.

Nevertheless, housing was still in short supply and the potential demand increased. The supply of housing was in a bad shape and house prices skyrocketed with rampant speculation to blame. Thus, the central government set up the Two Million Housing Construction Plan and started new town developments in order to expand the housing supply and stabilize housing prices.

2) Major Contents

In order to solve the serious housing problems in the capital region, the government took urgent action. In September 1988, plans for the development of new towns in Pyungchon and Sanbon were announced and further plans for new town developments in Bundang, Ilsan, and Jungdong followed in April 1989. The new town plans were part of the Two Million Housing Construction Plan that was promoted in 1988.

Bundang, Ilsan, Pyungchon, Sanbon, and Jungdong were selected because they had available land for large-scale development with reasonably low land prices, and were easily connected to the existing urban infrastructure. Also, they were located within 20~25 kilometers from the urban center in Seoul, allowing less than one hour of commuting time. In November 1989, housing sales for new town development started with a model complex in Bundang. Sanborn was completed in January 1995 and Bundang was the last newly constructed town completed in December 1996.

3) Significant Effects

The five new towns in the capital region made it possible to produce houses on large-scale sites in a short period of time. This resulted in several positive effects such as a stabilization of rising house prices and consequently the alleviation of housing problems in the capital region.

First, the construction of five new towns contributed to stabilizing the housing market and the improvement in housing standards for low- and middle-income families. The house prices in the capital region which had led to the rise in real estate prices for the whole nation began to stabilize after the supply of 294,000 units in five new towns.

New towns in the capital region were crucial in solving the problem of housing shortages and rising house prices which were caused by increases in population and households.

Second, the construction of five new towns increased the capacity of the metropolitan infrastructure. They also contributed to overcoming Seoul's infrastructure capacity by providing subway lines and stations, expressways, arterial and branch roads, water supplies and drainage, garbage incinerator plants, and cogeneration plants.

Third, new town construction relieved the overcrowding levels in Seoul. In particular, Bundang and Ilsan played a significant role in mitigating overcrowding and over-concentration in Seoul.

Fourth, new town construction contributed to economic revitalization and further job creation in the capital. New town development was a large-scale project that costed approximately a total of 15,000 billion won (13 billion USD) to supply houses to 1.18 million people (294,000 households). It is believed to have had a great ripple effect on the Korean economy in terms of production and job creation.

Table 15 ● Analysis of the derivative effects of new town construction in the capital region

Classification		Total	Bundang	Ilsan	Pyungchon	Sanbon	Jungdong
Effect on Production (100 mil won)	Nation Capital region	310,403 235,522	110,648 84,015	94,565 71,952	33,979 25,630	28,986 21,832	42,225 32,093
Effect on Creation of Added Value (100 mil won)	Nation Capital region	118,925 90,069	42,342 32,129	36,223 27,516	13,077 9,801	11,120 8,349	16,233 12,274
Effect on Employment (Thousand)	Nation Capital region	1,738 1,249	619 445	529 382	191 136	162 116	237 170

(Source: Korea Research Institute for Human Settlements, 1990, Analysis of the derivative effects of new town construction in the capital region)

Fifth, the construction of new towns contributed to the strengthening of finances in local government. New housing construction generated a sizable local tax income. The local tax income collected in new towns showed higher increase rates than the overall average of Gyeonggi-do (where five new towns are located) and most of the income came from acquisition tax and registration tax for housing construction and purchase. This implies that the new housing construction was beneficial to local public finance.

Finally, public facilities were made available. The five large-scale new towns became a provider of various public facilities such as department stores, general hospitals, large size parks, and cultural facilities. The expansion of major infrastructures like roads and subways contributed to the improvement of the metropolitan transport infrastructure and to the diversification of metropolitan spatial structures.

Despite the positive results of the new town constructions, several problems such as disorderly housing developments in the outskirts of new towns accompanied the new towns. In January 2003, the introduction of the National Land Planning and Utilization Act, which combined the Urban Planning Act and the National Land Use Management Act, covered the entire nation, including both urban and rural areas to tackle disorderly development around urban areas.

3.3. Housing Finance

3.3.1. Role of Housing Finance

Housing finance plays a significant role in controlling housing supply and demand, stabilizing house prices, and improving housing standards. Housing finance helps to revitalize the housing market through the intervention and control of housing supply and demand. The National

Housing Fund was raised to increase housing supplies (construction) through governmental funds, fiscal loans, deposits, national housing subscription savings deposits, and national housing bonds. The raised fund supported the home-buyers purchasing power and increased the effective demand for houses while it supported the home-builders and enhanced the supply capacity of housing in this sector.

The financial support for construction companies and producers of building materials improved the production capacity of the housing construction industry both in quantity and quality. Potential house buyers were encouraged to save money to buy a home in the future. This also helped the home-builders to raise funds for housing investments and, as a result, enabled them to predict the future housing demand in the housing market. (i.e. the amount of housing subscription savings reflected the housing demand)

In addition, housing finance enhanced the housing stability and fairness in income distribution through financial supports for low- and middle-income households. It also supported low-income households through the financial support of rental housing construction. This in turn contributed to the stability of the housing market by alleviating the funding burden of house purchases with long-term, low-interest rate housing finance.

3.3.2. National Housing Fund

1) Background

The government established the National Housing Fund to secure the necessary funds required to promote more efficient housing construction. The main goal was to improve housing market stability and the quality of residential environments. Under the Housing Construction Promotion Act (from 2015 the National Housing and Urban Fund Act), it was established in April 1981 and launched in July 1981.

2) Major Contents

① Operating Institution

The operating institution of the National Housing Fund (currently National Housing and Urban Fund, NHUF) is the Ministry of Land, Infrastructure and Transport. The operation and management administration of the fund was first entrusted to the president of the Korea Housing Bank (currently Kookmin Bank), secondly to the president of Woori Bank, and finally since 2015 to the president of Korea National Housing and Urban Guarantee Corporation.

② Raising Financial Resources

The National Housing Fund consists of government budgets and deposits, deposits from the public funds including the national pension fund, first and second-grade national housing bonds[8], funds from the housing lottery, housing subscriptions savings deposit, loan deposits, loans recoverable and interest earnings of the national housing fund, profits from the operation of the national housing fund, incidental profits from national housing business operation, and loans from Korean banks or finance organizations.

Table 16 ● The sources of national housing fund

Sources	Content	Interest rate(Yearly)	Period
The first grade national housing bond	Issued at registration, enrollment, and approval of real estate development and transaction	3.0%/year (5.0% /year before'01.7.31)	5 years
The second-grade national housing bond	Issued for houses, larger than 85 m^2 and under a price cap is applied. (bond bidding system)	0%/year (3.0% /year before'99.7.15)	10 years (20 years before'99.7.15)
Housing subscription savings	Savings deposit, a requirement to be eligible for purchase of public housing	4.5%/year - Below 2year : 3.5% /year - Below 1year : 2.5% /year	Until the time of winning the voucher of house
Public fund management balance	The balance of a public fund Managing budget	National bond interest rate +0.01%p	7,10 years
Lottery fund	Transfer from lottery fund	-	-
General account	Transfer from the general account	-	-
Collection of excess earnings from reconstruction	Collection of excess earnings from reconstruction (legal expenses)	-	-
Trusted fund	Fund from government officer's pension, Private school pension and National pension	An interest rate of regular savings	Within 3 years

8 See 2.2.2

Sources	Content	Interest rate(Yearly)	Period
Loan withdrawal	Withdrawal of expired loans	-	-
Interest receipt	Interest receipt from loans	-	-

* 1. An interest rate of the first-grade national housing bond has been lowered consistently according to the financial market situation and government policy. As of Jan. 1, 2017, the rate was set at 1.75%.
2. The second-grade national housing bond was abolished in 2013.

③ Operation Uses and Supporting Conditions

The purpose of the national housing fund is to provide loans to develop land and construct houses, as well as for individuals who are provided with the right to purchase national housing. The uses of the national housing fund are classified into the construction business and other businesses.

The construction business classification includes public sales, private sales, worker welfare, redevelopment and reconstruction, public rental, medium-sized rental housing, national rental housing, employee rental housing, redevelopment of rental housing, rental demanders fund, bankruptcy normalization fund, acquisition facilitation fund, multi-family housing, and rural housing.

Other businesses classifications include the residential land development fund, residential environment improvement fund, low-income rental deposit fund, sale intermediate payment fund, housing purchase fund for workers and low-income households and rental deposit (Chonsei) fund for workers and low-income household.

Table 17 ● Operational status for funds (as of Aug. 2011)

Classification		Contents
Fund operating expenses	Fund management budget	Administration fee for the fund management
	Operating budget	Research and other operational expenses
Ordinary business	Capital transfer to purchasing housing for rent	Assistance for purchasing multi-family housing for rental (Loan amount: 45% of the whole budget)
	Ordinary assistance for leasing(Chonsei)	Maintenance fee and registration fee for the lease project
	Governmental budget for public-rental housing	Governmental budget for construction of public rental housing (supporting 10~40% of the whole cost)
	Capital transfer of rebuilding surplus profit	The building surplus profit is given to local governments
Finance business	Rental housing construction	Loan to construction Smaller than 60 m^2: Loan amount 55 million won, Interest rate 3%/year 60 m^2~85 m^2: Loan amount 75 million won, Interest rate 4%/year Repayment period: Payable in 20 years with 10 years grace period
	Housing for sale construction	Loan to public-selling housing construction: A. Public housing construction for sale (to build) - Smaller than 60 m^2: Loan amount 55million won, Interest rate 5%/year - 60 m^2~85 m^2: Loan amount 75 million won, Interest rate 4%/year B. Public housing construction for sale (after completion) - Smaller than 60 m^2: Loan amount 60 million won, Interest rate 5%/year - 60 m^2~85 m^2: Loan amount 80 million won, Interest rate 4%/year
	Leasing(Chonsei)	Loan to low-income people for Chonsei (Leasing house): A. Loan to low-income people: Loan amount 70% of Chonsei, Interest rate 2%/year Repayment period: Installments over 15 years B. Laborer or wage earner: Loan amount 60 million won, Interest rate 4.5%/year Repayment period: Payable in 2 years

Classification		Contents
	Purchase housing	Loan to low-income people for home buying: - Loan amount: 100 million won, Interest rate 5.2% per year - Repayment period: Payable in 19 years with a one year grace period or Payable in 17 years with a 3 year grace period
	Housing improvement	Loan for improvement of residential environments and residential improvements for rural housing A. Loan to housing for multiple dwelling: Loan amount 120 million won, Interest rate 3%/year Repayment period Payable within 1 year B. Loan to detached house or multiplex house: Loan amount – 60 million won, 3%/year Repayment period: Payable in 17 years with 3 year grace period
	Others	Loan to city restructuring, land site development and purchase of rental housing project, Loans to purchase housing for lease: Loan amount 60 million won, Interest rate 5%/year, Repayment period: Payable within 5 years
Internal government expenses		Repayment for the principal and interest of deposit from special budgets and funds
Repayment of loans		Repayment for the principal and interest of issuing national housing bonds and housing subscription savings loans
Administration of excess cash		Administration of surplus profits after administration of fund (such as deposits bank)

(Sources: Ministry of Land, Transport and Maritime Affairs, Handbook for Housing Affairs)

Table 18 ● The amount of raised National Housing Fund (1981-2009)

(Unit: billion won, %)

Classification	1981~2000		2001~2009	
		%		%
Total	56,455	100	202,741	100
1st grade bond	14,183	25.1	70,017	34.5
Loan withdrawal	14,174	25.1	53,862	26.6
National bond management fund	9,982	17.7	27,416	13.5

Classification	1981~2000		2001~2009	
		%		%
Net profit	3,258	5.8	19,906	9.8
2nd grade bond	3,236	5.7	10,606	8.2
Others	11,622	20.6	14,938	7.4

(Source: Ministry of Land, Transport and Maritime Affairs, Handbook for Housing Affairs)

3) Results

The national housing fund has supported over one-third of the total housing construction carried out from 1981 to 2009 and 40% to 50% of the total housing construction in the late 1990s. This means that the national housing fund contributed greatly to increasing the housing supply. Moreover, houses supported by the national housing fund showed an improvement in housing standards, such as size expansion, modernization of housing facilities, and alleviation of residential density.

In conclusion, it is believed that the national housing fund has significantly contributed to an increase in the number of new houses as well as improving the quality of houses.

3.3.3. Korea Housing Finance Corporation

1) History and Background

(1) The Purpose of its Establishment

The Korea Housing Finance Corporation (KHFC) is a public housing finance company that aims to improve public welfare through the supply of reliable, long-term housing finance. Korea Housing Finance Corporation Act was enacted on 31 Dec 2003.

(2) Main Business

- Supply of long-term housing mortgage loans by raising funds through the issuance of mortgage-backed security bonds
- Housing Finance Trust Guarantee
- Housing Pension (Reverse mortgage or Home Equity Conversion Mortgage)

(3) History

- 1999.01: Establishment of mortgage-backed bond securitization corporation (KoMoCo)
- 2004.03.01.: Establishment of KHFC
- 2004.03.17: Taking over the KoMoCo
- 2004.06.15: Issuance of MBS
- 2005.10.11: Launch of Bogeumjari (home mortgage) loan for low-income and non-homeowners

- 2006.02.01: Launch of Bogeumjari (home mortgage) loan with the fixed interest rate on a 30-year mortgage loan
- 2007.07.12: Launching of Housing Pension (Reverse Mortgage)

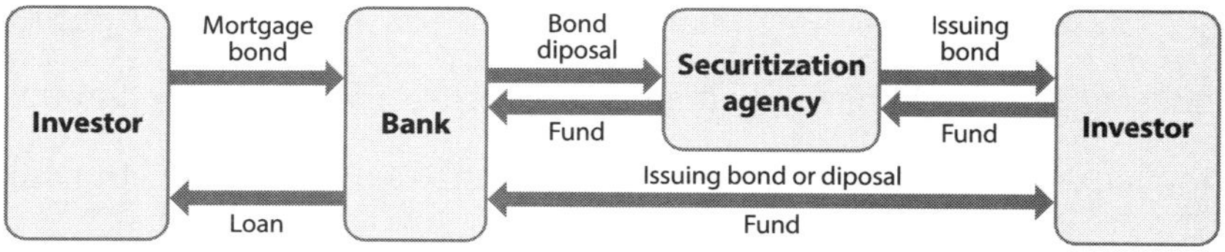

Figure 5 ● Securitization of mortgages

2) Main Business and Performance

(1) Securitization of Mortgage-backed Bonds and Supply of Long-term Low-Interest Rate Mortgage Loans

① Securitization of mortgage-backed bonds

By issuing mortgage-backed bonds and securities based on mortgages collateralized by financial institutions, the KHFC provided stable long-term low-interest funding to the housing purchasers.

Table 19 ● Issuance of mortgage-backed securities (MBS) (Unit: billion won)

MBS	Issue date	Amount of issued securities	Outstanding
KoMoCo		2,876	259
MBS 2004-1~7	2004	3,016	534
MBS 2005-1~9	2005	3,861	1,044

MBS	Issue date	Amount of issued securities	Outstanding
MBS 2006-1~5	2006	1,753	593
MBS 2007-1~6	2007	2,188	997
MBS 2008-1~7	2008	2,648	1,254
MBS2009-1~14	2009	494	242
MBS 2010-1~18	2010	431	342
Sum		17,267	5,265

* Mortgage-Backed Securities (MBS): A housing bond that is secured by foreclosure rights by the bank based on the borrower's house is called mortgage-backed bonds (MBB). MBS is the beneficiary certificate securitized by KHFC based on the mortgage debts from the bank (2011.6.30. KRW 1,067/USD)
(Source: KHFC, Housing Finance Magazine)

② Supply of mortgage loans with long-term low-interest rates

The purpose of a mortgage loan is to help people to own homes, manage the risk of variable interest rates, and enhance the stability of the financial market by implementing a fully amortized mortgage loan with long-term (over 10 years) and fixed interest rates.

- Basic type: fixed interest rate from the start of loan to end of the repayment (for customers who want to avoid the risk of the variability of interest rate)
- Mixed type: fixed rate plus variable rate, but the low rate at an initial stage
- Designed type: variable interest rate at the initial stage (for customers who expect a decrease in interest rate)
- Preferential type: the interest rate of 1% lower than the average for people of low-income levels and non-home ownership (income

under 20 million won yearly)

- Affiliation type: affiliated to intermediate payment, suitable for customers expected to make sufficient payment at the middle of the loan

Table 20 ● Sales records of Bogeumjari (Home Mortgage) loan (Unit: billion won)

Year	Sales Amount	Accumulated Balance
2004	3,332	2,874
2005	4,219	6,799
2006	1,387	6,354
2007	3,595	8,182
2008	4,244	10,731
2009	5,943	13,051
2010	5,848	16,010
Sum	28,568	64,001

* Sales amount: Figures are aggregated by data from financial institutions in charge of Bogeumjari Loan sales.
* Accumulated balance: Figures are the sum of basic and holding assets for the issuance of MBS
(Source: Ministry of Land, Transport and Maritime Affairs, Handbook for Housing Affairs)

(2) Housing Finance Credit Guarantee

The KHFC provides guarantee services to individuals who want to obtain loans from financial institutions as follows:

- Individual guarantee service for payment of installments for house purchases, leases, constructions, and renovation loans
- Guarantee services for home builders who need to obtain loans to build housing for sale and lease

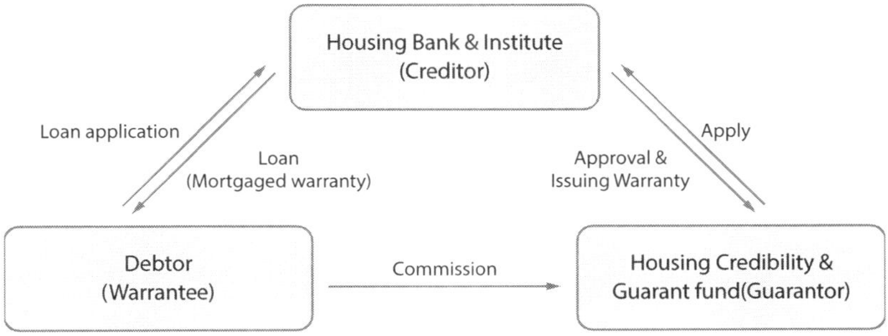

Figure 6 ● Flows of house credit guarantee fund

Table 21 ● Housing finance credit guarantee origination by type (Unit: billion won)

Year	Total		Individual		Home-builder	
	Households	Amount	Households	Amount	Households	Amount
2007	20,653	5,089	20,130	4,479	524	610
2008	21,558	6,760	20,650	5,856	908	904
2009	26,211	9,655	25,550	8,704	661	951
2010	29,511	11,490	28,952	11,140	560	350
Sum	97,933	32,994	95,282	30,179	2,653	2,815

(Source: KHFC, Housing Finance Magazine)

(3) Supply of Housing Pension (Reverse Mortgage) Guarantee

Housing Pension (Reverse Mortgage) is a program to provide monthly pensions to senior citizens who own homes but do not have any income source, by taking their houses as security. Both the borrower and his/her spouse can keep their home and receive pension through the rest of their lives.

Table 22 ● Reverse mortgage guarantee origination by payment type

(Unit: billion won)

Year	Total		Tenure		Modified Tenure	
	Case	Amount	Case	Amount	Case	Amount
2007	52	603	42	493	10	110
2008	70	863	34	409	36	454
2009	112	1,747	55	862	57	886
2010	2,02	3,036	122	1,879	80	1,159
Sum	436	6,249	253	3,643	183	2,609

* Tenure type: A fixed amount is paid out each month until the termination of the guarantee period (death).
* Modified Tenure type: Lump sum withdrawals are allowed within a certain limit, and the remaining amount is paid out in equal installments each month or if requested.

(Source: KHFC, Housing Finance Magazine)

3.4. Housing Supply and Demand Control

3.4.1. Housing Supply Methods (Sale and Rent Methods)

1) Background

Every year the central government draws up a housing construction comprehensive plan and allows local governments, the Korea National Housing Corporation (presently the Korea Land and Housing Corporations, LH), and private housing companies (in some cases) to build houses according to the plan. In May 1978, the Housing Supply Regulation was enacted to avoid speculations and to provide housing to those who are actually in need of homes. The Housing Supply Regulation set down the conditions and methods of housing supply including the supply process.

2) Major Contents

(1) Classification of Housing

Newly-constructed houses are classified into national housing or private housing depending on the type of support provided by the national housing fund. National housing is a house that has a net house size of less than 85 m^2 and is constructed by public corporations and private housebuilders with the financial support of the national housing fund.

Private housing includes all other houses except the national housing mentioned above. In other words, it includes houses larger than 85 m^2, built by public corporations without the support of the national housing fund or houses of any other size, built by the private sector without the support of the national housing fund.

Table 23 ● Types of houses

National Housing	• Net house size is smaller than 85 m^2 with the financial support of the national housing fund. - Constructed by the public sector or private builders with the support of the national housing fund. - The house smaller than 85 m^2 constructed by public corporations is considered national housing. - In the local area (excluding Metropolitan), housing size could be smaller than 100 m^2.
Private housing	• All houses except the national housing - Any size constructed by a private owner - Constructed by public sector larger than 85 m^2

(2) Targets for Housing

National housing, including rental housing and privately constructed national housing, is provided to households without homeownership.

Private housing is provided to a person aged 20 years or older (including people aged 19 years or younger in the case of a separate household) who live in the corresponding construction areas at the time of resident recruitment.

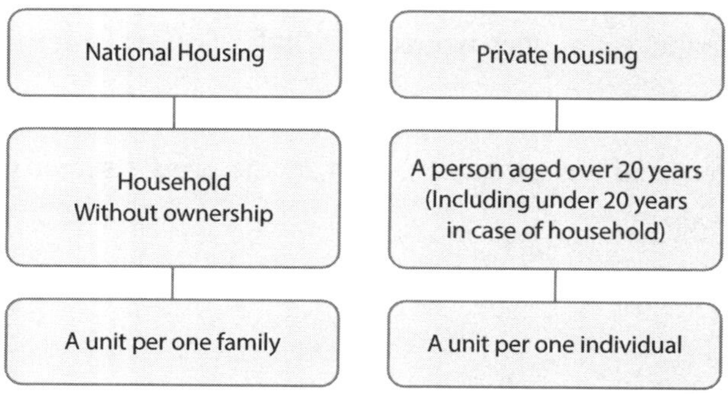

Figure 7 ● Targets and criteria for new housing supply

(3) Supply (Sale or rental) Methods[9]

When a developer (or project owner) sells (or rents) newly constructed houses of more than 20 units (30 from 2014) after receiving project approval from the local government, the developer should get approval for the sale (or rental) method (supply method) from the Mayor, County Governor or Chief of Borough (District area in Korea).

There are three different types of supply (sale) methods for housing, which are general supply, special supply, and group supply. General supply is the most common method for residents to be selected based on their ranking (category). This is determined by the date and amount of their savings accumulated in a housing subscription deposit account.

After the successful candidates are selected by the general supply method and competition among candidates in the same rank, the remaining housing units available are allocated on the basis of additional points and a random draw takes place among the candidates with the same point (rank) category. The system for additional points was first introduced in September 2007 and is applied to 75% of public housing smaller than 85 m^2 and 50% of public housing larger than 85 m^2. The remaining housings are distributed to the applicants according to a lottery system.

The additional points system for subscription counts total scores

9 Housing supply means administrative procedure or method for new housing sale or rent.

(total of 84 points) from the duration of non-home ownership (32 points), number of household members (35 points), and duration of housing subscription savings deposits (17 points) and selects the home purchasers with the highest points where there is competition in the same rank.

Table 24 ● Selection methods for owner-occupied units

<table>
<tr><th colspan="2">Type</th><th>Public Housing</th><th>Private Housing</th></tr>
<tr><td rowspan="3">Smaller than 85 m²</td><td>Savings type</td><td>Subscription saving</td><td>Subscription deposit or installment</td></tr>
<tr><td>Resident selection rule</td><td>Based on Ranking system</td><td>Based on the Ranking system</td></tr>
<tr><td>In case of competition in the same rank</td><td>Head of the household without a house for more than 5years and person with the highest deposits among those who paid more than 60 times</td><td>Additional points system 75% +
Lottery system 25%</td></tr>
<tr><td rowspan="3">Larger than 85 m²</td><td>Savings Type</td><td>-</td><td>Subscription Deposits</td></tr>
<tr><td>Resident selection rule</td><td>-</td><td>Ranking system</td></tr>
<tr><td>In case of competition in the same rank</td><td>-</td><td>Bond bidding system (more bidding amount)</td></tr>
</table>

(Source: MOLIT, Handbook for Housing Affairs)

The special provision for housing is a way of providing a house for persons of national merit, the disabled, small- and medium-sized company workers, etc. without being subject to competition with the general public. The group provision method is to provide houses to housing associations that have more than 20 members within 40 percent of total national housing built. The group provision method is an exceptional supply method and is rarely used.

(4) Main Achievements

The housing supply system promoted homeownership for people without a house while putting restrictions on housing supply targets. It played an important role in helping non-homeowners to get a new affordable house.

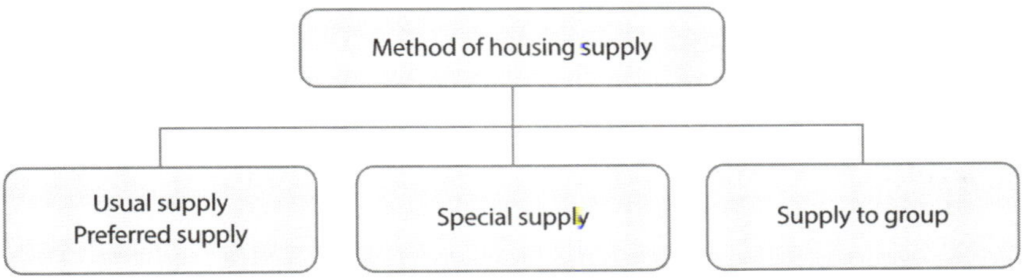

Figure 8 ● The methods for housing supply

3.4.2. Price Control on New Apartments

1) Background

Since the mid-1970s, the chronic imbalance of housing supply and demand had resulted in a rise in the existing house prices, which had become higher than the prices of new houses. To make matters worse, speculation in the housing market had led to a rise in sale prices for new houses as well.

Thus, in August 1977, the price control measure that restricts sale prices of new apartments was implemented in order to maintain housing prices at a certain level so that the buyer could purchase the housing unit at a reasonable price. Since then, home-builders were required to include the housing prices in the housing construction plan and obtain approval from local governments. This led to the regulation of the sale price of newly-built houses.

2) Major Contents

① Direct Price Control

The regulation of a ceiling on sale price was implemented in order to regulate the maximum price per square meter based on net floor area. From 1977 till 1981, the government (Seoul City Mayor) regulated a maximum price per square meter regardless of the size of a house or its actual cost.

Table 25 ● Changes of upper limit for newly-built apartment price

(Unit: ten thousand won/3.3m^2)

Classification	1977	1978	1979	1980	1981	1982	1985	1988	1989.11~
Smaller than85 m^2 in net floor area	55	68	78	90	105	105	115	126.8	Cost-based price control
Larger than85 m^2 in net floor area	55	68	78	90	105	134	134	134	Cost-based price control

(Source: Yoon & Shin(1994), Study of Market Effect on House Price Control)

② Cost-Based Price Control

The cost-based price control system started from November 1989 onwards and was in effect until December 1998. It was a regulatory method that set the maximum construction price for private housing against the construction cost including land cost and optimal profits. This method regulated the sale price but reflected the actual cost and raised the standard construction cost, if necessary.

National housing units smaller than 60 m^2 in net floor area which was approved and built under the Housing Construction Promotion Act (currently Housing Act) and supported by the national housing fund were restricted as per the sale price calculation method. The sale price of such housing consisted of the sum of the construction cost and the land cost. The Ministry of Construction and Transportation (later Ministry of Land, Transport and Marine Affairs and finally Ministry of Land, Infrastructure and Transport) decided on the construction costs based on high rates of inflation.

On the other hand, in the case of serviced land developed by the public sector, land supply price was determined according to the cost of land. The items included in the development costs were the prepayment of land cost interest, tax and registration fees, soft ground construction costs, rocky ground construction costs, and cutoff wall installation costs, which were added to the land price. Account book values or appraised values were applied to lands owned by a developer. The expenses that a project manager would be required to pay for under the Housing Construction Promotion Act such as installation costs of main public facilities and demolition costs for obstructions were also added to the land price.

In addition, there was an optional system that a home-builder could provide options (living room chest, indoor lights, wallpaper, etc.) instead of the basic specifications so that home-buyers could choose the options among them with additional costs incorporated. Such additional costs were limited to 15% of the construction cost.

③ Achievements

The sale price control policy contributed to housing stability for non-homeowners who were caught in a difficult situation under a supplier-oriented market and high land prices. Easier access to homeownership was the main contribution made by sale price controls.

Additionally, the sale price control policy indirectly resulted in the expansion of housing finance sources. Applications for housing subscription savings and deposits increased, and between 1981 and 1991, 26.3% of new financing for the national housing fund and 46.5% of new financing for the housing bank were raised under this system.

The bond bidding system linked with the sale price control policy helped with the sale of second-grade national housing bonds, which made up 13.3% of the national housing fund at 2,200 billion won. The funding to housing construction companies based on such financial resources largely contributed to an increase in housing supply.

3.4.3. Speculation Control

1) Major Methods

(1) Bond Bidding System and Designation of Speculation-Prone Districts

The bond bidding system was implemented to suppress excessive price speculation in large metropolitan areas, such as Seoul and Busan, and to use the proceeds of bond sales as a source of funding for public housing since May 1983. When a home buyer wanted to buy a new private apartment larger than a national housing unit (85 m^2 in net floor area) in a speculation prone district designated by the central government, he/she was required to purchase the second-grade national housing bonds (3% of annual interest rate, 20-year expiration-repayment).

While there was no maximum limit on bonds at the beginning of the bond bidding system, a maximum limit was introduced with an implementation of a cost linkage price system in November 1989. The maximum amount of bonds a purchaser can buy was set within 70% of the gap between a sale price of a new house and the price of an existing house depending on the house size.

The bond bidding system was implemented in areas where

speculation was predicted because the planned price for new housing was significantly lower than the market price for the existing housing. This system was abolished in July 1999 and was reintroduced in February 2006 again with an enactment necessary for the re-issuance of second-grade national housing bonds (0% of annual interest rate, 10-year expiration-repayment).

(2) Establishment of Repurchase Limitation Period

The huge difference between the prices of new housing and existing housing increased the purchasing demand for new housing. Therefore, in order to effectively distribute purchasing opportunities, it was necessary to restrict the re-purchasing or multiple-purchasing of houses for those who had previously obtained a purchase opportunity over a certain time period.

However, the stagnant housing market conditions which were characterized by a reduction of real income and housing demand continued on from the financial crisis of 1998 and were not easily recovered. In March 2000, the repurchase limitation period which prohibits a person (who has a purchase history of another house within the past 5 years) to apply for national housing was abolished. Therefore, regardless of past purchases, housing purchase opportunities were given to all applicants who were not homeowners at the time of the purchase application.

(3) Housing Resale Restrictions System

The housing resale restrictions system was introduced to restrict home resales, constructed or supplied, according to the Housing Construction Promotion Act (currently the Housing Act) for a certain period of time. There was an exception to this rule as a home resale could be approved by the head of the local government, such as a city mayor. This system prevented home buyers from seeking profits from a home resale instead of actually living in the purchased homes.

① Achievements

The housing resale restrictions and the bond bidding system were introduced to control probable demand and to secure national housing funds by the public sector by redeeming the difference between the sale prices and the market prices of a new apartment. The resale restrictions system made a positive contribution to the control of housing prices as well as the restriction of housing speculation.

The repurchase limitation period regulation was a positive measure to distribute house purchase opportunities in an effective and fair manner. The intensity of regulations was adjusted according to market conditions.

Measures such as the bond bidding system or the repurchase limitation system minimized adverse side effects by controlling new house prices in order to keep them at a certain level. Such measures were aimed at preventing speculative demand, setting up housing funds, and, consequently stabilizing housing prices.

3.4.4. Regulation on the Size of New Housing Supply

1) Major Contents

Newly-built housings are required to include a certain number of smaller-sized houses in order to provide a greater supply of housing for lower-income people. The mandatory small-sized housing supply ratio was implemented in 1990 and was applied to houses constructed on privately-owned developable land. However, in 1998, the regulation for privately-owned developable land was abolished and the small-sized housing supply ratio for publicly-owned developable land was categorized into metropolitan areas and other areas.

In addition, it was ordered that each unit of union housing built by the workers union or local union must be smaller than 85 m^2. Furthermore, housing reconstruction associations were allowed to build any size of houses on their own while residential environment improvement projects were required to construct 90% of their houses smaller than 85 m^2.

2) Achievements

The mandatory small-sized housing supply ratio was aimed

at offering opportunities for low-income classes to obtain homeownership. The high increase in small-sized housing supply contributed to improving the housing supply ratio and stabilizing housing prices.

3.4.5. Resident Savings

1) Major Contents

Under the resident savings system, an applicant for homeownership subscribes to the purchase of a house in advance and saves money in the subscription account. It was originally created to raise funding for housing finance, but currently, the residential savings is mainly used to assign qualifications and rank for housing subscription applicants.

The resident savings system consists of four different types, which include comprehensive subscription savings, subscription savings, subscription installment deposits, and subscription term deposits. There is no qualification limit (restriction) to apply for comprehensive subscription savings. The subscription savings are meant for non-homeowners applying for public housing whereas subscription installment deposits and the subscription term deposits are meant for individuals aged 20 years and older to apply for private housing.

Table 26 shows the qualifications for applicants and the characteristics of different resident savings. The subscription term deposits were differentiated by regions and house sizes, depending on housing prices and the regional economic status. A higher amount of deposit is required for individuals in bigger cities or requiring larger size housing.

Table 26 ● Types of resident savings

<table>
<tr><th>Classification</th><th>Comprehensive Subscription Savings</th><th>Subscription Savings</th><th>Subscription installment Deposit</th><th>Subscription Term Deposit</th></tr>
<tr><td>Qualification</td><td>No qualification restrictions</td><td>Non-homeowner</td><td colspan="2">Anyone over20 years old (regardless of homeownership)</td></tr>
<tr><td>Savings Method</td><td>Monthly payments of specific amount along with deposits</td><td>Monthly payments of a specific amount</td><td>Monthly payments of a specific amount</td><td>Lump-sum deposit</td></tr>
<tr><td>Payment Amount</td><td>20,000-500,000 won/ month or one time deposit of less than 15,000,000 won</td><td>20,000-100,000 won/ month</td><td>50,000-500,000 won/ month</td><td>2,000,000-15,000,000 won/month (varies depending on size and location of a house)</td></tr>
<tr><td rowspan="2">Supplied Housing</td><td rowspan="2">All housing</td><td>Housing constructed by public corporations smaller than 85m²</td><td>Private housing smaller than 85 m²</td><td>All private housing</td></tr>
<tr><td colspan="3">Mid-sized (60-85m²) National housing built by private companies</td></tr>
</table>

Table 27 ● Types of subscription term deposits and deposit amounts

(Unit: 1million won)

Net floor area region	Smaller than 85 m^2	Smaller than 102 m^2	Larger than 102 m^2- smaller than 135 m^2	Larger than 135 m^2
Seoul and Busan	3	6	10	15
Other large cities	2.5	4	7	10
Other cities	2	3	4	5

* Once the applicant changes the number of deposits, he/she is not able to change the size of a house again within two years.

(Source: Ministry of Land, Transport and Maritime Affairs, Handbook for Housing Affairs)

2) Achievements

The resident savings system[10] played a significant role in securing housing finance and housing construction funds during periods of the housing shortage.

3.5. Rental Housing Promotion

3.5.1. Backgrounds

In the 1960s and 1970s, the government focused on housing policies that provided more houses for sale and promoted homeownership. However, in the 1980s, the housing policies of the government were geared towards the promotion of rental housing and affordable homes for low-income earners.

3.5.2. Types of Rental Housing

1) Newly-constructed Rental Housing

Newly-constructed rental housing is built with the purpose of providing rental housing. This consists of publicly constructed and

10 Resident Savings - Comprehensive Subscription Savings, Subscription Savings, Subscription Installment Deposit, Subscription Term Deposit

privately constructed rental houses, depending on a government's financial support. Publicly-constructed rental housing is further divided into:

- Constructed rental housing with funding from national or local governments.
- Constructed rental housing with the support of the national housing fund.
- Constructed rental housing on land developed by the public sector.
- Privately-constructed rental housing constructed on land owned (except publicly developed land) by private companies.

2) Purchased Rental Housing

Under the purchased rental housing scheme, housing units built by the private sector are purchased by the public sector lessor and rented out to people in need.

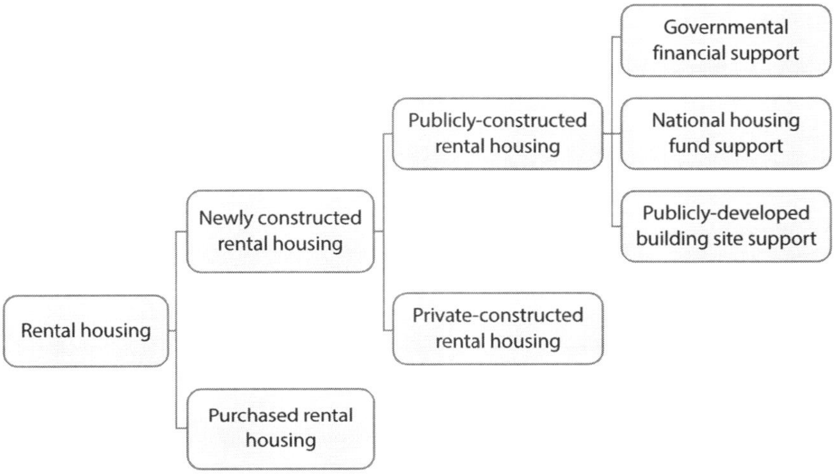

Figure 9 ● The classification of rental housing

3) Major contents

The public sector or private companies with the support of the national housing fund are permitted to build public rental housing. Public rental housing is different from private rental housing as it regulates renters' qualifications, renter selection methods, rent levels, and the terms of its sale after the lease of the housing unit for a certain period.

(1) Regulation Method

Only the head of a household without homeownership is qualified to apply for public rental housing from the announcement date of recruitment until the date of its occupancy. (This regulation was relaxed to give an equal opportunity to all household members in February 2015)

The Regulation on Housing Supply is applied to the tenant selection method for public rental housing. It is up to the private rental business to decide on the lessee's qualification and selection method for private construction rental housing.

Table 28 ● Types and regulations of rental housings by the Rental Housing Act

Classification	Constructed Rental Housing		Purchased Rental Housing
	Publicly-Constructed	Privately-Constructed Rental	
Security deposit and Monthly Payment	"Standard security deposit and monthly payments," limitation on security deposit depending on location (Capital region and the rest of the country) ※ Monthly payments are excluded for medium-sized public rental housing (>85 m^2) and 10-year rental housing built by private construction companies on public building land (< 85 m^2).	Decided by housing rental business entity (no restrictions)	Decided by Housing rental business entity (no restrictions)
Rental Period	5,10,30,50 years	5 years	5 years
Lessee qualification and selection	non-homeowner in accordance with the Regulations on Housing Supply	Decided by Housing rental business entity (no restrictions)	Decided by Housing rental business entity (no restrictions)
Preferential Sale of Rental Housing to Lessee	Household occupying rental housing from the beginning of the lease to sale of rental housing	Decided by housing rental business entity (no restrictions)	Decided by housing rental business entity (no restrictions)
Criteria of Sale Price	In accordance with the Rental Housing Act (Appendix 1) ※ Monthly payments are excluded for medium-size public rental housing (> 85 m^2) and 10-year rental housing built by private construction companies on public building land (< 85 m^2).	Decided by housing rental business entity (no restrictions)	Decided by housing rental business entity (no restrictions)

Classification	Constructed Rental Housing		Purchased Rental Housing
	Publicly-Constructed	Privately-Constructed Rental	
Assistance of National Housing Fund	55~75mil. won/unit, 8mil. won/unit intermediate payment	No assistance	Up to half of house price within 60 mil won/unit
Housing Maintenance	Obligatory maintenance for rental housing with over 300units With elevator and central heating installed		
Extraordinary Repair Allowances	Obligatory maintenance for rental housing with over 300units With elevator and central heating installed		

(Source: Ministry of Land, Transport and Maritime Affairs, Handbook for Housing Affairs)

Table 29 ● The source of finance and occupant qualifications for rental housing

Classification	Types (Business entity)	Bearer of Expenses	Rental Period	Subject(lessee)	Size (net floor area)
Public* Rental Housing	Permanent or 50-year Public Rental Housing (Central and local governments, LH)	Government, local governments, and LH (over 85%) ※ 15% of expenses shared by the occupant	Per-manent	- Low-income recipients of aid under the National Basic Living Security Act - Fatherless families, men of national merit, etc. - other subscription savings depositors	Smaller than 40 m^2
		- Projects from '92-'93: budget 50%, housing fund 20%, lessee 30% - Projects from '94: funding support depending on size	50 years	- Subscription savings depositors - Other special supply recipients ※ Men of national merit, household of deportation, disabled person, etc.	Smaller than 60 m^2

<table>
<tr><th>Classific ation</th><th>Types (Business entity)</th><th>Bearer of Expenses</th><th>Rental Period</th><th>Subject(lessee)</th><th>Size (net floor area)</th></tr>
<tr><td rowspan="3">Public* Rental Housing</td><td>National Rental Housing (LH, Local governments)</td><td>- Budget 10-40%
- Housing fund 40%-50%
- Business entity10%
- Lessee 10%-30%</td><td>30 years</td><td>- Smaller than 50 m^2: householder without home-ownership whose income is under 70% of urban-living worker's average income in the previous year (supply priority for those under 50% of above income average)
- 50~60 m^2 subscription savings depositor whose income is under 70% of urban worker's average income in the previous year (non-homeowner)
- Larger than 60 m^2: subscription savings depositor whose income is under 100% of urban worker's average income in the previous year (non-homeowner)</td><td>Smaller than 85 m^2</td></tr>
<tr><td>5-year, 10-year Public Rental (LH, Local institutes, Private companies)</td><td>- fund assisting depends on the size (smaller than 85 m^2) Small-sized (under60 m^2) 5,500 million won Medium-sized (60-85 m^2) 7,500 million won
- land supplied up to 149 m^2</td><td>5 years, 10 years</td><td>- Homeless householder (subscription savings depositor)</td><td>Smaller than 149 m^2</td></tr>
<tr><td>Employee Rental (same as above)</td><td>- Same as above</td><td>5 years</td><td>- Homeless householder employed in business entities with over 5 employees</td><td>Smaller than 85 m^2</td></tr>
</table>

Classific ation	Types (Business entity)	Bearer of Expenses	Rental Period	Subject(lessee)	Size (net floor area)
Private Rental Housing	Private-constructed Rental (private companies, individuals)	- Business owner and security deposit of lessee	5 years	- Depends on the business entity	No restrictions
	Purchased house to rent housing (individual, corporation)	- Business owner and security deposit of lessee - loans up to 60million won /unit	5 years	- Depends on the business entity	No restrictions

* In public rental housing, privately constructed house supported by the National Housing Fund is included. In this case, governmental finance was not offered to private companies.
(Source: Ministry of Land, Transport and Maritime Affairs, Handbook for Housing Affairs)

The transferor sublease of rental housing is allowed only under the agreement with the lessor while the transferor sublease of permanent or 50-year old public rental housing is prohibited. Constructed rental housing with more than 20 (currently 30) units after the project approval under the Housing Construction Promotion Act (currently Housing Act) can be sold after the compulsory lease period has expired (e.g., for 5 years, 10 years).

(2) Supports for Rental Housing

In developing residential land, over 20% of apartment construction sites are required to supply rental housing smaller than 85 m^2. Developable land for rental housing is supplied at 10% lower than the price of general land for sale.

Table 30 ● Criteria for the price of land supply

Classification	Seoul and Busan Metropolitan Regions		Other Large Cities		Other Regions	
	Sale	Rental	sale	rental	sale	rental
Smaller than 60 m^2	95%	70%	90%	70%	80%	70%
60~85 m^2	appraisal price	95%	appraisal price	80%	appraisal price	70%

* % means a proportion of the actual land development costs
(Source: Ministry of Land, Transport and Maritime Affairs, Handbook for Housing Affairs)

Financing and funding supports as well as various tax incentives for rental housing were promoted. Based on the 2010 national housing fund support statistics, 55 million won (the annual interest rate at 3%) per household were supported for the construction of small-sized (units smaller than 60 m^2) public lease, and 75 million won (the annual interest rate at 4%) per unit (household) were supported for the construction of medium-sized public lease. Additionally, 6 million won (the annual interest rate at 5%) per unit (household) was offered for the procurement of rental housing.[11]

Financial support for the construction of national rental housing includes 30% of governmental finance and 40% of the national housing funds (the annual interest rate at 3%) per unit. In order to lower the interest rate of funding that supports rental housing, the earnings from

11 Loan for rental housing has increased and is still increasing to provide for more assistance to the lower-income people.

the housing lottery issued are re-invested. The housing lottery (the lotto lottery since 2004) had raised funds worth 4,252 billion won until 2009 and the entire fund was used for the construction of rental housing.

The tax benefits for the building of national rental housing include the reduction and exemption of acquisition tax, registration tax (based on Local Tax Reduction Regulation), and capital gains tax (based on Tax Reduction Special Measures Act).

Table 31 ● Criteria of financial and funding support for national rental housing construction (as of 2010)

Year	Classification	Sum	Budget	Housing fund	Developer	Tenant
'98~'02	60~63 m^2	100%	30	40	10	20
'03	Type Ⅰ (46-50) Type Ⅱ (53-60) Type Ⅲ (63-66)	100% 100% 100%	30 20 10	40	10	20 30 40
'04	Type Ⅰ (46-50) Type Ⅱ (53-60) Type Ⅲ (63-66)	100% 100% 100%	40 20 10	40	10	10 30 40
'05~	Type Ⅰ (33-50) Type Ⅱ (53-60) Type Ⅲ (63-66))	100% 100% 100%	40 20 10	40 45 50	10	10 25 30

(3) Achievements

The major change in the rental housing policy was the supply of housing according to income levels based on the Two Million Housing Construction Plan. Figures for the supply of rental housing by the year

2000 show that local governments accounted for 9.3% of rental housing (117,000 households), while the Korea National Housing Corporation (at present LH) commanded 33.8% (427,000 households) and private companies garnered 56.9% (725,000 households), which indicates a high reliance on private companies.

However, recently, the trend has been changing and dependence on the private sector has been reduced while reliance on central government and public corporations has gone up. Between 2001 and 2009, publicly constructed public rental housing accounted for 85% of the total public rental housing, and only 15% of public rental housing was built by private companies. In 2011, privately-constructed rental housing resumed due to the price hike in rental deposits (Chonsei price).

4) Major Contents of the Private Rental Housing System

Since the early 1980s, construction of the private rental housing has been in existence. The over-speculation on the real estate begun in 1977 became more stable and a lot of houses remained unsold. Hence, the government announced the Housing Industry Promotion Program in 1982 as a part of counter-measures for the real estate market, and from this, the construction of private rental housing began.

In 1993, the Rental Housing Construction Promotion Act was rebranded to the Rental Housing Act. Features like the management of rental housing were introduced to protect rental households. The concept of rental housing and leasing business was defined. The rental housing was composed of constructed rental housing and purchased rental housing. The leasing provider was a business provider who rents out rental houses for more than a certain number of units and was required to register with the Minister of Land, Transport, and Maritime Affairs to receive a license for its business operations. Therefore, since 1993, private rental housing construction has increased dramatically and the role of the private sector was enforced.

In 1994, the house rental business system was also introduced to bring about residential stability for rental households. In April 1997, the regulations on tenant selection methods and sale conversion qualification standards for rental housing constructed without the support of the national housing fund were abolished in order to normalize the housing market which was hard hit by the financial crisis in 1997.

3.6. Upgrading of Substandard Housing(Improvement of Urban and Residential Environment)

3.6.1. Background and History

Since the 1960s, cities were faced with urban problems such as urban sprawls, long-distance commutation, traffic congestion, the rise of real-estate prices, lack of infrastructure and pollution due to industrialization and urbanization. To alleviate the side effects of urban sprawl and restore urban functions, a systematic and effective improvement of deteriorated and substandard houses in urban areas was needed.

① Since the mid-1970s, urban redevelopment projects had different legal grounds depending on the objects of the project. For instance, housing redevelopment projects and downtown redevelopment projects were implemented in accordance with the "Urban Redevelopment Law", while substandard housing improvement projects and house reconstruction projects were implemented by the "Residential Environment Improvement Law for Deteriorated Housing" and "Housing Act" respectively.

② In July 2003, the various laws above were consolidated into the "Urban and Residential Environment Improvement Law" to systematically manage redevelopment projects.

③ In March 2005, rental houses were required to be provided either for over 20% of total houses built in residential environment projects or for over 17% of total houses built in redevelopment projects in order to promote residential stability for tenants.

④ In September 2006, development charges were imposed on developmental gains in order to return profits gained by housing redevelopments to society.

⑤ In April 2009, mandatory construction of rental housing for reconstruction projects was abolished and regulations of floor area ratio were relaxed mainly in order to normalize a stagnated housing market.

3.6.2. Major Contents

1) Residential Environment Improvement Project

The Residential Environment Improvement Project renovates deteriorated houses in areas where people on lower incomes live and aims to improve residential environments and the welfare of low-income households. The two ways of implementing redevelopment projects are: 'self-help' approach and compulsory expropriation.

In the case of the 'self-help' approach, residents are expected to physically improve their homes while either a mayor, governor or the LH corporation provides adequate infrastructure including roads and other utilities to the area. The compulsory expropriation is carried out by either the mayor or the LH. However, in this case, at least two-thirds of landowners and half of the tenants must agree with the specific developer.

2) Housing Redevelopment Project

The Housing Redevelopment Project was introduced to improve residential areas with deteriorated housing issues and where significant infrastructure development is needed.[12]

It also defines a district's designation, project planning, action planning, regulations for developers, re-allocation of developed land, and project expenditures. The urban redevelopment project is known for its strict process guidelines and rules because it is regarded as an urban planning project. The project developers can be either:

- Housing association alone or
- The LH (when invited by landowners who own over half of the area in total or invited by over 2/3 of all owners of the area) or
- Housing association and LH, the local government, a builder, or a qualified registered company together.

The implementation process of the redevelopment project includes

12 A traditional redevelopment project was implemented in accordance with the Urban Redevelopment Law to rationally and effectively use lands in the district and to recover urban functions. It covers all businesses related to buildings, site clearance, residential land development, improvement of public facilities, and additional projects.

a comprehensive plan, a redevelopment plan with a district designation, approval from a committee, redevelopment union establishment, selection of a developer, project permission, permission for land reallocation plans, sales, construction completion, and ownership transfer.

3) Housing Rebuilding Project

The housing rebuilding project includes demolishing old, dilapidated houses in a designated district and reconstructing new houses by local homeowners. In this case, the homeowners can work jointly with a home-builder after setting up a self-established association. Thus, the housing rebuilding project is different from the housing redevelopment project.

4) Urban Environment Improvement Project

The urban environment improvement project, which is similar to downtown redevelopments under the previous Urban Redevelopment Law, is undertaken in commercial or industrial areas.

Table 32 ● Comparison of housing improvement projects

Classification	Residential Environment Improvement	Housing Redevelopment	Housing Rebuilding	Urban Environment Improvement
Subject	- Areas with a concentration of deteriorated and substandard low-income dwellings and severely deteriorated infrastructure	- Areas with a concentration of deteriorated and substandard individual housings and deteriorated infrastructure	- Areas with a concentration of deteriorated and substandard public housing with sound infrastructure	- Commercial and industrial areas with a need for recovery of urban functions or commercial vitalization
Developer	- Local Improvement: Mayor, local governor, LH, etc.	- Association	- Association	- Association or landowner
		- LH, etc.	- LH, etc.	- LH, etc.
	- Compulsory Expropriation: local governor, LH, etc.	- Association with local gov., LH, builder, or qualified registered company	- Association with Local gov. or LH	- Association with Local gov., LH or Builder
Size of housing	- Notice made by MLTM. Under 85 m^2: above 90%. Rental housing: above 20%	- Notice made by MLTM. Under 85 m^2: above 80%. Rental housing: 17%	- Notice made by MLTM. Under 85 m^2: above 60%	- No restrictions
Target	- Landowner - Tenant: rental housing - Remaining lots: regular sale	- Landowner - Tenant: rental housing - Remaining lots: regular sale	- Association member (building and included land) - Remaining lots: regular sale	- Landowner
Measures For tenant	- Construction and supply of rental housing for tenants - Support for moving expenses	- Construction and supply of rental housing for tenants - Support for moving expenses	- None	- Support for expenses of moving and compensation for businesses closing temporarily
Public support	- Supported by central and local governments - Free to state- or public-owned land	- Land and building provided by dwellers	- None	- Privilege for disposal of state- or public-owned land

Classification	Residential Environment Improvement	Housing Redevelopment	Housing Rebuilding	Urban Environment Improvement
Land	- Compulsory expropriation (Public housing)	- Land and building provided by dwellers	- Land and building provided by dwellers	- Land and building provided by dwellers

* MLTM: Ministry of Land, Transport and Maritime Affairs (MLTM was renamed as Ministry of Land, Infrastructure and Transport in 2013)

3.6.3. Achievements

1) Performance

As of Dec 31, 2009, there were a total of 2,129 residential improvement projects (917 redevelopment projects, 552 reconstruction projects, 172 urban environment improvement projects, and 488 residential environment improvement projects). From 2001 to 2009, the total area under redevelopment projects was 58,936,584 m^2; 211,000 houses were demolished and 533,000 houses were newly constructed. From 2001 to 2009, there were reconstruction projects for 2,821 associations, 694,800 existing housing units, and 905,000 newly-constructed houses (based on association approval).

2) Effects

(1) Relieving the Housing Shortage in Metropolitan Areas

Housing redevelopment and reconstruction projects resulted in twice as many newly-built houses being built as houses demolished.

(2) Improving Deteriorated Residential Environments

Housing redevelopment projects played a significant role in improving residential environments. In terms of the improvement of the residential environment, the quality of housing was greatly improved. As poor housing areas were redeveloped, the negative image of smaller houses with poor-quality bathrooms altered. Also, the redevelopment of poor housing areas had contributed to the improvement of the residential environment in surrounding areas. Redevelopment attracted more convenience facilities to the areas concerned, for example, small- and medium-sized clinics and supermarkets were introduced, which improved the residential environment.

(3) Increasing Land and House Prices

Once the district was redeveloped, the price of land and houses in the district increased due to speculation in the real estate market.

(4) Revitalizing the Housing Construction Industry

Due to the shortage of available land for houses, redevelopment of old and deteriorated houses contributed to improving the physical environments of existing towns, thereby increasing housing supply and revitalizing the housing market.

3.7. Utilization of Housing Association

3.7.1. Background

In December 1977, the housing association system[13] was created when the workers' union without home-ownership were allowed to construct their own homes under Article 44 of the Housing Construction Promotion Act (currently the Housing Act).

The Housing Construction Promotion Act, revised in 1980, provided legal grounds for housing association organizations, and it helped to facilitate home building. Afterward, related articles in the Act were revised to focus mainly on criteria for qualifications for a member of a housing association. In the beginning, only district associations and workers' associations were institutionalized, but in 1987, the reconstruction association system was introduced. This change to the housing association system was included in the state policies designed to revitalize the housing industry.

3.7.2. Major Contents

The housing association system allows residents and employees without home-ownership to purchase homes by establishing a housing

13 Housing association system: Housing Act #32 - #34 (Currently #11 - #14)

union and building homes regardless of subscription savings accounts. There are different types of associations including workers' associations, district associations, and reconstruction associations.

Workers with no homeownership working for the same company or more than 20 owners of small-sized housing can establish a workers' association for housing. Tenant households in the same or neighboring cities or districts or groups of more than 20 owners of small-sized housing can establish a district association for housing. More than 20 owners of old sub-standard houses can set up a reconstruction association to demolish the existing houses and construct new houses.

To become a member of a local association, the head of a household has to be either a tenant from the date of the application for approval of the establishment of an association until the move-in date or an owner of a house smaller than 60 m^2. In addition, the membership is limited to those whose repurchase limitation period has already lapsed. Besides, the residence requirement should be fulfilled, i.e. he/she has to reside in association establishment approval areas or in adjacent cities or districts on the date of the application for an association establishment approval.

In the case of the member of a workers association, almost all the requirements are the same as above. However, instead of a residence requirement, there is a worker status requirement, i.e. he/she to be employed in the same governmental entities, local autonomous entities, or corporate entities in the city or district in which the association is located.

The reconstruction association is meant for old substandard house owners including land attached to the additional facilities (when one household owns more than 2 homes or more than 2 persons have joint ownership for one house, they are considered as one member of the housing association).

When the employer of an association or employees constructs houses for its members or employees, the housing association or the employee by themselves cannot alone be the main developer and they must construct houses together with a legitimately registered developer.

3.7.3. Achievements

The housing association system is either for small-sized homeowners or tenants to provide opportunities to have their own homes. It provides houses for members of workers' or local associations established. The housing associations system has contributed reasonably to the improvement of residential environments and in providing home-ownership for low-income households since the 1970s.

In the housing association, the tenants have the advantage of relatively affordable house prices compared to the general house prices, and favorable subscription qualifications are given without a subscription savings account. The housing association system also contributed to the facilitation of home-ownership for low- and middle-income homes.

3.8. Supply of 'Bogeumjari Housing' and 'Urban Lifestyle Housing'[14]

3.8.1. Bogeumjari Housing

1) Background

In September 2008, the Bogeumjari Housing[15] construction program was introduced to provide various types of houses to meet the demands of different income levels instead of a supply-side housing policy. Bogeumjari Housing includes all the publicly-built small- and medium-sized houses for sale and rental houses. The public sector builds Bogeumjari houses with financial support from budgets and the NHF and then sells or rents them to eligible applicants.

2) Major Contents

The Bogeumjari Housing plan was scheduled to build 600,000 housing units in the Capital Region by 2012 and to provide a total of 1.5 million housing units by 2018, which includes 1 million units in the

14 Bogeumjari Housing' and 'Urban Lifestyle Housing'are discussed in more detail in Chapter 5, 5.2.2.

15 Bogeumjari housing: Houses for sale or rental houses supplied by the LH with the support of budget and National Housing Fund in order to solve the housing problem for the low income class in large cities like Seoul.(Bogeumjari means nest or home in Korean)

capital region and 500,000 units in the rest of the country.

The provision plan is comprised of 700,000 housing units under 85 m^2, the national standard housing size, for sale and 800,000 housing units for rent. The housing units for sale are provided at a lower price than those in the surrounding areas mainly through the construction of houses in the green-belt zone. The provision plan includes 100,000 permanent rental housings for low-income households, 400,000 national rental housings, and 100,000 long-term rental housings.

A new subscription method under which 80% of the houses for sale are sold with an advance reservation was introduced[16], and this helps expedite the process, which is faster than the existing selling method.

In 2009, the Special Law on Bogeumjari Housing Construction was enacted to streamline the process for land development and housing construction. Consequently, this laid the foundation of a fast Bogeumjari housing supply.

3) Achievements

As of 2010, Bogeumjari Housing has provided a total of 185,000 housing units, including 39,000 units in the first Bogeumjari

16 Advance reservation: When the public developer such as the LH announces a comprehensive plan combined with the construction of several complexes, the subscriber is requested to choose 3 houses in the order of his/her preference to enroll in an advance reservation. Advance reservation is available within one year before a regular subscription.

development site (model complex), 3,000 units in Ui-rea New Town (Southeast area of Seoul) and 41,000 units, 86,000 units, and 16,000 units respectively in the second, third and fourth Bogeumjari development sites. The 2011 housing provision plan aims for 97,000 rental housing units and 53,000 housing units for sale.

Bogeumjari Housing relieved development restrictions on the green-belt zone to provide lower land prices than the market price and contributed to the stabilization of the housing market with promotion of homeownership for low-income households. However, there was criticism that Bogeumjari Housing led to the increase in lease deposits (Chonsei) due to the long list of families waiting for the Bogeumgari housing subscription.

3.8.2. Urban Lifestyle Housing

1) Background

In May 2009, in order to supply affordable housing for 1 or 2 person households in the city, the Urban Lifestyle housing became available with either loosened building codes and installation criteria for additional facilities or exemptions from these codes and criteria.[17]

17 Urban Lifestyle Housing is allowed only in urban areas.

2) Major Contents

Urban Lifestyle Housing is composed of less than 150 units of houses smaller than 85 m^2 of net floor area, equivalent to the size of national standard housing. It also consists of three different types: multi-family units in a complex (smaller than 85 m^2 of net floor area), studio type (12~30 m^2), and dormitory type (7~20 m^2).

- A multi-family unit in a complex should be smaller than 85 m^2 of net floor area and lower than 4 stories, and the total area of the complex should be less than 660 m^2. However, an additional floor could be built if approved by the construction committee.
- A studio type has a net floor area between 12 m^2~50 m^2 equipped with an individual kitchen and bathroom in the unit, but the unit is to be constructed as one main room for living and sleeping beside the bathroom.
- A dormitory-type has a net floor area between 7~30 m^2 equipped with a communal kitchen, bathroom, laundry, and lounges.[18]

18 Dormitory type Urban Lifestyle Housing was abolished in July 2010.
The Urban Lifestyle Housing is different from a general apartment building in a sense that several housing regulations are not applicable. For example, it is exempted from construction supervision under the Housing Act, sales price limit, regulations on subsidiary facilities such as management offices, play grounds, senior citizen centers, noise standards, distance between buildings and roads and landscape in the complex, etc.

Chapter 4

Achievements of Housing Policy in Korea

4.1. Alleviation of Housing shortages

Korea has achieved economic growth and urbanization in a short span of time, resulting in a concentration of population in urban areas and a high increase in the number of households, and consequently shown acute housing shortages. In 1960, the housing supply ratio was rather high at 84.2%. In 1985, the ratio was reduced to 69.8%. The housing problem was getting worse due to persistent problems in housing shortages.

However, the Two Million Housing Units Construction from the late 1980s and continuous housing provision in large quantities helped to relieve the problems associated with an absolute shortage of housing in the nation. Thus, the housing supply ratio was greatly improved to 105.9% (98.3% as per new housing supply ratio) in 2005 and 111% (101.2% as per new housing supply ratio) in 2010, and the housing problem was eased to a great extent. The Two Million Housing Units Construction Plan played a significant role in alleviating problems caused by the housing shortage.

Table 33 ● Changes in housing supply ratio

Years	1960	1970	1975	1980	1985	1990	1995	2000	2005	2010
%	84.2	78.2	74.4	71.2	69.8	72.4	86.0	96.2	105.9 (98.3)*	111 (101.2)*

* Housing supply ratio = number of housing units/ number of households,
* New housing supply ratio=number of housing units (including multi-family housing) / number of households (including one-person households) used for 2005 and 2010.
(Source: Ministry of Land, Transport and Maritime Affairs, Handbook for Housing Affairs)

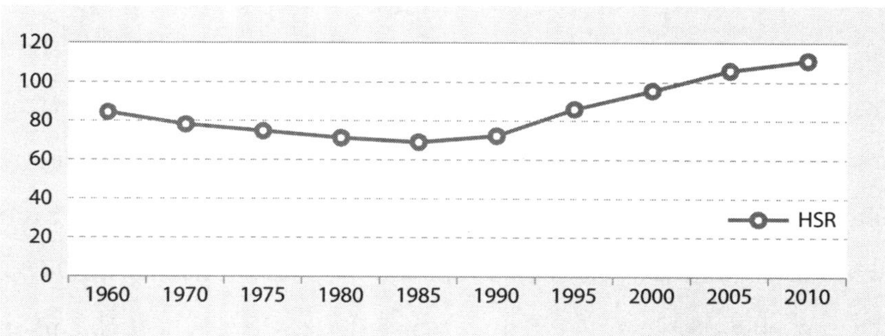

Figure 10 ● Changes in housing supply ratio
(Source: Ministry of Land, Transport and Maritime Affairs, Handbook for Housing Affairs)

The percentage of housing construction was only approximately 37% to 44% of housing requirements in the 1960s, about 61% to 75% in the 1970s, and 62% in the early 1980s. In the late 1980s, the percentage of construction reached 95% of housing requirements and rose to 151% of requirements in the early 1990s. It, thus, alleviated the housing shortage largely. In the late 1990s, housing construction percentage rose to approximately 110% (114.3% in the early 2000s) and the quantity of housing supply exceeded the housing requirements. Therefore, the period of the 2000s can be regarded as a housing over-supply period as against the period of housing shortage prior to the year 2000.

Table 34 ● Housing built vs. housing requirements[1] (Unit: thousand / %)

Classification	'61~ '66	'67~ '70	'71~ '75	'76~ '80	'81~ '85	'86~ '90	'91~ '95	'96~ '00	'01~ '05
Housing* requirements (A)	1,039	931	1,180	1,523	1,647	2,180	2,069	2,121	2,357
Net Increase of household	806	673	897	1,215	1,602	1,783	1,604	1,354	-
Loss of Housing	233	258	283	308	345	397	465	598	-
Housing built (B)	386	410	721	1,136	1,017	2,062	3,126	2,333	2,709
B/A (%)	37.2	44.0	61.1	74.6	61.7	94.6	151.0	110.0	114.9

* Housing loss ratio is assumed to be 1.3% a year
(Source: Ministry of Land, Transport and Maritime Affairs, Handbook for Housing Affairs)

1 Housing requirement: Number of housing net increased loss of housing

4.2. Improvement of Housing Quality

The quality of housing has been improved along with the alleviation of housing shortages. Since the 1980s, a large number of apartments, fitted and decorated with modern interiors, were constructed in big cities. Through housing redevelopment projects, the existing old substandard houses were demolished and new houses were built. A series of urban redevelopment projects, such as housing redevelopment projects, reconstruction projects, and residential environment improvement projects, contributed to the improvement of housing standards.

The table below shows the annual changes in dwelling standards between 1975 and 2005 including average size per housing, dwelling area per person, number of rooms used, bathroom, toilets, etc. The number of housing per 100 people increased from 13.7 units in 1975 to 27.9 units in 2005 and the average house size increased by 1.8 times from 47.7 m^2 in 1975 to 83.8 m^2 in 2000. The dwelling area per person increased by 2.8 times from 8.2 m^2 in 1975 to 22.8 m^2 in 2000 and the number of rooms used per person increased from 0.43 in 1975 to 0.8 in 2000.

Table 35 ● Changes in dwelling standards by year

Classification	1975	1980	1985	1990	1995	2000	2005
Number of houses per100 persons (unit)	13.7	14.2	15.1	17.9	20.7	23.7	27.9
Average size per housing (m^2)	47.7	68.4	75.7	80.9	82.8	83.8	-
Dwelling area per person(m^2)	8.2	10.1	11.8	14.3	17.2	20.1	22.8
Rooms available per person(unit)	0.43	0.47	0.51	0.71	0.9	1.1	0.8
Bathtub installation (hot water, %)	-	10.0	20.0	34.1	75.1	87.4	95.8
Flush toilet (%)	-	18.4	33.6	51.3	75.0	86.9	94.0
Stand-up type kitchen (%)	-	18.2	35.1	52.4	84.5	93.9	97.9

(Source: National Statistical Office, Population and Residence Census, Each year)

Housing facilities were also significantly improved. The installation of hot water in the bathroom increased greatly from 10% in 1980 to 95.8% in 2005, and the installation of flush toilets rose from 18.4% to 94.0% during the same period. In 2005, 97.9% of housing had stand-up kitchens, showing a great positive shift in the housing facilities and dwelling units.

4.3. Stabilization of Housing Markets and Housing Prices

4.3.1. Housing Market Stabilization

Over the past several decades, Korea had experienced a housing supply shortage which has been one of the reasons for the high price of housing in many big cities. The housing speculation tendency has been also another reason to exacerbate unstable housing prices in the market. Therefore, several measures to stabilize the housing market had been continuously implemented. On November 29, 1967, the Special Measures for Real Estate Speculation Prevention Act was enacted to increase housing market stability. Additionally, economic policies such as 'Contingency Policy for Price Stabilization' on November 3, 1969, and 'Economic Stability Policy' on January 7, 1970, were implemented.

However, housing prices skyrocketed in the late 1970s due to real estate speculation. The government introduced the housing sale price control system and put into effect to stabilize housing price in 1977. On May 10, 1978, the Housing Supply Regulation was also enacted and the government began to involve in regulating the housing sale more directly. Despite such efforts, stabilizing the housing prices was still difficult. As a result, the 'Real Estate Speculation Prevention Measures' (also known as 8/8 measures) were announced on Aug. 8, 1978.

The main contents of the 8/8 measures are:

① License system on the real estate agent.

② Improvement of property registration.

③ Heavy tax on capital gain by property transfer.

④ Heavy tax on non-business purpose property.

⑤ Establishment of a Land Development Corporation.

The implementation of these regulations brought the stabilization of housing prices to some extent, on one hand, it resulted in a decrease in housing supply on the other hand. Hence, the government introduced various approaches to expand the market and boost the level of housing transactions. These are housing market revitalization measures on June 5, 1980, taxation relief measures on June 26, 1981, extension of the capital gains tax exemption period and improvement of housing funding loans on January 4, 1982, and reduction of the resale limitation period for the national housing (from 2 years to 6 months).

However, due to such measures, the housing market became overheated again. Less than a year since the revitalization measures were taken, the resale limitation period for the national housing was again extended from 6 months to 2 years in Seoul and other specific regions on December 22, 1982. In April 1983, new measures like the national housing bond purchase system for private housing and the designation of an overheating speculation zone were introduced.

The Regulation for National Housing Priority Supply, the precursor of Housing Supply Regulation, was enacted in August 1977 which prohibited the simultaneous purchase of two new houses. In 1978, the above clause in the regulation was temporarily relaxed and modified to no more than two housing purchases in 3 years. In 1983, the limitation period was extended in order to prevent subscribers to purchase new houses more than twice in 5 years for national housing and 3 years for private housing. In November 1984, the limitation period was extended to no more than one housing purchase in 10 years for the national housing and 5 years for the private housings. In 1989, the prohibition period for purchasing new housing more than once was extended to every district in all cities and the regulations became stricter by preventing the purchase of new housing with the name of the spouse within 10 years.

The government maintained such regulations for more than 10 years but in the late 1990s, the level of unsold houses increased and the housing market became stagnant which in a way prevented the government to keep these regulations. In 1997, the restriction on multiple-homeownership was no longer applied to districts except the Capital region. In 1998, after the restriction on multiple-homeownership was maintained for 15 years, the restriction period was revised again from 10 years to 5 years for purchasing the national housing and from 5 years to 2 years for the private housing in an attempt to increase housing demand.

In March 2000, the restrictive period of purchasing multiple housing for the national housing was abolished. Furthermore, an opportunity for housing purchase was granted to households without homeownership regardless of their housing purchase history. Such actions are due to a decreased level of housing transaction in the market and a low level of housing demand after the Asian financial crisis in the late 1990s.

In summary, a number of measures against real estate speculation were aimed to prevent the real estate market to be overheated and to achieve housing market stability. While these measures were implemented temporarily and partially based on the conditions of the housing market, such effort did help expand the housing supply and stabilize house prices for the Korean public.

4.3.2. House Price Stabilization

The housing market has remained unstable since the 1960s. As a chronic housing shortage led to the increase in housing price, it confirms that housing shortage moves in tandem with the instability in housing price. Furthermore, since the government's much effort to prevent speculation aimed to stabilize housing prices, it partially hindered the revitalization of the housing market and led to a vicious cycle of housing problems and a decrease in housing supply.

The housing prices became stable since 1990. The Two Million Housing Units Construction Plan began to be implemented in several stages from 1988 and showed successful outcomes since 1990. The rise of housing prices since 1960 became stable, which resulted in the stabilization of the housing market.

One of the key elements to stabilize the house price was the large provision of houses and the government's effort to maintain the demand-side housing policy, such as establishing policy priorities to supply for first-time buyers and speculation prevention measures through the setting up of computerized housing network. For example, table 36 shows that, while the housing sales price rose 11.5% in 1988 and 19% in 1990, it declined by an average of 0.8% annually from 1990 to 1997. Although there was an abrupt change in such trends at the end of the 1990s due to the financial crisis, the market remained stable in the long term at least until the mid-2000s. Such results show that the Korean government's effort contributed to the stability of housing prices.

Table 36 ● Changes in housing price

Classification	'88	'89	'90	'91	'92	'93	'94	'95	'96	'97	'98	'99	'00	'05	'10
Selling price	78.8	90.3	109.3	108.7	103.3	100.3	100.2	100.0	101.5	103.5	90.7	93.8	94.2	128.1	148.4
Leasing price	59.9	70.4	82.2	83.8	90.1	92.3	96.5	100.0	106.5	107.4	87.6	102.3	113.7	136.8	158.1

(Source: Ministry of Land, Transport and Marine Affairs, Handbook for Housing Affairs)

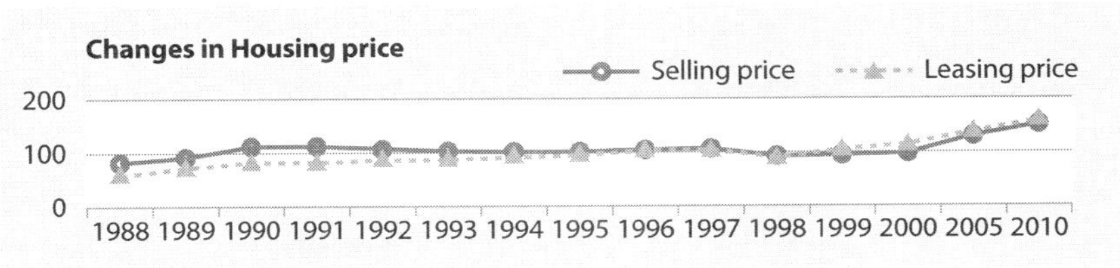

Figure 11 ● Changes in selling and leasing price of housing

4.4. Housing Supply and Demand Control through Supports and Regulation

The ultimate goal for housing policy is to stabilize the housing price and maintain a healthy demand-supply relation in the housing market as well as providing affordable housing to residents. To that end, the Korean government aimed to provide sufficient housing to alleviate the housing shortage, stabilize house prices, and provide a number of small-sized houses for first-home buyers.

4.4.1. Financial Supports and Land Development

1) Financial Supports

One of the key financial supports to achieve housing policy goals is support for housing construction through the national housing fund. The maximum rate for a loan per housing unit was varied depending on the type and size of houses. From 1981 to 2009, the national housing fund supported 4,234,000 housing units, taking account of 32.5% of new houses constructed over time.

Table 37 ● The number of housing built through the support of the National Housing Fund (Unit: number of houses, %)

Period	Housing built supported by NHF (A)	Total houses built (B)	ratio A/B
1981-1990	1,007,886	3,078,316	32.7
1991-2000	2,089,148	5,458,606	38.3
2001-2009	1,137.845	4,487,585	25.4
Sum	4,234,879	13,024,507	32.5

(Source: Ministry of Land, Transport and Marine Affairs, Handbook for Housing Affairs)

In the 1980s, almost 1/3 of newly built housing (1,008,000 units out of 3,078,000 units of housing) was constructed with the national housing fund scheme. It supported 2,089,000 units out of 5,459,000 units of housing in the 1990s and 1,138,000 units out of 4,488,000 units in the 2000s, which accounted for 38.3% and 25.4% of the total number of houses constructed respectively. Thus, the national housing fund contributed to achieving the goal of the government's policy to alleviate housing problems significantly.

In addition, the dwelling standards have been improved with the support of the national housing fund. The net floor area of houses supported by the national housing fund was 3.8 m^2 larger than that of previously-built houses and the number of private rooms increased by 0.4%. Houses supported by the national housing fund also showed improvements in interior facilities: setting up of modern-styled kitchen by 33.2%, flush toilet by 33.9%, hot water bathroom by 49.5% and modern heating system by 50.5%, in consequence, the dwelling standard also greatly improved.

2) Support for Developable Land

In addition to financial supports for newly constructed houses, the public sector also took the responsibility of providing necessary developable land for housing construction which laid the foundation for efficient housing construction. To do this, the Developable Land Development Promotion Act was enacted and came into force.

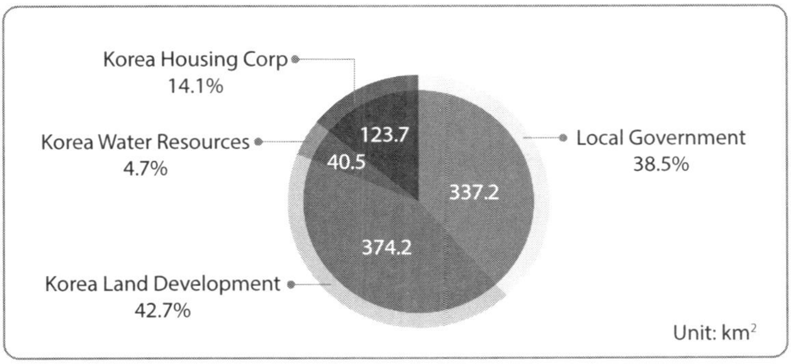

Figure 12 ● Supply of developed land by respective business entities (1982~2009)
(Source: Ministry of Land, Transport and Marine Affairs, Handbook for Housing Affairs)

The total land developed between 1982 and 2009 (for 28 years) after the enactment of the Housing Land Development Promotion Act, was 875.6 km^2 with an average annual land development of 30.2 km^2. Such a land development by the public sector contributed to the massive construction of houses within a short period of time.

The land readjustment, previously used in land development, was not able to meet a high demand due to the lengthy process of land readjustment. However, public development made a large quantity of housing construction possible by across-the-board land purchase and prompt land development within a short period of time. The public sector has provided an annual average land development area of 30.2 km^2 for 28 years. It is estimated that the quantity of land provided by the public sector accounted for approximately 30% of the land required for housing construction. In other words, the role of the public sector in obtaining the basic element for building houses for the public was very crucial.

4.4.2. Sale Price Control and Regulations on Project Approval

1) Sale Price Control

The housing market before the 1980s was relatively geared towards the supplier due to the constant imbalance in the housing supply and demand. As a result, the central government intervened actively in the market with regulations for sale price control and with policies to promote home-ownership and protect the rights of consumers in the supply chain and allocation of houses.

The regulations for sale price control for newly-built housing played a significant role in providing affordable houses for low- and middle-income non-homeowners who experienced difficulties in purchasing a house due to the supplier-oriented housing market and high land price. Since the regulations offered the opportunities to purchase a house for low- and medium-income households with a lower price than the actual market price, it benefited those groups of people (without houseownership) significantly. On the other hand, some critics argued that the regulations for sale price control generated sale premiums for new houses and created speculative demand for houses and thus resulted in an abnormal housing market for homeownership. However, others viewed that due to the fact that such speculative demand was there, the dramatic increase of housing construction was possible.

The regulations also helped to expand financial resources in the housing market. With the extra support from the government, people actively applied for housing subscription savings, deposits, and installments to purchase a house that was supplied at an affordable price. By the end of 2009, 13.910 million accounts (23.2383 trillion won; USD 20.2 billion) were opened, which accounted for 30.2% of the newly-raised national housing fund.

In addition, at the time of bidding for bonds under sale price regulation, the compulsory purchase of second-type national housing bonds was implemented and, through this, the national housing fund raised 3,236.3 billion won between April 1983 and July 1999 and 1,802.9 billion won between 2006 and 2009 (This program was available between in April 1983 and July 1999 and reintroduced in February 2006). Such kinds of support allowed construction companies to obtain funds for house construction and to build more houses.

2) Project Approval

The housing developers were required to get project approval from the government when they planned to build more than 20 units (currently 30 units) of apartments or houses. Once the project was approved, they needed to adhere to several regulations such as regulations of the sale price, size regulations, housing construction standards, and supply method regulations under the Housing Construction Promotion Law (currently Housing Act). The approval included the changes in land use under the law on urban planning, and obtaining 44 different permissions and approvals under 24 different laws.

When the project developer intended to build houses that exceeded a certain size of land area, a comprehensive project plan was required to be prepared and receive preceding approval since various subsidiary and welfare facilities should be installed together in this case. It was also expected to include the organizations of a housing complex in the project plan.

Initially, the plan approval aimed at the projects with more than 100 households, but it gradually expanded to the projects with more than 20 households. It also was reinforced to regulate the installation of subsidiary facilities. Such modifications of the law reflected social changes and improving residential environments as well as raising the standard of individual housing.

While the main facilities, except for facilities in the housing complex, are supposed to be installed or built by the local government, local governments with insufficient finance at the time of project approval allowed the private housing developers to install or build main facilities in the form of land donation.

4.5. Residential Stability for the Low-Income Class

By reflecting housing policy in the 1960s and 1970s, those policies were not designed to benefit the low-income class. Even though the Public Housing Act was enacted in 1963 with the purpose of improving public welfare and stabilizing resident's life by providing affordable houses to the tenants, it was replaced by the Housing Construction Promotion Act (currently the Housing Act) in 1972 which it did not play any substantial role for the low-income households.

In 1984, the Rental Housing Construction Promotion Act was enacted, which was totally revised and replaced with the Rental Housing Act in 1993. This law played a significant role in providing affordable housing for the low-income class. The public sector was in charge of rental housing supply for the low-income class while the private sector provided rental housing focusing on the middle-income class. The first housing supply plan established for the low-income class was the 250,000 permanent rental housing construction plan announced as part of the Two Million Unit Construction Plan. As a result, 190,000 permanent rental housing units were constructed.

From April 1989, more affordable housings for the low-income households were provided in major cities with rental housing for tenants in housing redevelopment districts and residential environment improvement districts. From 1990, rental housing for workers without homeownership began to be built, and approximately 73,000 housing units were constructed until 2008. The provision of rental housing was one of the most effective programs for the low-income class. Approximately 2.1 million rental housing units were constructed from 1982 to 2008, accounting for 16.6% of total housing.

Table 38 ● Rental housing construction performance (1982~2008)

(Unit: number of a house)

Housing construction performance In total		Rental housing			
		Sum (Component ratio)	Public-rental	Permanent-rental	Employer-rental
12,792,883 (100%)		2,117,258 (16.6%)	1,850,729	190,077	76,452
Rental housing	Public org.	1,264,545	1,074,468	190,077	-
	Private company	852,713	776,261	-	76,452

* Public rental housing: long-term rental housing from 1982 to 1991, public rental housing since 1992 (Except Chonsei rental housing)

(Source: Ministry of Land, Transport and Marine Affairs, Handbook for Housing Affairs)

4.6. Development of Housing Industry

In order to solve the chronic housing shortage, the government enacted the Housing Construction Promotion Act in 1972. This law played a crucial role in breaking down old practices of building his/her own house individually and promoting the building of modern houses for both the private enterprises and the government-provided housing units. This means that the central and local governments, public corporations, and private businesses participated in housing construction altogether. While each one of them had relatively different roles and goals, their efforts all added up to tackle the housing problems. In particular, with different goals, the public and private sectors in a way constructed different housing units and had their own roles and contributions.

The public and private sectors together built 16,350,000 housing units from 1973 to 2009 since the Housing Construction Promotion Act (currently the Housing Act) came into force. The public sector constructed 5,510,000 units accounting for 33.7% of the total number of houses, and the private sector constructed 10,840,000 units, accounting for 66.3% of all.

In particular, during the Two Million Unit Housing Construction Plan period between 1988 and 1992, 2,717,000 housing units, an average of 543,000 housing units per year, were constructed. Out of this, the public sector built 905,000 housing units (33.3%) and the private sector built 1,812,000 housing units (66.7%). This clearly shows the important role of the private sector in housing construction and their contribution.

Moreover, 543,000 housing units were newly built every year after the implementation of the Housing Construction Promotion Act, which was 3.8 times more than the houses built before 1987 (prior to the Two Million Unit Housing Construction period), 142,000 units. This suggests the contribution of a great amount of housing supply from the national housing construction industry and housing market.

Table 39 ● Housing construction by period (Unit: thousand)

	1973~2009	1988~1992
Total	16,350 (100%)	2,717 (100%)
Public sector	5,510 (33.7%)	905 (33.3%)
Private sector	10,840 (66.3%)	1,812 (66.7%)

(Source: Ministry of Land, Transport and Maritime Affairs)

PART II

Main Issues of Housing Policy in Korea: (2011~)

Chapter 5

Housing Demand and Supply

5.1. Housing Market and Demand in Korea

5.1.1. Market Changes and Its Effect

In the housing market, there are large numbers of suppliers and buyers and these market players play important roles to determine the optimum price and quantity by mutual agreement. Excessive demand or supply often brings an unstable market characterized by either a sharp increase or a sudden drop in housing prices. In other words, the 'discrepancy or imbalance between supply and demand' causes market instability.

The process of supplying houses is inflexible or slow compared to the shift of demand for housing. This can be due to various accounts including population growth, migration, and even the preference of people. Such different features of housing demand and supply often produce an imbalance in the housing market. Furthermore, domestic and foreign economic fluctuations in recent years have become another influential factor amplifying the agitation of housing supply and demand. If this kind of instability continues for a substantial period of time, it can cause various problems such as personal economic damage, ill effects on the national economy and society, and so on.

For example, if demand is larger than supply, i.e. D > S, then housing prices and rents will rise, which causes hardships, particularly for low-income people. On the contrary, if demand is smaller than supply, i.e. D < S, then housing price will drop and the market will be stagnated, and this situation will lead to hardship for homeowners and small-scale businessmen.

5.1.2. Changes in Housing Market and Demand in Korea

As explained in the Housing in Korea section, there was a prolonged housing price surge, especially from the end of the 1980s for 20 years. To cope with this hike in housing prices, the Korean government intervened actively with various approaches in the housing market. However, there were limitations in this active intervention, which caused various side effects. Hence, this period is often labeled as 'the age of active but inefficient government intervention'. At that time, the government introduced a variety of policy measures including taxation, financial support, regulation, and direct supply of land and housing. Furthermore, demand restraint or control policies were sometimes used as a key policy measure.

Meanwhile, housing demand in Korea was strongly influenced by the expected appreciation of properties and speculation in addition to the usefulness of housing consumption (e.g. convenience of living). Housing demand tended to be dominated by speculative investment to a great extent in this period. This excess speculative demand sometimes made an abnormal demand curve as seen in Figure 13.

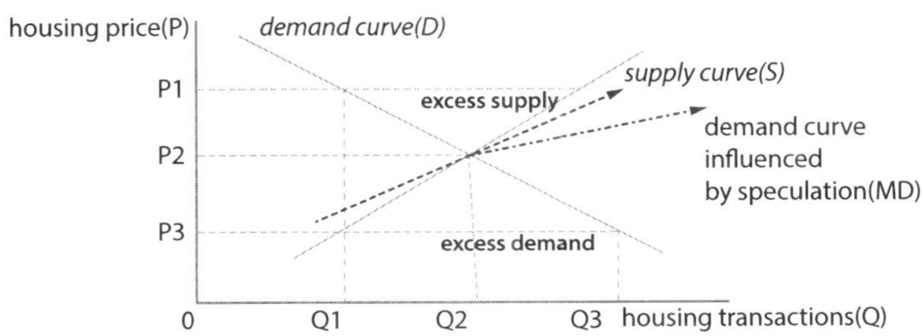

Figure 13 ● Reversed demand curve

This graph exhibits how the abnormal demand curve appears. The solid line is a normal demand (ND) curve. However, there is another demand curve (dotted line) representing the speculative demand (SD) and SD increases sharply with the rise of housing price or even with the possibility of price rises. By the influence of SD, the slope of the demand curve becomes flattened, presenting with a double dotted line in the graph. When the demand reaches a certain point, SD becomes bigger than ND, and then the modified demand (MD) begins to rise once again despite the high price. In short, the force of speculation makes the demand curve out of normal trajectory showing the increase, not decrease, of demand with the growth of the price.

This phenomenon can be appeared in various markets in the forms of value in use and value in exchange. Analysts have explained these terms with commodity market and asset market (Cooper, 2008). The market consists of commodity market (CM) and asset market (AM), i.e. M= CM + AM. Here AM refers to either the possibility of investment or the value expected to be obtained through investment. If the weight of AM is bigger than CM (i.e. AM> CM), then due to the imbalance between supply and demand, the price of a commodity can be twisted.

5.1.3. Recent Demand Changes and Challenges in the Korean Housing Market

After the global economic crisis in 2008, housing prices and transactions rate fell in the Korean housing market for several years. Such a situation has prompted the concern of the chain reaction given that the decline of housing prices could lead to a decrease in housing transactions and consequently lowering housing demand. This contraction of housing demand also increased the demand and price of rental housing as a side effect. Such a situation was thought to lead to additional pressure accelerating the precipitation of housing prices. If this process continues for a substantial period, then the endless negative loop can take place which will impair not only the housing market but also the national economy.

Another phenomenon worth noting was that Chonsei housing was changing into monthly rental housing. Due to this change in the rental market, the housing situation of low-income families was exacerbated as they had to move from Chonsei, guaranteed by lump-sum deposit, to monthly rent requesting a low deposit or no deposit but asking for a higher monthly rent.

Furthermore, speculative demand continued to remain as an obstacle to market stabilization. When the housing market is stagnating, the middle- or higher-income people who can afford to buy a house would not purchase unless they can expect a substantial amount of profit from the housing price hike.

However, things have changed since the end of 2015. The housing market began to boil since that time. In particular in Seoul, the market showed an exceptional surge in housing prices. The main reason for this boom can be summarized as the shortage of housing supply in the city center, and the expectation of floor space ratio increase by housing rebuilding. On top of that, speculative demand was added especially in the Gangnam housing market.

Facing this new housing market situation, the Korean government made a series of housing market stabilization policies. A series of policy packages including the 8.2 policy package (2017), 12.16 package (2019) 6.17 package (2020), etc. have been announced by the Korean government. These packages consisted of various fiscal, financial, tax, and regulative measures such as:

- Increase of capital gains tax rate, strengthening of the conditions for mortgage loans, lowering of LTV and DTI levels;
- Tightening of regulations on the rebuilding of apartment sites;
- Designation of Speculation Control Areas in Seoul and neighboring localities.

In short, Korean people had to confront another overheating housing market, even at the beginning of the 2020s.

The following two graphs show the changes in the sales price and

Chonsei price in Seoul and the whole nation. Here, Chonsei price means the amount of Chonsei deposit. In these graphs, we can find that, in the depression period between 2010 and 2014, Chonsei price was rising, while sales price was stable. However, conversely, in the booming period since 2015, housing sales price has been rapidly rising especially in Seoul, while Chonsei price was showing no significant movement.

Figure 14 ● Changes of the sales price and Chonsei price in the whole nation
(Source: MOLIT, Korea Appraisal Board)

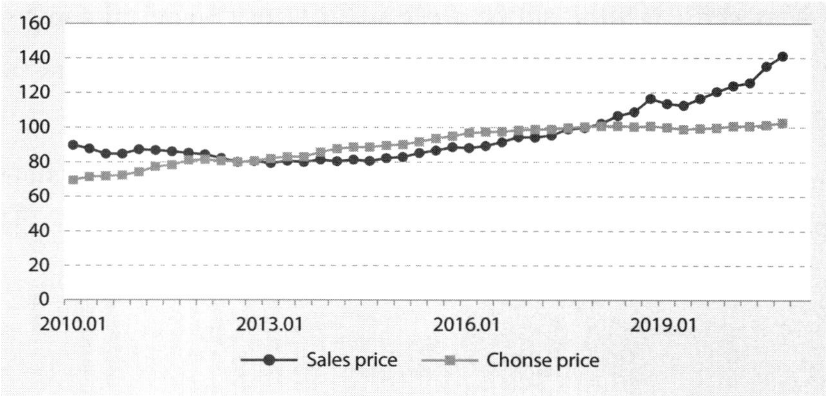

Figure 15 ● Changes of the sales price and Chonsei price in Seoul
(Source: MOLIT, Korea Appraisal Board)

5.2. Housing supply policy

5.2.1. Necessity

Housing supply includes the supply of newly-built houses and existing houses for a transaction. In that aspect, housing suppliers consist of developers who provide newly-built housings and the owners of existing housings. The numbers of demolished housings for substitution should be subtracted from existing housings. Between the two housing markets, the government tends to intervene more frequently in the newly-built housing market.

Policy measures to affect the supply of housing are often considered to be vital as they can adjust housing market imbalance and subsequent price fluctuations. They can also help to stimulate or tranquilize the macro-economy in time. For example, when the economy is in a downturn, the government tends to try to boost the economy by spending more money on housing. As a result, the housing supply policy through the government expenditure tends to show the reverse movement against a general economic cycle.

Then what can be the main drivers that the government uses housing supply policy as a tool to boost or stabilize the national economy? The main reason can be a high multiplier effect of expenditure on housing. The government can expect additional effects of job creation and production growth by supporting housing construction.[1] The effect of job creation and the enhanced production by a certain amount of investment is much higher in the construction industry including house building than in other industries. Specifically, the production increase in the construction industry per unit expenditure was 1.95, while that of the whole industry was 1.79 in 2019 in Korea. As for job creation, the construction industry created 10.8 jobs with an investment of 1 billion won, compared to 10.1 jobs for the whole industry in 2019 (Bank of Korea, Input-output table). For this reason, the Korean government

---

1 This seems to be true for most of countries since the house building necessitates various kinds of inputs such as materials, labor, electric devices, water resources, and so on.

has tended to count on a housing supply policy to boost or restrain the economy. Therefore, such a policy is often shown when the status of the economy is uncertain or in a downturn.

As explained in previous chapters, housing policy in Korea has focused on massive supply over the past few decades. On average 500,000 housing units are planned to be built every year. However, the effect of policy measures during this time has been relatively different from what has been presumed. This is partly due to the price limit on newly built housing. It is often viewed that the restriction on house prices brings excessive demand. Excessive demand naturally results in the pressure of price increase in the market, and this situation leads to another strengthened price limit. This process as a whole causes a different type of vicious circle.

5.2.2. Housing Construction and Supply - Past Efforts and Results

1) Overview

Since the 1980s, Korea has experienced rapid urbanization and an increase in small-size households, resulting in a sharp increase in housing demand and prices. Due to the housing price hike, low-income households were particularly suffered from chronic residential instability.

The Korean government exerted huge efforts to build housings to the greatest extent for the stabilization of the housing market. The most representative case would be the Two Million Housing Unit Construction Plan during the five-years from 1988 to 1992. After implementing this plan, the government reported that a total of 2.7 million housing units were built under the plan, and the construction of housing continued to expand thereafter.

Table 40 shows the number of housing construction between 1995 and 2020 in Korea, which remain more or less stable even though there were visible reductions during the times of the financial crisis in 1998 and the global economic crisis in 2008~2010.

Table 40 ● Annual housing construction (based on permission)

Year	1995	1998	2000	2005	2008	2010	2012	2013	2015	2018	2020
Housing Units(000s)	619	306	433	464	371	387	587	440	765	554	458

(Source: Ministry of Land, Infrastructure and Transport (MOLIT))

To finance the housing construction, the national housing and urban fund (NHUF)[2] and private banks housing funds have been developed and provided to house builders and purchasers. Table 41 illustrates that the amount of the housing fund provided by NHUF has been growing

2 The national housing fund (NHF) has changed to the national housing and urban fund (NHUF) in 2015.

consistently since 2008 when the financial and economic crisis hit the Korean economy. By all the efforts made by the government and industry, the housing supply ratio reached 100% in 2009 and went up to 104.8% in 2019, and 103.6% in 2020.[3]

Table 41 ● Funding amount of and loans originated by NHUF

Year	2008	2010	2012	2014	2016	2017	2018	2019	2020
Funding(bil.won)	22,098	34,515	45,372	64,689	57,329	66,529	69,321	74,594	100,303
Loan (bil. won)	9,503	15,156	15,852	15,914	14,086	17,680	22,510	23,093	18,870

(Source: MOLIT)

Furthermore, it is important to note that the low-income households without home ownership have been benefited the most through the housing supply policy. For the improvement of the residential condition of this group of people, various policy measures including housing price limit or control policy (1977~), housing size limit, housing subscription system, etc. were implemented. Also, the low-interest loan was provided and low-cost residential land was developed by the public sector to provide extra support for low-income people.

3 The method to calculate housing supply ratio was changed in 2015 from field survey method to residence registration census method to mitigate the duplication, omission, operator mistakes, etc. during the survey. As a result the housing supply ratio has been lowered by around 1.5%p compared to the previous ratio in each year.

2) Supply of Public Housing

Back in 2008, the Lee, Myoung-bak (MB) administration announced a plan to construct another 2 million housing units, supported by public funds between 2009 and 2018. These public housings were named Bogeumjari Housing.[4] Out of 2 million housing units, around two thirds of them (1.5 million units) were planned to be built by the public sector and the rest (0.5 million units) was planned to build by the private sector.

The Park, Geun-hye government which started in 2013 continued to take the MB government's plan and did not provide any other plan encompassing various types of housing to be supplied. According to the supply plan mentioned above, the public sector including the Korea Land and Housing Corporation (LH) and local government corporations were to build 1.5 million housing units during 2009~2018.

Spatially, 1 million units (67%) were to be built in Seoul metropolitan region (SMR), while 0.5 million units (33%) in non-SMR. In the total public housing units, small-sized public housing for sale made up 0.7 million units, while public rental housing (PRH) took 0.8 million units. In the PRH, 0.1 million units were planned as permanent public rental housings to provide to those in the lowest income level. For these housing units, the government covers 85% of the expenses to

4 Bogumjari means the nest.

build.

The main progress for the Bogeumjari housing was:

· Special Act on the Construction of Public Housing was enacted in 2009 and 78.8 km^2 of land in the SMR including the land in the green belt (GB) zone was designated and secured as the land for public housing. The table below shows the provision of public housing during the period.

· The supply of public housing has shown a pattern of declining in the first half of the 2010s compared to 2010 mainly due to the stagnated housing market condition and excessive supply of housing. However, the supply of public housing has begun to recover slowly since the mid-2010s. The number of permissions granted was 94,000 units in 2019 and 82,000 units in 2020. Among those, public rental housings for low-income tenants took 56,000 and 44,000 units respectively.

Table 42 ● Provision of public housing

Stage	Type	2010	2011	2012	2013	2014	2015	2016	2017	2018	2019	2020
Permission	Total	159	126	113	74	63	76	76	77	81	94	82
	(Rental)	85	70	61	69	59	73	71	68	63	56	44
Completion	Total	137	123	79	104	127	141	148	86	82	79	81
	(Rental)	108	90	56	80	102	124	125	65	63	58	63

(Source: MOLIT)

3) Diversification of Supplied Housing

(1) Urban Lifestyle Small Housing

The introduction of urban lifestyle small housing was based on the growing number of small member households compared to the dwindling number of small-sized housing mainly due to urban redevelopment. This mismatch brought about an imbalance between supply and demand of small size housing and consequently the residential instability of low-income households. The following tables show the trend of the rise in the number of 1~2 member households and the demand for newly-built housing.

Table 43 ● 1~2 person household ratio by region

	1990	1995	2000	2005	2010	2015	2020
SMR (%)	21.0	26.2	31.1	38.3	44.0	50.4	56.9
Non-SMR (%)	24.1	32.2	37.6	45.5	51.9	56.1	62.5

(Source: Statistics Korea, Population and Housing Census)

Table 44 ● Demand for newly-built housing by size

	2011			2015			2020		
	~ 60 m^2	60~85 m^2	85 m^2~	~ 60 m^2	60~85 m^2	85 m^2~	~ 60 m^2	60~85 m^2	85 m^2~
Numbers(000s)	197	129	106	187	121	96	179	111	82
Ratio (%)	45	30	25	46	30	24	48	30	22

(Source: Korea Research Institute for Human Settlements (KRIHS) A Study on Housing Policy Paradigm Shift for Social and Economic Structural Change (2011))

To expedite the construction of this type of housing, the government loosened various regulations including parking lot size, convenience facilities, etc. Urban lifestyle small housing is largely classified into several groups: complex-type tenement house; complex-type multi-unit house; and studio-type houses. With the deregulation of building standards, especially parking lot size, the number of houses built in this type increased exponentially. The number of studio-type building permission had increased from 1,125 in 2009 to 18,416 in 2010, 72,361 in 2011, and then to 102,554 in 2012

Figure 16 ● Pictures of urban lifestyle small housings
(Source: Korea Land and Housing Corporation (LH))

The sudden increase of this type of small housings, however, brought about several problems such as a shortage of parking spaces leading to roadside parking, increase of unsold housings, limited housing space for ordinary 3~4 member households, etc. To solve these problems caused by the continuous supply of small-size houses, the government decided to bring the regulation back in 2013 for the small-size housing, and thereafter their numbers began to decline. However, with the recovery of the housing market since 2014 and the continuing growth of small member households in metropolitan cities, the supply of this type of housing bounced back in 2015. The number of permits issued has been from 69,119 units in 2013 to 63,628 in 2014 and 95,532 units in 2015.

However, with the increase of the request for decent housing among would-be housing purchasers, the number of permits issued for building urban-life-type small housing has begun to diminish since then.

Table 45 ● Urban lifestyle small housing construction (based on permission) (000s)

Types	2010	2011	2012	2013	2014	2015	2016	2017	2018	2019	2020
Total	**18**	**72**	**103**	**69**	**64**	**96**	**78**	**68**	**47**	**41**	**35**
Studio-type house	-	-	-	43	29	35	27	29	20	17	14
Complex-type multi-unit house	-	-	-	22	30	51	41	31	23	18	16
Complex-type tenement house	-	-	-	4	5	10	10	8	4	6	5

(Source: MOLIT)

(2) Quasi-housing

Despite the increased supply of housing, the converted housing which was supposed to be built for other purposes has remained continuously. The main reason for the increase of this type of accommodation is the lower rent than ordinary housing. Hence, lower-income people want to reside in this type of accommodation. However, these facilities are not properly managed according to the relevant regulations including safety rules. Consequently, there are many risks to live in this kind of structure such as fire, downfall, or even collapse.

For this reason, a new type of dwelling, called quasi-housing was introduced to strengthen the safety standard and to enhance dwelling conditions for low-income people. The revision of the Housing Act and Building Act was made in 2010 for this. As a result, quasi-housing consisting of officetel[5], elderly housing and private dormitory became legalized and regulated by the laws. The process of building permission and standard check of quasi-housing are stipulated in the Building Act, not in the Housing Act which has more complicated and higher level of health and safety rules, for the invigoration of quasi-housing.

(3) Green Home (Eco-friendly housing)

The MB administration drew up a plan to build 1 million units of Green Home in 2008. For this, action plans including facilities and building standards followed in May 2009. Besides, the notification of facilities and building standards for eco-friendly housing was released in September 2010.

5 This is a studio type apartment used for either dwelling space or office.

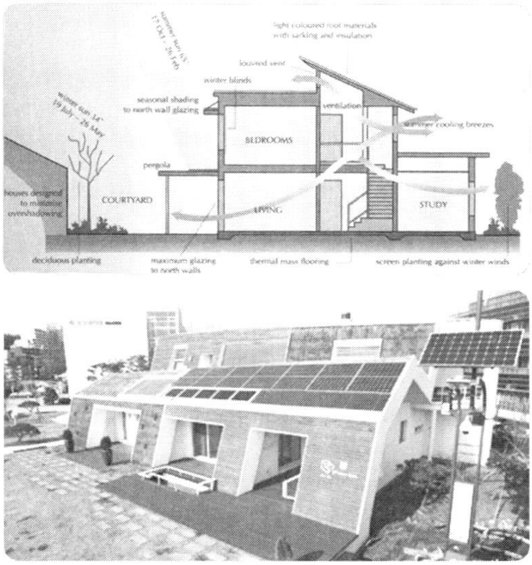

Figure 17 ● Use of clean energy and eco-friendly construction
(Source: MOLIT)

The green home is featured by energy efficiency (i.e. reduced energy consumption), the use of renewable energy, and eco-friendly construction. In particular, when the permanent public rental housings are renovated with financial support from the government, the concept of green home ought to be applied in various parts including balcony chassis and external windows.

(4) Happiness Housing

Happiness Housing (HH) is one of the ambitious projects announced by President Park, Geun-hye in 2012. The basic idea of HH is to build public rental housings by making use of unused rail beds, public land, etc. to lower the building costs, mainly to support younger generations.

LH and the public corporations set up by provincial or local governments are the main providers. These housings are supplied preferably to the youth including newly-wed couples, new employees, and college/university students. The HHs constructed are distributed to the youth (60%) and the elderly (20%). And the remaining 20% is distributed to low-income people based on recipients' income level.

HH is attractive in that its rent level is significantly low (60~80%) compared to other houses in neighboring areas. Along with these housings, social enterprises for jobs, government office buildings, and community centers are induced to locate in the same sites to make the happiness housing sites vibrant and lively for the residents, most of whom are low-income people.

As many as 200,000 units were planned to be supplied during 5 years from 2013 to 2017. Actual construction began in 2014 with the permission of 26,000 housing units and further 38,000 units in 2015 within major metropolitan cities.

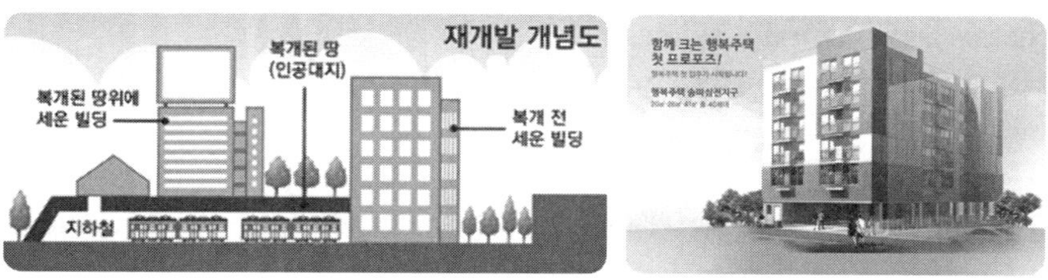

Figure 18 ● Concept design of Happiness Housing
(Source: MOLIT)

Supply of completed HH began in 2015. With the strong demand of the younger generation and the active participation of local governments, the construction and supply of HH are smoothly under way.

Table 46 ● Supply of Happiness Housing completed (000s)

	2015	2016	2017	2018	2019	2020
Number of housing units	38.0	38.2	28.2	30.2	31.0	25.9

(Source: MOLIT)

(5) New Stay and Public Support Private Rental Housing - Promotion of Private Rental Housing

The brand of ‘New Stay’ referring to a new type of private rental housing was introduced by the Park, Geun-hye administration. This policy was announced to provide the residential stability of the middle-income group at the beginning of 2015. The goal of this new policy was to address a fast-changing market situation from Chonsei to monthly rental and a shortage of registered rental housing.

In 2014, the number of total households was 18 million, whereas that of rental households was 8 million (44.4%) and the number of households living in registered rental housing was only 1.6million, 20.1% of rental households. In such a situation, not only low-income but also many middle-income households faced residential instability.

Therefore, the Korean government decided to promote private rental housing business and to increase the registered rental housing. The new type of housing was named New Stay housing. To promote the rental housing business and New Stay, various incentives have been provided for this scheme such as low-price land, tax reduction, increased amount of NHUF provision, and lower interest rate. In return, the supplier of New Stay housing ought to maintain the housing as rental housing for at least 8 years and follow the regulation including the restriction of rent increase over 5% per year.

For the effective implementation of this policy, the 'Special Act on the Private Rental Housing' was legislated in 2015. The photos below are the bird's eye view of the Dohwa New Stay site located in Incheon city which was the first site started for this project.

Figure 19 ● The bird's eye view picture of Inchon Dohwa New Stay site
(Source: MOLIT)

The actual supply of New Stay began in 2015 and the following table shows the result and plan of New Stay housing in 2017. With the active participation of private developers, New Stay housing was likely to be settled down in a short time. However, considering that the role of private rental housing had been increased in the housing market, the supply of New Stay housing and similar types of private housing needed to be further encouraged.

Table 47 ● The supply result and plan of New Stay Housing

Goal (2014~2017)	Permit Issued (000s)				2017 Plan
	Total	2014	2015	2016	
85	39	-	14	25	46[6]

(Source: MOLIT)

This "new stay housing" was changed to "publicly-funded private rental housing" in 2018 with the inauguration of Moon, Jae-in government who emphasized the role of the public sector instead of the private sector. This newly initiated housing type was characterized by the reduction of government incentives and the increase of responsibility for the private sector supplying private rental housings, named as publicly-funded private rental housing, changed version of the "New Stay" housing in Park, Geun-hye administration. Even though the incentives for private rental housing have been reduced, public support private rental housing, as well as New Stay, righteously exhibited

6 With the inauguration of the Moon, Jae-in government and the change of New Stay to public support private rental housing, the data on the permission of New Stay in 2017 has not been released.

the importance of private rental housings to solve housing problems, especially for the lower-income people. The government made a plan to supply 33 thousand units of this housing each year or 165 thousand units in total during 2018-2022.

5.2.3. Expanded Role of the Public Sector

1) Changes in Circumstances

The Korean housing market began to show a drastic change since the beginning of the 2010s as the housing supply ratio exceeds 100% and the housing purchase demand has shown a cyclical change. As a consequence, the Korean housing market has moved back and forth between supplier-driven market and consumer-oriented market. In particular, the depression of the world economy from the financial crisis in the late 2000s led to stagnation in the housing market and unappealing conditions for housing construction and supply.

Housing builders suffered from a massive loss due to the decline of housing purchase demand and construction laborers lost their jobs. This situation continued until mid-2014. After the introduction of a series of policy measures in 2013 and 2014, the housing market turned around escaping from the depressed market. At the end of 2015 and 2016, the housing market began to show a sign of recovery and since 2017 the housing market has changed to a booming market and then to an overheated market. To stabilize house prices soaring consistently, the Korean government has mobilized various policy measures including heavy taxation, restriction on housing loans, tighter qualification for house subscriptions, etc. However, the effect of these government efforts has been assessed as weak, since the supply of housing in Seoul and other metropolitan cities has been blocked by the strong regulations on reconstruction and redevelopment.

Even after the recovery of the housing market began in 2015 the homeownership ratio has not elevated substantially since the demand for housing is mainly coming from landlords rather than aspiring home owners.

Table 48 ● Changes in housing supply ratio and homeownership ratio

	2010	2012	2014	2015	2016	2017	2018	2019	2020
Housing supply ratio	100.5	101.1	101.9	102.3	102.6	103.3	104.2	104.8	103.6
Homeownership ratio	54.3	53.8	53.6	56.8	56.8	57.7	57.7	58.0	57.9

(Source: MOLIT)

In the rental market, the preference of Chonsei led to the decline in housing prices and the rise of Chonsei deposits or prices in the depressed market, and vice versa. The residential stability of low-income people has been worsened due to the rise of Chonsei prices. For example, the continuing instability made the low-income group move from Chonsei to monthly rental housing with a lump-sum deposit and then move to rental housing with small or no deposit requesting higher monthly rent in the worst case.

2) Housing Supply Policy of Moon, Jae-in Administration

The directions and measures of housing policy of the Moon, Jae-in administration which started in 2017 were reflected in the Long-Term Comprehensive Housing Plan (LTCHP) for the period from 2013 to 2022 revised in 2018. The new vision of LTCHP is 'better residential life of all the people without worrying about housing' and its objectives are 'to reduce housing cost burden, to create the end user-centered housing market and to promote a safe and pleasant residential environment.' For this purpose, LTCHP listed various policy measures including customized housing assistance, the increased supply of public housing, improvement of the quality of public rental housing, expansion of housing loan, promotion of transparency in the rental market, upgraded management of apartment houses, improvement of the residential environment through urban renewal and regeneration, etc.

LTCHP depends on housing supply with various types and channels to achieve the objectives of the plan. Firstly, the housing supply will be expanded for low-income levels and end-users. During the period between 2013 and 2022, a total of 1 million units of public housings including public rental housing (PRH), public housing for sale (PHFS), and public-support private rental housing (PS-RH) will be supplied. (Table 49)

Table 49 ● Supply of public housings (000s)

Types	Total	Annual average	2018	2019	2020	2021	2022
Total	1,002	200	190	199	199	205	209
PRH	652	130	132	130	130	130	130
PHFS	150	30	18	29	29	35	39
PS-RH	200	40	40	40	40	40	40

(Source: MOLIT)

A total of 650,000 units of PRH will be provided through not only the development of residential sites but also the mixed-use development of old public buildings and small-scale redevelopment as a part of urban regeneration to increase the supply of housings in the inner-city areas.

The supply of public housing for sale with low price will reach an average of 30,000 units per year and middle-size units with the size between 60 and 85 m^2 will also be supplied taking into account the demand of multi-child households.

A total of 200,000 units of private rental housing supported by the public sector (PS-RH) will also be supplied. Initial rent, qualification of tenants, etc. of this housing type are regulated by the government in exchange for public support mainly in the forms of tax reduction and a low-interest loan.

Secondly, until the end of 2022, the government aims to secure 2 million units of PRH and PS-RH stock for the residential stability of low-income tenants by regulating initial rent, annual growth of rent, etc.

Thirdly, the annual supply of newly-built housing will be determined based on the estimation of housing demand for newly-built housing. LTCHP estimated that the annual demand for newly-built housing will be 386,500 units during 5 years between 2018 and 2022. However, actual supply volume will be managed flexibly considering the economic cycle, the supply of public housing, the number of unsold housing, etc.

Fourthly, the enhancement of the quality of housing is pursued by introducing or expanding long-lived housing, modular housing, smart home, etc. To this end, the government will support R&D activities of related industries, and smart home technologies will be mobilized in developing smart cities.

All in all, housing supply will be taking an important position in the housing policy in Moon, Jae-in administration like previous administrations by affecting all the related fields encompassing market equilibrium, housing welfare of low-income people, quality of housing, and so on.

5.3. Necessity of Continuous Housing Supply

5.3.1. Current Situation

1) Why Does It Matter?

Under various policy measures introduced in 2013 and 2014 including the reduction of housing supply and enhanced assistance, the housing market began to recover from 2015. At that time the government included the reduction of housing supply in a policy package to maintain the balance between housing demand and supply. However, leaving the actual effects aside, several concerns were expressed. Firstly, people wonder whether the long-term housing market stability can be maintained with the reduced supply and, secondly, what the desirable housing construction and supply policies are. Also, the reappearance of the booming market in the latter half of the 2010s made the idea of reducing housing supply to maintain a balance between supply and demand meaningless. However, the intentional reduction of supply can be suggested whenever the housing market faces the situation of oversupply. Therefore, the necessity of continuous supply of housing even in the depressed housing market seems worth discussing.

2) Issues to be Reviewed

First of all, until 2022, the average annual housing demand is estimated at around 400,000 units (400,300 in 2018 and 366,900 in 2022) according to the estimation in the LTCHP announced in 2018. Accordingly, it has been strongly argued that the continuous housing supply is indispensable for the stability of the housing market for a substantial time.

The argument for claiming continuous housing supply can be summarized as follows:

Firstly there has been a strong demand for redeveloping old houses and moving into new and better housing, and this tendency will continue more in the future. Secondly, housing demand has increased with the rise of double occupancy households seeking jobs and good education elsewhere. Finally, it also has been worried that if the Korean economy loses its capacity to supply enough housings to meet the housing demand, it would be impossible to cope with the future housing shortage.

Table 50 is the comparison of the housing supply ratio between Korea and foreign countries. We can find that the housing supply ratio in Korea is still lower than in many advanced countries and that further construction and supply of housing is needed for a while.

Table 50 ● Housing supply ratio and the number of houses per 1000 persons

	Korea (2020)	Japan(2019)	USA(2020)	UK(2020)
Housing Units (A)	21.7mil	62.4mil (2018)	140.5mil	29.5mil*
Households (B)	20.9mil	53.3 mil (2015)	128.5mil.	27.8mil(19.9)**
Population (C)	51.8mil	126.4mil (2019)	331.4mil	67.1mil
A/B	103.6%	117.0%	109.3%	106.1(148.2)**
A/C (X 1,000)	420.4	493.7	424.0	439.6

* Estimated by applying the annual increase rate between 2000 and 2012
** Excluding one-member households (7.9 million)
(Source: Statistics Korea (Korea), Japan Statistical Yearbook 2021, US Census Bureau (USA), Office for the National Statistics (UK))

Moreover, in 2011 and 2012, over 500,000 units of house construction would not have been possible without the help of the massive construction of studio-type houses, an average supply of 8,000 units per month. These facts illustrate that it is important to build housings for ordinary families continuously in the medium to longer-term, although the volume of housing construction can be reduced flexibly during the economic downturn. Another thing we have to pay attention to is how to provide a consistent housing supply in major cities without any disruption or fluctuation. The table below shows the housing supply ratio of metropolitan cities in Korea during 2010~2020. The housing supply ratios in Seoul and Incheon are a little bit lower than other metropolitan cities implying that further construction and supply of housing is needed in the Seoul metropolitan region.

Table 51 ● Housing supply ratio in major cities

	Housing Supply Ratio (%)						
	2010	2015	2016	2017	2018	2019	2020
Whole nation	100.5	102.3	102.6	103.3	104.2	104.8	103.6
Seoul	94.4	96.0	96.3	96.3	95.9	96.0	94.9
Busan	99.7	102.6	102.3	103.1	103.6	104.5	103.9
Daegu	101.5	101.6	103.3	104.3	104.0	103.3	102.0
Incheon	99.8	101.0	100.9	100.4	101.2	100.2	98.9
Gwangju	101.8	103.5	104.5	105.3	106.6	107.0	106.8
Daejon	101.0	102.2	101.7	101.2	101.6	101.4	98.3
Ulsan	105.1	106.9	107.3	109.3	110.3	111.5	110.2
Sejong	-	123.1	108.4	111.5	110.0	111.4	107.3

(Source: MOLIT)

5.3.2. Constraints in Housing Supply and Measures to Overcome

Commonly indicated constraints of housing supply are housing land, finance, labor, construction materials, regulations, and low demand. Among these, securing enough sites for housing is a crucial factor for housing supply in small countries like Korea. In general, it takes at least 2~3 years from the designation of residential land to the completion of site development before housing construction, and this becomes one of the main reasons for the time lag between housing demand and supply. Also, it becomes harder to find suitable housing land inside or in the vicinity of major cities. The growing opposition from land owners of developable lands and the high price of raw land are major reasons for this. Consequently, the newly supplied housing land tends to have a distance from the town center.

A shortage of funds is another afflictive factor. To develop residential land and build houses, a large amount of funds needs to be raised in advance. The burdens of developers and house builders have been doubled with a high-interest rate for loans and reluctance of financial institutions to participate in the project to finance due to high-risk and high-return characteristics of housing site development.

Labor and construction materials also can impede housing supply. Because of house price control, which was maintained for nearly three decades, house builders have tended to employ unskilled workers and to use low-price materials. This has become one of the causes of consumer dissatisfaction which is harmful to securing the effective housing demand. Administrative regulations also are hampering the housing supply. There are numerous administrative and bureaucratic procedures from making a development plan to allowing residents to move in, which can block the propitious development of residential sites and supply of housing.

A project of housing supply consists of various kinds of activities such as land acquisition, financing, construction works, collecting buyers, distribution of housing, negotiation with interest groups, etc. From these, small and large conflicts can emerge at any time before handing over.

Therefore, complex regulations such as land use control, NHUF loan guidelines, housing supply regulation, housing construction standards, building act, and environmental regulations have been enforced, while such regulations can become a significant obstacle for the timely supply of housing. Excessive interferences like price ceiling and heavy tax imposition on multi-home owners have been applied over a long time.

5.3.3. Policy Alternatives

To overcome the constraints discussed above, the Korean government has decided or is considering the introduction of various policy alternatives. To help relieve housing land shortage, high-density development in existing cities and the reservation or conversion of the lands acquired by LH have been contemplated. The need to expand transport and education infrastructure in the newly developed residential areas has been emphasized to provide suitable community facilities and promote land use in these areas.

To provide enough finance, the raise of LTV for the NHUF loan,[7] the participation of financial institutions in project financing (PF), and the

7 The raising and lowering of LTV and DTI are not determined solely from the housing standpoint, since these issues are closely related with the monetary policy and consequently national economic policy. Therefore, there have been frequent adjustments of these ratios according to the conditions of housing market and national economy.

diversification of the source of financing including REITs are pursued.

Regarding the labor and construction materials, training of workers and the timely procurement of materials are to be implemented. With complicated regulations, consistent deregulation in the housing sector is being sought for. This means that, for example, the concept of 'one house for each household', which began at the time of housing shortage and has continued for several decades thereafter, needs to be reviewed and modified reflecting the changed housing market circumstances. As an alternative, it is recommendable to allow the purchase of the second house in rural areas by residents and the subscription for the newly built housing by foreigners.

5.4. Conclusion

The increase of housing supply has been a prime objective of housing policy in Korea over decades. As the housing supply ratio exceeded over 100% recently, the request for the slash of housing supply seems to increase. However, from a longer-term point of view, the supply of adequate volume of housing needs to be continued to maintain the stability of the market as well as the residential life of people. The increasing number of households, demand for the redevelopment of old housing, and the improvement in the housing quality are the main reasons for the assertion of continued housing supply.

Chapter 6

Market Equilibrium - House Price Stabilization Policy

6.1. Introduction

6.1.1. Basic Housing Problems

Basic housing problems are twofold:

① Cyclical market instability caused by discrepancies between demand and supply;

② Insufficient support for the housing minority from the government.

Between these two, the first issue is reviewed and examined in this chapter, while the second problem will be discussed in the chapter on housing welfare.

6.1.2. Problems Caused by Housing Market Instability

There is an enormous number of suppliers and buyers participating in the housing market. Based on mutual consent and agreement between suppliers and buyers, transactions are supposed to occur at an optimum price. However, excess demand or excess supply can lead to a sudden price hike or drop in the market. In short, disequilibrium caused by differences between housing demand and supply often results in instability or fluctuation of the housing market.

As discussed previously, long-term market instability produces many victims and harmful side effects on the national economy and society. Specifically, if demand is stronger than supply, the housing price and Chonsei deposit will rise leaving more burdens on tenants.

In contrast, when demand is weaker than supply, the housing price will fall and home buyers with a mortgage loan and self-employed small business owners and construction workers will encounter a hardship. All in all, the long-term market instability can bring about a significant influence or impact on people's lives, and consequently on the national economy.

6.1.3. Difference between Theory and Reality

In analyzing the housing market instability and in exploring its countermeasures, we often recognize that theoretical frameworks or principles do not correspond to the circumstances we often face in the real world. When the excess housing demand appears, theoretically, problems can be solved by increasing the housing supply. However, increasing the housing supply cannot be easily achieved due to a shortage of land, insufficient funds, or any other reasons we discussed in the previous chapters. In the same vein, the excess supply can be tackled theoretically by reducing the supply. However, such an approach does often bring a strong adversarial conflict from house builders and long waiting buyers. Then what is a good way to resolve disequilibrium and to restore the balance between housing supply and demand?

6.2. Housing Market

6.2.1. Features of Housing Market

1) Imperfect Competition Market

The imbalance between housing demand and supply often comes from the location of housing more than any other factor. This is because locational fixity or spatiality becomes one of the most important elements when purchasing a house. By contrast, in a commodity market, identical goods are produced mechanically and supplied massively, and as a result, the locational fixity plays a minor role. Table 52 shows the differences between the housing market and commodity market.

Table 52 ● The housing market and commodity market

	Housing market	Commodity market
Price	· high price compared to household income · identical product, non-identical price	· identical product, identical price
Substitution	· imperfect substitution	· perfect substitution
Trader	· traders with regional basis	· myriad of traders(no regional basis)
Quality	· non-identical	· identical
Mobility	· immovable, traders move	· movable
Transaction	· influence of many laws and regulations · mediators are needed	· minimal influence of laws and regulations
Accessibility to Information	· limited accessibility · needs time and cost	· full accessibility
Scope of Market	· regional market · exists in a specific space	· regional, national and international market
Types of Market	· owners' housing market · rental housing market · newly-built housing market · secondhand housing market	· myriad markets according to types and quality · limited secondhand market

(Source: Ha (2010), modified)

2) The Role of Existing Housing Market

Housing markets consist of two kinds of housings, newly-built housings and existing housings or secondhand housings. The newly-built housing market is undoubtedly affected by various macro- and micro-level factors including interest rate, income, housing production capacity, and technology. Additionally, in recent times, various other factors influence the newly-built housing including market size, the shortage of housing in the region, infrastructure, migration of population, etc.

The existing housing stock accounts for a huge proportion of the housing market. However, the values of housing vary with age, quality, and condition. Due to this, housing-related industries such as safety inspection, management, maintenance, and repair services have developed.

In general, the existing housing market is much bigger than the newly-built housing market. In Korea, the total housing stock is well over 21 million units in 2020, and only 0.4 or 0.5 million units (2%) are newly built annually. Housing transactions made in the Korean housing market are around one million units every year, of which 30% or 40% is newly built housing. However, regardless of its size, the market for newly-built housing takes a significant part in the housing market and the national economy as it creates jobs and provides a substantial influence on the price of existing houses.

3) Subordinate Housing Market

As has been stressed, a housing market is spatially based and consisted of numerous subordinate markets. In other words, the housing market is a regional market with limited boundaries comprising various subordinate markets. For example:

- The Korean housing market is the aggregation of the housing markets of the Seoul metropolitan region (SMR) and non-SMR region;
- SMG housing market consists of housing markets inside of Seoul and around Seoul in SMG;
- Seoul housing market can be defined as the sum of housing markets of Gangnam, non-Gangnam in Seoul, and sometimes new towns located adjacent to Seoul.

The reason why people are interested in subordinate markets can be summarized as:

① Substantial differences can be found in the size and quality of housing stock between regions and sub-regions. For example, Seoul's housing market is quite different from that of Suwon city, the capital city of Gyeonggi-Do province, although both cities are located in Seoul metropolitan region;

② There is a diverse consumer demand in housing depending on region based on its historical and cultural context;

③ Factors causing disequilibrium in the housing market vary region by region. Therefore, housing market indexes tend to be strongly influenced by specific subordinate markets.

6.2.2. Housing Market Equilibrium

1) Analytical Methods of the Housing Market

Some scholars have analyzed and explained the housing market equilibrium based on their viewpoints.[1] The main examples are:

① Classicism sees the housing market as a perfect competition market filled with suppliers and buyers, all of whom are assumed to be equipped with perfect knowledge, information, and rational behavior. In this perspective, the importance of interaction between supply and demand in the market is highlighted and the theories of microeconomics provide a theoretical basis.

② Institutionalism emphasizes the role of institutions such as government, banks, and developers in the housing market.

③ Macroeconomic analysis focuses on the relationship between the housing market and macro-economy including employment and

1 Ha, 2010. On the other hand, Lund (2006) classifies the theories of housing policy into five categories based on their standpoints: 1) Laissez-faire economics or neoclassical economics, 2) Social Reformism including Social Liberalism and Fabian Socialism, 3) Marxist political economy, 4) Behavioral approaches mainly based on underclass behavior theories, and 5) Social constructionism derived from post-modernism thinking.

economic cycles.

④ Urban housing model tries to analyze housing issues within the context of urban space. In this model, given the spatiality factor in housing, people want to minimize the access cost.

⑤ Political economics emphasizes the distortion and conflict caused by capital. This perspective often goes hand in hand with structuralism in explaining or criticizing capitalism.

None of these theories is likely to explain how the housing market operative in the real world inclusively but it does explain in part. This means that the actual housing market should be understood with all the possible perspectives suggested in these theories. Nonetheless, classicism based on microeconomic theory, i.e. an approach focusing on the demand, supply, and pricing, is the most commonly touted as a basic analytical tool.

2) Housing Market Equilibrium

In general, housing market equilibrium is explained with the theoretical framework of neoclassical economics. According to this theory, the supplier of housing requires the highest price (asking price), while the buyer wants the lowest price (bidding price). The interaction of asking and bidding price determines the sales price. Buyers (households) are supposed to act rationally in the housing market. Considering the diverse range of buyer's income, it is presumed that they choose to consume services either from housing or from other goods to maximize their satisfaction or utility.

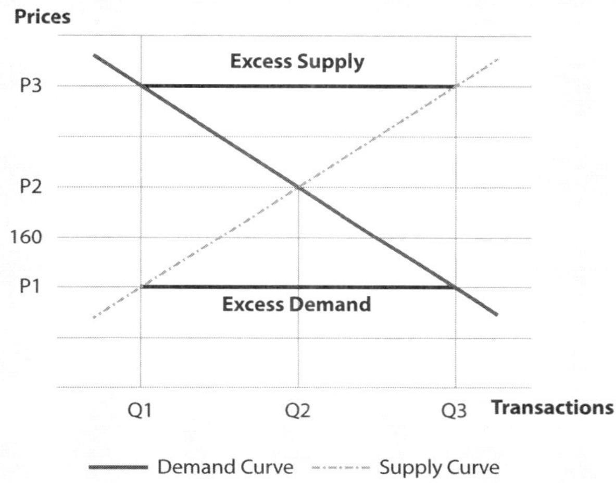

Figure 20 ● Housing market equilibrium and excess demand

Figure 20 shows the relationship between housing price (P) and the number of housing transactions (Q). When the housing demand curve and supply curve cross each other, the equilibrium can be achieved with the 'agreed' quantity and price of housing. At the point (P2, Q2), optimum price and quantity of transaction are determined. However, if the price rises, then demand will be reduced and the level of supply subsequently increases, resulting in excess supply. Conversely, if the price goes down, it results in excess demand.

It is difficult to achieve equilibrium in the housing market. Partly it is also due to the specific characteristics of housing. Housing is different from other goods in nature. House is one of the essential needs for people's lives and this affects people to own their housing. Housing is not also readily accessible to purchase due to the high price. Furthermore, Housing is not goods to be producible easily and immediately. It takes a long time to supply housings, while housing demand tends to change within a short time due to various reasons. Therefore, unlike the economic theory, long-term adjustment processes are necessitated to reach equilibrium between demand and supply.

3) Related Issues in the Market Equilibrium Discussion

(1) Location Factor in the Housing Market

The price of housing services varies according to their locations. Even if a row of identical houses are in the same size and built by one provider, their prices may differ depending on the location of the houses, etc. According to economic theory, the function of market rent shows a curve that slopes downward to the right illustrating the relationship between distance and rent. In other words, the price or rent of housing has a close relationship with the distance.

Considering the format of the mononuclear urban structure, the price of housing with easy accessibility to the city tends to be higher. In particular, when a city grows bigger and becomes populous, the external economy and diseconomy become coexist. Thus, people's income level and their preferences become important factors to choose their houses. In this situation, the location becomes a core element to decide the price of housing. However, there are some exceptions in advanced countries such as the USA where low-income households tend to live downtown, and high-income households choose to live in suburban areas with a sizable land.

(2) Quality of Housing Services and the Density and Style of Housing

An interesting finding is that the areas where the land price is relatively inexpensive and rent level is low tend to be filled with single-family houses or garden houses. This seems to be a common phenomenon both in developed and developing countries. Another finding is that the location factor tends to have a different influence between different levels of income groups. For example, people at the high-income level are fond of living in suburban areas, while people at the super-high income level tend to reside in the city center. However, these cases are likely to be found only in the countries having almost perfect housing market equipped with abundant available land, no restrictive regulations, etc. such as the USA in a specific period (Boelhouwer, 2011).

Then, how about in Korea? Koreans tend to want to live near the city center regardless of their income level. Therefore, interestingly, there is no clear spatial division between the residential areas for high-income levels and those for low-income levels. By contrast, in Washington D.C., USA, the division seems to be clear and a kind of gentrification, i.e. encroachment of residential areas by high-income people where once low-income people lived, takes place.

(3) Validates the Economic Cycle Theory?

In economics, Kondratiev waves (also called K-wave or long economic cycle) are supposed to be cycle-like phenomena in the modern economy. It is argued that the period of a wave ranges between forty and sixty years, and the cycles consist of alternating intervals between high sectoral growth and intervals of relatively slow growth. Many debates ensued surrounding the validity of this long-term economic cycle. By comparison, Juglar explains the economic cycle as four stages, namely stages of expansion, crisis, recession, and recovery, suggesting an economic cycle extending 7~11 years. On the other hand, in the case of the Kuznets Cycle, a cycle extends 15~20 years, while Kitchen Cycle is only 40 months.

If a long-term adjustment period is required to reach an equilibrium in the housing market, then can we find one of these cycles in Koreas' housing market? It is widely discussed by scholars in Korea that the cyclical movement of the housing market tends to show 10-year long-term cycles and 5-year short-term cycles for decades. This means that Juglar's cycle in conjunction with the more frequently appearing

Kitchen cycle may explain Korea's housing market better than Kondratieff's or Kuznets' cycle.

6.3. Current Housing Market Situation in Korea

6.3.1. Restructuring of the Rental Market

After the 2008 global economic crisis, the price of housing and property transactions declined in the housing ownership market. In the rental market, a complicated situation occurred. Since monthly rent is higher than the interest income generated from Chonsei deposit, landlords prefer monthly rental to Chonsei. This has brought about a rise in the Chonsei deposit, the increase in transactions and the supply of monthly rental, and the drop of monthly rent due to the increase of supply. The imbalance between Chonsei demand and supply and the subsequent hike of Chonsei price brought the flash point of a drastic change in the rental market. Such a change can be labeled as the 'restructuring of the rental market'. Even after the recovery of the housing market in 2015, the transfer of Chonsei to monthly rental continuously increases due to the requests of landlords.

The structural changes which are characterized as the fast shift of the rental market from Chonsei housing to monthly rental and the stagnancy in the ownership market have accelerated the imbalance between supply and demand in the Chonsei market. For example, the ratio of monthly rentals in the whole rental market changed from 45.0% in 2008 to 59.6% in 2015, and again 60.5% in 2016. The ratio of monthly rentals has leveled off at about 60% since then.[2] On the other hand, the ratio of Chonsei price to house sales price showed a continuous rise in the first half of the 2010s (62.5% in 2013, 63.7% in 2014, 66.6% in 2015, 67.5% in 2016, and 69.6 in 2017) and then, after the peak year of 2017, there appeared a gradual descent (67.8% in 2018, 66.31 in 2019, and 65.9 in 2020) mainly due to a huge surge in house prices in the latter half of 2010s. The following graph shows the reversed occupancy rate between Chonsei and monthly rental in the housing market.

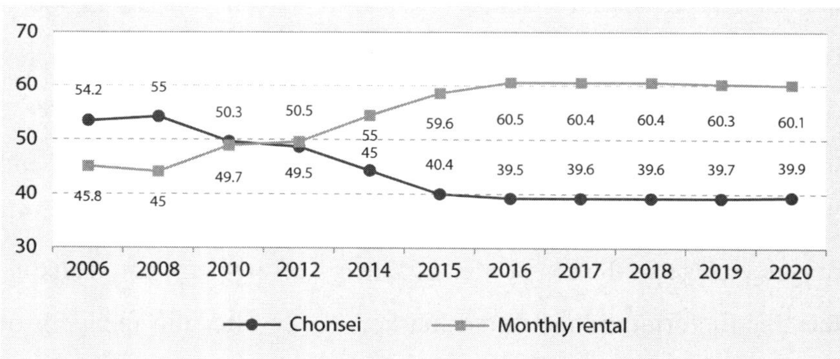

Figure 21 ● The proportion of Chonsei and monthly rental in the rental market
(Source: Statistics Korea)

2 The housing occupancy type data was not published in 2020.

6.3.2. Revitalization and Booming of Ownership Market

The global economic crisis that occurred in 2008 affected property transactions and the level of housing demand. Due to the growing uncertainty on housing prices and the burden on additional loans, many people postponed purchasing housing. Besides, the cost burden in purchasing and extra cost to maintain their housing became another contributing factor for people to remain in the rental market especially Chonsei, to house ownership.

In this circumstance, the Korean government diagnosed that the normalization of the rental market depends upon the recovery of the ownership market. They thought the continued slump in the housing market can cause the accelerated growth of Chonsei demand. On the other hand, house owners found it difficult to return the Chonsei deposit money to the tenant once the contract terminates. This difficulty pressured the house owners to change their rental housing from Chonsei to deposit-based monthly rental housing, or monthly rental with a variant deposit (MRVD), as an intermediate stage.

Thus, several packages of policy measures have been introduced and implemented since 2013 and the Korean housing market began to show the sign of recovering at the end of 2014. Also, property transactions have started to increase from the newly-built housing market from the second half of 2014, partly due to the prolonged rise of Chonsei prices.

As a result, Korean people have witnessed a relatively robust market since 2015

The housing market in Korea began to revitalize in 2015 and further entered into a booming market resulting in various effects and side effects on people's lives and the national economy. The rapid rise of house prices started in Seoul and surrounding cities spread all over the country. In the case of Gangnam the price of apartment houses more than doubled within two or three years at the end of the 2010s. Speculative investments added to the boiling market made matters worse. Facing this situation, the Korean government tried to quell down house prices by introducing various policy measures centering on heavy taxation, restriction on lending, tight qualification for housing subscriptions, etc. through the several announcements of policy packages. However, the upward trend of house prices continued until the early 2020s.

Furthermore, the rental market went from bad to worse due to the amendment of the Housing Lease Protection Act in July 2020 to introduce the extension of the rental period from two to four years and the rent control restricting the increase of rent within 5% every two years. With this legislation, landlords were forced to change their houses from Chonsei to monthly rental or exit from the rental market for good to make up the loss inflicted by new restrictions. Consequently, low-income tenants have fallen victim to this disturbance in the rental market.

Regarding the fundamental cause of the instability in the ownership market and rental market, scholars have pointed out that the supply of housing in major cities especially in Seoul has long been dwindled mainly due to severe restrictions on redevelopment and reconstruction and this has worked as a pressure pushing up both house prices and Chonsei. Problem is that reconstruction and redevelopment projects in metropolitan cities have to go through complex processes including the purchase of properties, the compromise between house owners and tenants, etc. Therefore, a substantial supply of housing in these reconstruction and redevelopment sites necessitates a prolonged time to be realized.

6.3.3. Comprehensive Analysis

By examining the housing problems in the past, we can conclude that excessive demand has resulted in housing and Chonsei price hike. However, the changes in the 2010s characterized by the bounce back from years of decline in the housing prices and the continued strong Chonsei showed rather complicated and unexpected circumstance.

All in all, the Korean government faces significant challenges to stabilize ownership and the rental market simultaneously. Considering the housing supply ratio currently exceeding 100% with the incessant supply of housing in the future, it is likely that customized strategies meeting the various demands specified by regions, types, income levels, etc. need to be introduced instead or on top of the previous type massive supply of housing in a few huge sizes of housing sites developed by the public sector.

On the other hand, the housing market which was formerly controlled by the government due to the several housing price hikes with a high housing demand recently shows a gradual shift toward the market looking for more convenient and economically bearable houses. Certainly, the Korean housing market is going through a transitional period. In other words, the extent of people who prefer to live in a convenient place which causes small housing expenses tend to increase significantly and this seems to bring a big change in the housing market in Korea.

Here, it is worth comparing the advantage and disadvantages of housing ownership. Owning a house incurs various expenditures including the financial cost to purchase, tax, management expenses, depreciation, etc. On the other hand, housing ownership provides benefits such as convenient life, dignity, social prestige with good neighborhoods and community, and the possibility of a price appreciation. People compare the cost and benefit from both sides, and try to maximize their welfare from home ownership. In the case of Chonsei, the financial cost is small with no taxes and no risks of losing their actual capital. Since Chonsei is profitable and substantially convenient for tenants especially when housing price is fluctuating, the

Chonsei market will continue to be strong.

Recently, some people prefer special housings such as apartment houses endowed with a sound living environment, country homes, or duplex homes. This means that people began to recognize the value of "invisible profit" and search for the houses embracing this feature. However, people's inclination for pursuing profit from speculation still significantly affects the housing market. A long queue in front of a model house where the location of housing is sound explains such an aspect.

In short, a complicated market situation has been produced at the beginning of the 2020s by various factors and forces in Korea.

6.4. Analysis of Housing Market Pricing in Korea

6.4.1. General Causes of Market Instability

The housing market in Korea has shown instability for a long time mainly due to the imbalance between demand and supply. The nature of the housing supply is such that it needs a long period, at least 6 months to 1 year for building a detached house and 3 to 5 years for apartment houses. By contrast, changes in demand occur frequently.

As a result, there have been discrepancies between demand and supply almost all the time. Furthermore, the fluctuations in the global economy have begun to influence demand and supply in Korea's housing market as experienced in the global economic crisis that occurred in 2008. The following table shows the factors affecting housing demand and supply.

Table 53 ● The factors affecting housing demand and supply

Demand		Supply	
Population	population density and growth rate	Land supply	new residential sites, floor area ratio
Purchase Capability	income, employment, savings	Development system	easy procedure, profitability (retrieving development gains)
Financing Condition	interest rate, loan control	Financing condition	interest rate, financing methods
Expenses for acquisition & maintenance	tax, maintenance expenses	Supply cost	land price, tax, building materials, wage
Supply system	price control, subscription system, resale allowance	Supply system	price control, subscription system, resale allowance

Population density and economic growth rate are influential on housing demand. The purchasing capacity of people formed by their income, employment, and savings also affects housing demand. Financial conditions including the interest rate and loan control affect both housing demand and supply. Tax and maintenance expenses incur the cost and tend to decrease housing demand.

Supply system such as price control, subscription system, and resale allowance affects housing demand and supply either in boosting or reducing ways. In contrast, land supply, convenient development system and low supply cost positively affect housing supply. Here, the factors affecting both demand and supply are financial condition and supply system.

However, many other factors do affect demand and supply in various ways. These different factors and functions of demand and supply interact with each other and, frequently, create the instability of the housing market. This means that to stabilize the housing market, the investigation of the exact reasons or factors resulting in the instability of the market should be carried out beforehand.

6.4.2. Causes of Market Instability in Korea

The Korean housing market has unique characteristics making it difficult to achieve equilibrium. The factors usually indicated as influencing demand are macro-economy, education, politics, the pursuit of diversified style, frequent changes in trend, etc. In contrast, supplying housing takes a long time. Spatial factors, especially the shortage of housing lands, also have worked as the main factors impeding the housing supply.

The imbalance in the housing market has been derived from the interaction or integration of various factors related to the structure of the market, regulation, behavior of participants, etc. The factors contributing to the market imbalance can be classified into two groups, i.e. internal factors and external factors.

First, there is a group of internal factors.

① The price of second-hand housing is higher than that of newly-built ones in Korea. This odd phenomenon is resulted from the price control on newly-built housing not to go beyond a certain level. Even though the regulation has been indicated as a major barrier to normalize the housing market over years, this regulation has not been fully abolished until now. At the end of 2014, an agreement was reached between political parties to abolish price control. However, this agreement was applied only to the private housings built on the privately developed sites which are transacted at market price. The house price limit has applied to housings built on publicly developed sites consistently. Moreover, facing a steep rise in housing prices from the mid-2010s, the Korean government decided to expand this price control to private housings built on private lands in the speculation control areas such as Seoul in 2019.

② Secondly, a high level of housing price and speculative demand has been the main driving forces resulting in the housing market imbalance. In Seoul, speculative demand particularly accelerated the housing price hike which led to a further rise in housing demand and, consequently, a reversed demand curve. As described in the preceding sections, the demand curve influenced by speculation is different from the normal demand curve. Accordingly, once market price begins to rise, it is difficult to return to the market equilibrium.

③ The excess flow of money into the real estate sector due to the undiversified investment instruments in the financial market has become another main factor preventing the balances in the housing market. Koreans invest 70% of their assets in real estate mainly through the purchasing of housings by themselves. This investment pattern often leads to an irrational speculative investment. New investment instruments such as real estate investment trusts (REITs) and real estate funds were introduced at the beginning of the 2000s to help invest in real estate based on careful calculation of cost and benefit and rational decision. Yet, these advanced investment channels have not been fully developed compared to those of Japan and Singapore where REITs were introduced around the same time. No tax incentive for corporate type REITs and strict listing requirements of financial authorities are indicated as the main obstructions for the development of REITs.

④ Copycat investment exists. If some people invest in housings and lands in certain areas or types, other people tend to follow such an investment pattern without careful consideration or calculation. This tendency is due to either speculative demand, or lack of information.

⑤ Rule of thumb style business of the construction and house building industry is indicated as another problem. Being accustomed to the 'high risk, high return' type business for a long time, this industry has been failing to respond to changes in demographic and household structures and the evolving preference of people and to create new housing demand.

⑥ Unbalanced development between regions is closely related to a high population in specific areas. Industries in Seoul Metropolitan Region (SMR) have also been a contributing factor to the imbalance in the housing market. Furthermore, socio-economic factors have affected the concentration of population and industry and the lack of residential sites in SMR.

Three external factors have been contributing to the instability of the housing market.

⑦ Irrational and immature politics and conflicts between different ideologies or different groups' interests have prevented the government to introduce appropriate policy measures at the right time.

⑧ There have been mismatches or collisions between policies. Specifically, without the proper implementation of related policies such as transportation, education, taxation, etc. it has not been possible to reach the goal of a stable housing market.

⑨ Financial industry has also contributed to the instability in the housing market. Inflexible implementation of debt-to-income ratio (DTI), loan-to-value (LTV), and project financing by financial intermediaries and oversight agencies hamper the stability and development of the housing market.

6.5. Housing Market Stabilization Policy of Korea

6.5.1. Major Policy Measures

In the periods of the booming housing market with a housing price hike, specifically during the end of 1980s~1990s, 2002~2003, 2005~2008 and from 2016 to the present, all or some of the following policy measures have been mobilized:

- As taxation measures, higher capital gains tax, acquisition tax, and comprehensive property tax are levied.
- As financial measures, the reduction of DTI and LTV and tighter lending criteria of mortgage loans are applied.
- As regulation measures, tighter housing subscription qualifications and the expansion of special zones assigned to prevent speculative transactions are applied.
- As supply measures, the development of residential sites and new towns and the increase of housing supply are pursued.

In the periods of housing price fall, i.e. during 1997~2001, 2011~2014, the exact opposite policy measures, the reversal of the above measures, were implemented.

6.5.2. Policy Measures in Depression in the 2010s

Since the 2008 global economic crisis, the housing market in Korea has suffered a stagnancy with the decrease in housing price and the subsequent accumulation of empty apartments and houses. To confront the situation, the Korean government introduced various policy measures, aiming to improve the market condition.

1) The Policy Package I (April 1, 2013)

The reduction of public housing for sale was announced to lead and induce the adjustment of housing supply in the market. The government also implemented the alleviation of the tax burden, increasing the financing assistance and deregulations. Specifically, temporary exemption of acquisition tax for the first-time buyers and the exemption of capital gains tax for 5 years were carried out. The government also allowed the vertical extension of buildings or upward remodeling, which had been controversial over time due to the safety issue.

2) The Policy Package II (Aug. 28, 2013)

This policy package was announced to cope with the instability in Chonsei market. At that time, housing prices plunged with excessive supply in the sales market, while the Chonsei deposit or price rose sharply in the rental market. To tackle this situation, a series of policy measures were introduced by the government as follows:

① To promote homeownership, house price and maintenance costs were set to be lowered through the reduction of an acquisition tax rate, etc.

② To increase of the supply of rental housing, were intended to be supplied. For this purpose, financial support through interest cuts and increasing the borrowing limit of loans, more reductions in capital gains tax, income tax, and corporation tax, etc. were sought.

③ To support tenants suffering from the increased housing rent (monthly rental households), the deduction of income tax on monthly rent was expanded and the "housing voucher" system was decided to be introduced.

3) The Policy Package Ⅲ (Sep. 1, 2014)

Another package of policy measures was announced in September 2014 with two objectives: the revitalization of the housing market through deregulation and, based on the revitalization, the residential stability of low-income households.

(1) Revitalization of Housing Market

Firstly, as deregulation on renewal projects, the regulations to limit redevelopment became eased down by shortening the age of housing from 40 to 30 years old, and the obligation imposed on developers to provide small-sized housing and rental housing in the same building site was also deregulated.

And secondly, as a reform of the housing subscription system, the discrimination against multiple homeowners in supplying housing according to the housing subscription merit system is abolished. Household members, as well as the head of household, are allowed to apply for housing subscriptions.

(2) Enhancing the Residential Stability of Low-income Households

To invigorate private participation in the rental housing market, private investment in Rental Housing REITs was encouraged through consistent tax incentives.

Also to mitigate the burden of low-income households, non-recourse mortgage loan was introduced for lower-income households having no ownership.

4) The Policy Package Ⅳ (Sep. 2, 2015)

Another policy package was announced by the Korean government due to rental market instability, especially the Chonsei market in 2015. The main contents of this package were:

Firstly, stronger measures were put forward to support the low-income non-homeowners such as low-income aged people living alone and college students.

Secondly, with the promulgation of the Special Act on Private Rental Housing (Aug. 2015), the construction of New Stay housing was activated.

And thirdly, the government pursued to support urban renewal through deregulations and enhanced transparency of housing policies to improve the residential condition in downtown areas.

6.5.3. Policy Measures in the Boom Years in the 2010s

The housing market has turned around since the end of 2015. In particular, reconstruction sites in Seoul led an exceptional hike. The Korean government facing this situation has begun to introduce strong anti-speculation measures since the latter part of 2016.

1) Policy package I (Nov. 3, 2016)

To prevent speculation and to stabilize housing prices, the government designated Subscription System Adjustment Area (SSAA) applicable to 25 districts in Seoul, 5 districts in Busan, and 7 Cities including Sejong and Gwachon. In the same vein, regulations or guidelines related to the purchase of housing also were strengthened such as requirements for multiple subscription and resale of housing purchased, etc.

2) Policy package II (Jun. 19, 2017)

As housing prices continued to rise, the Korean government announced another policy package. Firstly, SSAA has been expanded by adding Gwang Myoung City and 2 districts in Busan.

Secondly, regulations related to the purchase of housing in SSAA has strengthened once again by including the extension of the resale restriction period in Seoul to the time of property ownership transfer (i.e. title registration), the tightened mortgage loan by lowering the LTV and DTI rate by 10%p.

3) Policy package III (Aug. 2, 2017)

Another bundle of housing market stabilization policies was released to bring down house prices. The specially managed areas, Speculative Overheating Areas (SOA), were newly introduced to apply to 25 districts in Seoul, Gwachon city, and Sejong City where a surge of house price led by speculation continued. In these areas, in addition to all the regulations applying in SSAA, a 40% limit on LTV and DTI was newly introduced.

On the other hand, other policy measures such as the expansion of housing price control on the housing built in privately owned land, the implementation of excessive capital gains charge applying to reconstruction sites, tighter regulation on the transfer of property right in redevelopment and reconstruction projects in SOAs were introduced.

4) Policy package Ⅳ (Sep. 13, 2018)

Housing prices in Seoul and the vicinity continued to rise sharply differently from other main cities mainly by the infiltration of speculative investment to harness the shortage of available housings.

To address speculative investments, the government raised the comprehensive property (real estate holding) tax rate imposing on the owners of high price houses. The restriction on lending loans to multi-home owners purchasing additional houses in speculation-ridden areas was also announced. These measures, higher taxation and loan restriction, began to apply to rental business operators by this policy package.

5) Policy package Ⅴ (Dec. 16, 2019)

Housing prices in Seoul and neighboring cities which showed a decline in the first half of 2019 have begun to rise again since July of that year. The concern of the market was that the lack of housing supply in Seoul caused by heavy regulations on reconstruction and redevelopment has worsened the situation

Confronting this situation, the Korean government decided: first, to tighten the control on the mortgage loan to prevent speculative investments, secondly, to raise the comprehensive real estate tax rate and to expand the cases of levying transfer income tax and, thirdly, to investigate the source of money buying houses in the speculation-ridden areas.

6) Policy package Ⅵ (June 17, 2020)

Housing prices in Seoul and Gyeonggi-do which showed stability after the announcement of the policy package V began to rose again in the mid-2020 and spread out to neighboring provinces.

A new housing market stabilization policy package was announced to tackle the situation with the following policy measures:

- To regulate the booming areas, SMR, Daejon, Cheong-ju were designated as special regions to prevent speculation;
- To prevent speculative transactions, areas near the International Trade and Cooperation Center in Gangnam district were included in the land transaction permission area;
- To prevent the speculative investment by private rental housing businesses an intensified monitoring of their activities and the

reduction of tax incentives were decided to implement.

6.6. Future Directions

To return the housing market to normal, it is important to increase the resiliency or force of restitution of the housing market. A cyclical upswing or downswing needs to be managed and restored by the market principle formed by the supply and demand of housing with the participation of numerous suppliers and buyers.

Unfortunately, the Korean housing market has failed to show development in that direction. Looking at the recent changes in the 2010s in the Korean housing market, achieving the goal of market stability through the normalization of supply and demand in a short time is strongly unlikely. Especially in the booming years, implementing various policy measures like those introduced in a series of policy packages in the 2010s is important. Besides such kinds of direct interventions in the market, many diversified indirect measures also need to be introduced and implemented simultaneously. Balanced regional development through e.g. decentralization of population and industry, upgrading of new towns in SMR though the supplementation of education and transportation facilities can be included in this kind of measures, and these indirect fundamental solutions should be carried out consistently from a longer-term perspective.

Chapter 7

Distribution of Housing

7.1. Introduction

As the Korean government has emphasized for several decades, building as many new houses as possible is important, but this cannot solve all the problems in the housing market. Although the housing supply ratio exceeds 100%, there remain many issues unsolved. Together with the increase of housing stock the advancement of housing market systems is necessary to solve persistent problems such as the instability of the rental housing market or the ordeals of people on low incomes.

In parallel with increased housing supply, the appropriate distribution of newly built housing together with the utilization of existing housing stock needs to be systematized. In Korea, for the proper distribution or supply of newly-built housing, strict regulations on housing supply have been applied.[1] On the other hand, for the utilization and improvement of current housing, rebuilding and remodeling programs for housing have been encouraged.

7.2. Institutional Framework

7.2.1. Housing Supply Policy

In general, housing policy targets either housing or households, in other words, the physical factor or the human factor. This means that housing policies can be classified into either policy to improve housing or policies to offer assistance to households. Between the two, the

1 The term 'distribution' is likely to be more suitable than 'supply' in aptly explaining Korea's housing policy. A large number of people have waited for decades to purchase new houses supplied by house builders according to the laws and regulations, since the supply falls far short of the demand. Against this backdrop, the Korean government made a series of rules to decide on the orders or the ranking of potential buyers of newly supplied housings. In other words, it is the distribution of the right to purchase newly built houses for people on waiting lists. Therefore, this term 'distribution' implies that there is a semi-compulsory allocation of houses among people, which can be described as being bureaucratic. Here, these two terms are used interchangeably.

household has been the main target for housing policy in most countries including Korea.

In Korea, supports for households are made by the levels of household income or housing expenditure. For people in the lower 40% level of income bracket, full support is provided, while partial support is given to people in the 40~60% level of income bracket. Virtually no support is offered to those above the 70% threshold or higher income level. The table below shows the various policy measures to achieve these housing policy goals, i.e. support for housing and support for households.

Table 54 ● Policy measures to achieve the housing policy goals

<table>
<tr><th colspan="3">Targets & levels</th><th>Methods</th></tr>
<tr><td rowspan="2">Support for Housing</td><td colspan="2">Substandard Housing</td><td>Housing improvement fund with a low- interest rate</td></tr>
<tr><td colspan="2">Deteriorated housing</td><td>Support for housing management or Remodeling</td></tr>
<tr><td rowspan="4">Support for Households</td><td rowspan="2">Full support (lower 40 % income level)</td><td>Those unable to bear the minimum housing expenses</td><td>Support for housing management or public rental housing (permanent or 30 year (Kookmin)[2] public rental housing)</td></tr>
<tr><td>Those capable of bearing minimum housing expenses</td><td>30 year or Kookmin or rented or purchased public rental housing</td></tr>
<tr><td colspan="2">Partial support
(40~60% income level)</td><td>Support for housing purchase
• subscription to public housing
• support for the first home-buyer and Chonsei tenant
• 5 or 10 year-public rental housing</td></tr>
<tr><td colspan="2">Self-support
(over 70% income level)</td><td>Increase of housing supply, supporting housing sites, financing, tax incentives</td></tr>
</table>

2 'Kookmin' has the meaning of 'people' or 'national'.

As a measure to improve the quality of substandard or dilapidated housing, the government mobilizes a housing improvement fund with low-interest rates, housing management supports, and remodeling supports.

In contrast, various policy measures are mobilized to support households. For people whose income is in the lower 40% income bracket, full support is given. Among this group of people, those who are unable to bear even minimum housing expenses, either housing management support or permanent or 30-year (Kookmin) public rental housings are provided.

For those who are capable of bearing minimum housing expenses, 30 years (Kookmin) public rental housing or rented-public rental housing, or purchased-public rental housing are provided. For those within the 40~60% income level bracket, a first home-buyer and Chonsei tenant will be provided with a 5 or 10 year-public rental housing or a right to subscribe to public housing.

All these measures are mobilized to help people on lower incomes. For people in the 70% or more income level bracket, indirect support measures are considered such as increases in housing supply, support of lower-priced housing sites developed by the public sector, financial assistance, and tax incentives.

7.2.2. Housing Distribution Systems - Housing Supply Regulations

1) Outline

(1) Necessities

Excess housing demands can increase house price speculation and distort house ownership which can directly affect the housing stability of people on lower incomes. To avoid such a situation, conditions, methods, and procedures of supply need to be stipulated in the associated laws and regulations.

In most countries, governments apply a legislated public housing supply system only to public housing for those in a lower-income bracket. In Korea, by contrast, the housing supply system has been applied to those even in high price private housing. The main reason for this is to promote fairness in the distribution of the limited housing units available for those awaiting the opportunity to purchase a new house. In basic terms, the housing supply system is directly connected to the pricing of houses supplied.

As competition-based pricing of newly-built housing often results in house prices skyrocketing to unsustainable levels, it leads to adverse predicaments for lower-income households. To counteract these adverse effects all newly-built housings price levels in Korea have been decided upon by the preset price limit system, a system that has been in situ for many years.

In the case of existing housing, the price is determined in the market without any interference from the government. Therefore, the Korean housing distribution system can be said to be a supply-order system of newly-built housing that complies with strict laws and regulations.

One thing to note is that the final decision regarding the distribution of newly-built houses is often made based on an applicant's waiting time and the amount they have contributed to the national housing and urban fund (NHUF). In Korea, a huge amount of financial resources for countrywide mass house-building programs and for helping those on lower incomes to purchase housing has accumulated through sources such as:

- Subscription savings, subscription deposits, subscription installments and comprehensive housing subscription saving for NHUF;
- Government budgets, transfers from lottery funds, etc. for NHUF;
- Down payments and intermediate payments of home buyers paid to house builders before moving into housing. This is a type of advance payment by purchasers to relieve house builders' shortages of funds under the guarantee of the government;

(2) Special Features of Korean Housing Distribution System

One of the most distinctive features of the Korean housing distribution system is the cooperative linkage in place between the subscription of newly–built housing and the fundraising that exists to build large quantities of housing. By contrast, most advanced countries' housing distribution systems if any depend heavily on the housing market system.

Another important feature is the provision in place for impoverished non-homeowners, which include public rental housing, loan guarantees, and low-interest rate loans. Interestingly enough, the Korean housing distribution system shows a similarity in part with the housing distribution or allocation system used for social (public) housing in socialist countries or planned economies, although the market context in Korea has changed dramatically in recent years.

(3) Status and History of Housing Distribution System

Figure 22 illustrates the status of the Housing supply regulation in the enforcement system of the Housing Act. This regulation is one of the five enforcement regulations to execute the Housing Act and its presidential decrees.

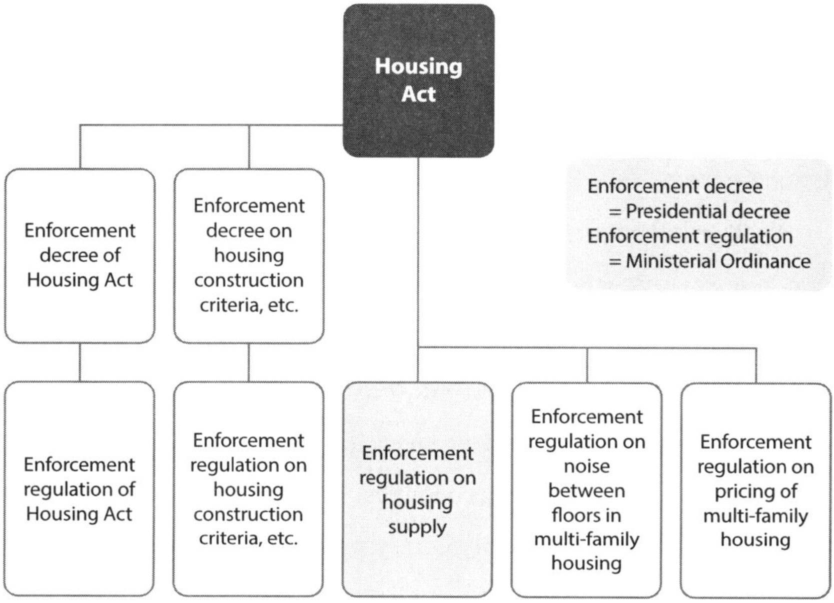

Figure 22 ● Housing Supply Regulation in the enforcement system of the Housing Act

In August 1977 the 'Regulation on the Preferred Supply of National Housing' was enacted. This regulation was applied to national housing only. In July 1978 the 'Housing Supply Regulation' on public and private housing was enacted. Since then the regulations have been revised many times. These revisions were made to reflect the changing circumstances of housing demand and supply and to assist aspiring homeowners taking off from lower-income backgrounds.

2) Point at issue - Is it still necessary?

Given the limited housing supply, the regulation is required for an appropriate and orderly distribution system to be in place. With the housing supply ratio exceeding 100% since the mid-2000s, a question arises is whether this type of regulation is still necessary or not. Some reasons as to why the regulation needs to be maintained at its current level are as follows:

- The intense competition that exists for housing built in good locations indicates the necessity for tighter regulation.
- There are numerous potential buyers or aspiring homeowners who have put their trust in government rules and regulations and have waited for decades for the opportunity to buy property. The abolishment of the Housing Supply Regulation before substantially fulfilling this demand could bring about a matter of trust between the government and the potential buyers.

3) Main Contents [3]

(1) Basic Principles

Housing suppliers must comply with the regulations in regards to the conditions, methods, procedures of subscription, and deposit amount.

3 The housing supply conditions, methods and procedures explained here are mainly based on regulations as of 2020. These are subject to changes announced by the government thereafter.

However, a special supply system is applied to patriots and veterans, the handicapped, and evictees from development sites. Candidates fulfilling these regulation criteria are allowed to subscribe and purchase newly-built housings.

The housing price limit (ceiling) system applies with some exceptions such as urban lifestyle small housings, and houses built on private land.[4] Therefore, if someone subscribes to and is successful in purchasing a housing unit, then he or she can exploit the potential margin between the market price and the controlled price, i.e. capital gain.

It is also required for the residential building developers to comply with regulations regarding the supply of adjunctive rental housing. This means that, if a developer wants to build housing for sale, then the developer should build rental housing concurrently on the same construction site at a rate stipulated in the regulation (30~60%). It is a type of precondition for housing construction permission. In short, the construction, distribution, and possession of housing have been carried out by a series of set plans and guidelines of the Korean government.

The following graph illustrates the procedure for subscription and a contract for newly-built housing.

4 The price limit regulation on the houses built on private land was eased in April 2015, but reintroduced in 2019.

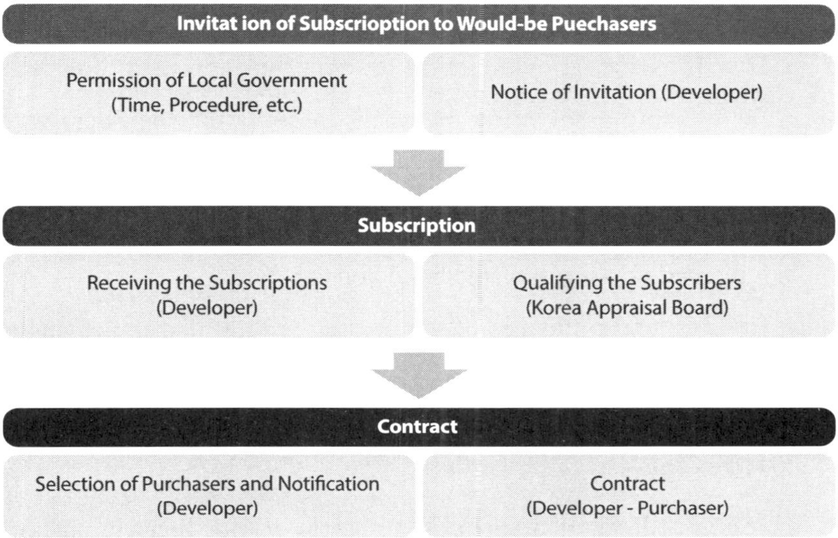

Figure 23 ● Procedure of subscription and contract of newly-built housing

(2) Application of Regulations

A developer who constructs more than 30 (20 until 2014) housing units should get permission for housing site development and house building from local government. However, there are some exceptions to this rule, e.g. in cases of urban lifestyle small housings and mixed-use buildings.[5]

Some parts of the regulation do not apply to special purpose housing

5 These buildings can be built according to the Building Code, not to the Housing Act which allows the development of housing site causing greatly a change in the category of land resulting in the increase of plot value.

as follows:

- Housings for redevelopment association members, housings for housing association members (association members who try to build houses by themselves), housings for evictees from residential or industrial development sites;
- Laborers' housing, callable bond housing;[6]
- Housing for employees of the institution relocated to provincial areas, foreigners' housing, and urban lifestyle small housing.

(3) Principles of Distribution

Housing is distributed under the principle of 'one housing unit per one household' and in principle, the head of a family living in the same municipality where the housing construction site is located is eligible for a newly-built housing subscription.

The scope of the municipality was broadened from Shi, Gun (local) to Do (provincial) in 2012 to allow for residents living in a city to apply for a housing subscription for residential projects in other cities within the same province. This is to expand housing demand in a stagnated market. Also, there are special distribution cases exempt from the

6 These are special in that laborers and purchasers of callable bond are eligible for subscription of these housings without waiting in the long queues for subscription.

application of the regulation, which includes housings built-in Sejong[7] city, eleven Innovation Cities[8], and six Enterprise Cities. These cities are under construction in local areas to disseminate government ministries or public corporations and help induce private businesses to leave SMR.

(4) Subscriber Savings, Deposits, Installment

Savings and deposit schemes have been operated, firstly, to raise funds to help real buyers and house builders and secondly, to give priority to would-be buyers waiting for a longer time. In 2009, the 'comprehensive housing subscription savings'(CHSS) scheme was introduced in addition to the existing three savings systems.

Table 55 ● Subscriber savings · deposits · installment

	Subscription savings	Subscription (term) deposit	Subscription installment (deposit)
Qualification	Head of non-homeowning household subscribing to public (national) housing	Head of household subscribing to private housing	Head of household subscribing to private housing below 85 m^2
Deposit or installment amount	20~100 thousand Won per month	Seoul, Busan/ metropolitan/city below 85 m^2: 3/2.5/2mil.won below 135 m^2: 6/4/3mil.won over 135 m^2: 15/10/5mil.won	50~500 thousand Won per month

7 Sejong city is a multi-purpose administrative city being built at the centre of the Korean peninsula to disperse the function of the Korean government concentrated in Seoul metropolitan region.

8 Innovation cities are 11 cities being built all over the country to send many government corporations to disseminate industry and population for the balanced regional development.

	Subscription savings	Subscription (term) deposit	Subscription installment (deposit)
Usage	National Housing and Urban Fund	National Housing and Urban Fund	Bank housing account

※ Based on the Housing Supply Regulation.

Subscription saving is necessary for the head of a non-homeowning household (houseless family) subscribing to public (national) housing[9]. The subscriber has to open a bank saving account and put 20,000~100,000 Won per month in the account. All the money collected in these accounts becomes an important source of NHUF. A subscription (term) deposit is necessary for the head of a household subscribing to private housing. The subscriber has to put a designated amount of money at the time of opening the deposit account. The amount collected in this account also becomes a source of NHUF.

Subscription installment (deposit) is required for the head of a household subscribing to private housing below 85 m^2. The subscriber has to open an account and put 50~500 thousand Won per month in the account. The amount collected through this account goes to the housing account of the bank, not to NHUF, and is used to support private housing builders and purchasers of these housings. Among these three account systems, subscription savings are the most suitable for people

9 Public (national) housing is the small housing or affordable housing with the size below 85 m^2 supported by the public sector either in fund or land. .

on the lowest incomes.

(5) Comprehensive Housing Subscription Saving (CHSS)

This saving system was introduced to integrate three subscribers' schemes, namely subscriber savings for public housing and subscriber deposits and installment for private housing. This scheme applies to both public and private housing. Anyone can open a CHSS account regardless of age or home ownership. A deposit of 20,000~500,000 Won must be paid into the account each month.

CHSS was introduced in 2009, 20 years after the initiation of housing installments in 1989. The introduction of this saving scheme is to expand the subscription opportunities for those in need of housing and to increase the size of the housing fund. From the 1st of September, 2015 new subscribers were not allowed to open any type of account other than the CHSS account. This can be said to be the beginning of the unification of diversified subscription account systems.

Table 56 ● Subscription accounts by types (as of Dec. 2020) (000 accounts)

	Total	CHSS	S-Savings	S-Deposit	S-installment
Total	27,224(100%)	25,559(93.9%)	438(1.6%)	1,049(3.9%0	179(0.7%)
Seoul	6,801(25.0%)	6,142	159	422	77
Incheon & Gyeonggi-Do	8,910(32.7%)	8,286	163	403	58
5 Metro-politan cities	5,353(19.7%)	5.138	50	137	28
Others	6,161(22.6%)	5,993	65	87	16

(Source: MOLIT)

The total number of housing subscription accounts opened at the end of Dec. 2020 was 27.2 million. Almost all households in this country have at least one active housing subscription account. Among the account types, CHSS, the newest one, took the largest portion (94%, 25.5million) followed by S-Deposit, S-Savings, and S-Installment.

Spatially, SMR took the lion's share of all accounts. As many as 15.7 million accounts or 57.7% of the total accounts were opened in SMR, which was higher than the ratio of population in SMR, 50.0%. This means that SMR residents generally hold more than one account and are more ready to subscribe to newly-built housings.

4) Suppliers' Housing Subscription System

To build and supply housings, a supplier has to comply with conditions to enter into the subscription process, namely securing land ownership and guarantees as stipulated in the housing supply regulation. Before inviting subscribers the supplier should fulfill the precondition of completing over 60% of the skeleton construction work together with two contractors' joint liabilities on a guarantee. If the supplier has a construction guarantee issued by the Korea Housing Guarantee Co.[10] or insurance companies, the supplier can begin the process of subscription upon the first phase of development.

---

10 This organization was changed to Korea Housing and Urban Guarantee Co. (HUG) in 2015.

If the housings are constructed by the central government, local governments, LH, and local public corporations, subscription may proceed when construction work reaches 40% completion instead of 60% of the total work. In all cases, the right of pledge should be cleared before entering into the subscription process. Among the subscribers applying for housing, the winners or would-be homeowners will be chosen by a lottery system.

Then why these kinds of complicated regulations related to housing subscription and distribution are necessary? To alleviate the financial burden of house builders, the Korean government allowed them to sell the housing under construction before completion. Since the sale of housing before completion can cause problems of default and breach of contract, the house builders are required to get a housing completion guarantee from Korea Housing and Urban Guarantee Co. (HUG) or two contractors' joint liabilities on a guarantee. To prevent an unexpected loss of subscribers and, consequently, guarantors in case of the bankruptcy of house builders, a set of regulations like these are stipulated. In this regard, HUG has played an important role both in maintaining the housing supply system and in securing the needed financial resources for the massive supply of housing.

5) Methods of Housing Supply

(1) General Supply

As for national (public) housing, the ranking of buyers is determined by the number of deposit payments, i.e. the length of the payment period. To be included in the top-ranking group, one should have a record of 24 (12 until 2017) times of payment in SMR, and 12 (6 until 2017) times in non-SMR. In the same ranking group, an individual's ranking is determined by the total scores acquired by aggregating an individual's scores allocated to a period of non-home ownership, deposit amount, family size, etc.

In the case of middle-size (60~85 m^2) national housing built by private developers with the support of the NHUF, those who have a record of one year or twelve subscriber savings deposit payments are eligible for a subscription. To be eligible for private housing, either a certain amount of deposit or period of subscription savings and installments as stipulated in the regulations are needed.

(2) Special Housing Supply and Group Supply

10% of national or private housing units equal to or smaller than 85 m^2 are supplied preferentially to patriots, veterans, and newly-wed couples. Multi-child families and first home buyers also can benefit from this special supply.

Table 57 ● Special supply of housing

<table>
<tr><th colspan="2" rowspan="2">Objects</th><th colspan="2">Housing types</th><th rowspan="2">Special rules</th></tr>
<tr><th>Public Housing</th><th>Private Housing</th></tr>
<tr><td colspan="2">Recommended by authorities, etc. (evictees, disabled, etc.)</td><td colspan="2">10%</td><td>• Increase of supply at the discretion of Mayors or Governors
- (NH)10% → No limit
- (Private)10% → 15%(SMR), 20%(non-SMR)</td></tr>
<tr><td rowspan="5">Personal application</td><td>Newlyweds</td><td>15%</td><td>10%</td><td rowspan="4">• Local governments can increase or decrease the volume of each case within the limit of 10%p.
* The total volume (65%) and minimum volume (3%) should be maintained.</td></tr>
<tr><td>Multi-child</td><td>10%</td><td>5%</td></tr>
<tr><td>Living with an old parent</td><td>5%</td><td>3%</td></tr>
<tr><td>First home buyer</td><td>20%</td><td>-</td></tr>
<tr><td>Patriots</td><td>5%</td><td>-</td><td>-</td></tr>
<tr><td colspan="2">Total</td><td>Below 65%</td><td>Below 28%</td><td>-</td></tr>
</table>

※ Based on the Housing Supply Regulation.

6) Contract and Payment

Would-be homeowners should pay 10% of the housing price as subscription money, 20% including the subscription money as a down payment, and 60% as an intermediate payment. In the case of rental housing, 40% of a rental security deposit needs to be paid. The remaining amount will be paid during the moving-in period. As for the timing of payments, subscription money should be paid at the time of subscription, down payments at the time of making the contract and intermediate payments need to be paid before and after 50% of construction work.

7) Management of Would-be Occupants and Dwellers

There are restrictions in place on multiple subscriptions to prevent over speculation and to provide equal opportunity across the board for non-homeowners. For housing units equal to or smaller than 85 m^2 (national housing), multiple subscriptions are prohibited, particularly those in designated overpopulation control zones in the SMR for 5 years and in other areas for 3 years. This applies to individuals who have been selected as purchasers. In the case of housing units bigger than 85 m^2, it is prohibited in the overpopulation control zone in the SMR to apply for another subscription for 3 years after being selected as a purchaser, and in case of other areas for 1 year. In the case of land-leasing housing built on land leased from the public sector, reapplication for the subscription is prohibited for 5 years from the point of selection.

On the other hand, there are restrictions on the resale of newly-built housing purchased in SMR for 1 to 10 years for the same purpose. This restriction which was introduced in 1981 to control speculation was relaxed in 2014 to boost the real estate market but has been retightened since 2017.

Table 58 ● Resale restriction periods of the housings purchased (as of Dec. 2020)

Housing Land			Resale restriction period for buyers	
			Speculation ridden areas	Other areas
SMR	Housing on the sites developed by the public sector	Housing price over 100% of market price	3 years	3 years
		85~100% of market price	4 years	4 years
		70~85% of market price	6 years	6 years
		Below 70% of market price	8 years	8 years
	Housing on the sites developed by the private sector	Housing price over 100% of market price	3 years	1.5 years
		85~100% of market price	3 years	2 years
		70~85% of market price	3 years	3 years
		Below 70% of market price	4 years	4 years

※ Based on the Housing Supply Regulation.

A purchaser of newly-built housing cannot resell their housing during the periods stipulated in the regulations. If a house is built on a site developed by the public sector and the purchasing price from the house builder is lower than the market price, the purchaser should wait 3 years (formerly 1 year before 2019) before the resale of purchased housing. In the case of housing built on sites developed by the private sector, the restriction periods shrink. These restriction periods vary according to the differences between the purchased price and the market price and to whether the housing is built in the speculation-ridden areas or not.

Another restriction imposed on the purchaser of newly-built

housing is the residency requirement. The residency requirement applies to public housing in general and private housing built on the sites developed by the public sector. A purchaser of the newly-built housing meeting the above condition is obliged to live in the purchased house for up to 5 years before selling to others. The period of required residency is determined by the difference between the purchased price and market price as shown in this table.

Table 59 ● Residency requirement

Price of Purchased housing	Required residency period
Purchased price less than 80% of the market price	5 years
Purchased price equal to or more than 80% of the market price	3 years

8) Problems and Countermeasures

(1) Problems

In operating the housing distribution system one of the most difficult issues is how to identify and confirm the exact income of non-homeowner households (houseless families) considering that priority is always given to low-income households.

Besides, compared to newly-built housing, the support for and management of existing housing is a lot lower. Financial support and tax incentives are mainly targeted at newly-built housing, while no incentive for the deliberate management of existing housings is given. This tendency expedites the dilapidation of existing housing and shortens the overall lifespan of housing.

(2) Countermeasures

Efforts are currently being made to prevent housing subscriptions by high-income non-home owner households by mobilizing the social welfare management network. It is managed by the Ministry of Health and Welfare (MOHW) and contains various kinds of information on households and household members.

In regards to the dilapidation of existing housing stock, a sufficient supply of housings may prevent such a trend of housing dilapidation. However, replacing all existing housing incurs huge costs and is time-consuming and unrealistic, thus the revitalization of housing renovation programs is in place, to upgrade the condition of existing housing by the Korean government.

7.2.3. Improvement and Practical Use of Existing Housing - Rebuilding and Remodeling

1) Rebuilding

The housing rebuilding program aims to improve the conditions of housings and their environment in case the urban infrastructure for the dilapidated housings is well maintained. This is a part of urban redevelopment. The local government decides whether to rebuild or upgrade existing housings after reviewing the safety inspection report made by an expert in this field, looking specifically at urban planning in the area and local circumstances. Here, the safety inspection report plays a crucial role in determining the rebuilding of housing

(1) Requirements for Rebuilding

Rebuilding regulations define deteriorated buildings subject to rebuilding as being: 1) more than 20 years old, 2) physically dilapidated, 3) vulnerable to earthquakes and 4) economically and financially feasible to rebuild.[11] On top of this definition, the Seoul Metropolitan Government (SMG) strengthened these conditions in 2003 by extending the minimum age of housing eligible for rebuilding from 20 years to 20~40 years by city ordinances to prevent waste of resources.

In opposition to this inhibitory rule by the SMG, the central government eased rebuilding regulations in 2012 to promote housing rebuilding. It was stipulated directly in the law that "despite the

11 * 'Act on the Maintenance and Improvement of Urban Areas and Dwelling Conditions for Residents' stipulates the conditions and procedures of rebuilding in detail.

* Rebuilding is different from remodeling. In rebuilding, an old and dilapidated housing is demolished and a brand new housing is constructed on the site. By contrast, in remodeling, the main structures of old housing are maintained without demolition works taking place and other parts of the housing units are expanded, improved and strengthened.

strengthened ordinance of local governments [SMG], buildings that have 'important physical and structural defects (IPSD)' can be rebuilt." Most buildings, constructed before 1992 when earthquake-resistant design became compulsory, were able to be included as a part of the IPSD building classification. Through this legislation, the redevelopment process for houses built before 1992 became more simplified than in previous years.

The governmental difference between local and central administrations is the most notable in their conflicting points of emphasis, with the SMG concentrating its efforts on the urban landscape and its functions in dealing with housing rebuilding and the central government stressing the importance of the national economy and equitability.

(2) Increase of Small Housing Construction

In the case of rebuilding projects implemented in crowded areas in the SMR (overpopulation control zone), the floor space ratio can be raised to a maximum level as stipulated by law. This is another initiative of the central government to overrule potentially inhibitory ordinances of the SMG emphasizing the urban landscape.

However, the central government through its regulations has deemed that the margin between a maximum level floor space and that of a SMG's regulation should be used to build additional smaller-sized housing units. By increasing the number of small-sized housing in urban areas in this way, the Korean government aims to increase the number of original residents resettling in developed areas.

2) Remodeling

(1) Outline

Remodeling is used to prevent any further deterioration of housing older than 15 years and to enhance their function. As an incentive for remodeling, a developer can expand the total floor space by 30% in a multi-family housing unit and within the 30% of floor space expansion, the developer has the flexibility to increase the number of housing units. In this case, the increased housing units are required not to exceed 10% of the total housing units.

(2) Remodeling to Increase Floor Numbers

Remodeling to increase floor numbers or elevation of a building or so-called upward remodeling was allowed in 2013 after a long debate on the sensitive issues related to the safety of the housing after remodeling. Some scholars opposed the idea of upward remodeling because upward remodeling can change the overall main structure of an apartment building and during this process, unseen structural damages might become a future safety issue. In allowing upward remodeling, the Korean government strengthened the associated safety criteria.

For this purpose, remodeling-related regulations were changed in 2014 to incorporate safety inspections carried out by independent safety diagnosis institutions to streamline safety confirmation processes. The structural drawings must be submitted at the time of the remodeling applications, and the local government is obliged to set up a basic plan for remodeling in advance to permit upward remodeling.

7.3. Recent Changes in the Housing Distribution Policy

7.3.1. Changes in the Depression Period

Changes in the housing distribution system introduced in the mid-2010s to meet the structural changes of the housing market can be summarized as follows:

① Score-based subscription system, which was introduced to select the most appropriate subscriber by marking scores relating to important factors, was abolished in the case of housing exceeding 85 m^2 in size. In a stagnant housing market, the need to apply this system even to larger-sized housing was reduced and thus deregulated.[12]

② Strict rules on the subscription of homeowners were relieved.

12 Under the score-based subscription system, applicants with a longer houseless status and a lower-income get a higher score and are more advantageous in purchasing newly-built houses.

Leaving aside non-homeowner families, homeowners also were allowed to be involved with top rank subscribers applying for private housing.

③ Special housing supply to multi-child families was increased. To promote childbirth, a special supply ratio of private housing was raised from 5% in total housing units to 10%. In the case of public housing, a 10% limit had already been applied.

④ As discussed above, the ban on the redevelopment of relatively new houses was eased by shortening the age qualification of houses from 40 years to 30 years by law in 2014. As a result, the SMG's redevelopment ban on apartment houses aged less than 40 years was changed. Consequently, 248,000 housing units completed during 1989~1991 benefited from this change.

7.3.2. Changes in the Booming Period

The regulation for housing distribution has been strengthened in the booming period after 2015 to prevent speculative demand in the housing market centering on the apartment housings to be reconstructed. In this context, various measures to maintain housing stability have been announced.

A subscription account needs to be opened even for the 2nd ranking subscribers who are subscribing to leftover housings in subscription adjustment areas, which was not requested previously. In the case of the

1st rank subscription, a subscription account fulfilling the condition of the enrolment period, deposit amount, etc. is required.

The supplying method of land for public rental housing was also changed in 2017. The land for building public rental housing with the size of national housing, that is 85 m^2 or less, will be supplied by the public sector developer such as local corporations through a "lottery system" instead of a competitive bidding system to prevent the hoisting of land price.

As an effort to prevent speculative demand in reconstruction and redevelopment sites, the government tightened the regulations on the transferring of reconstruction association membership and clarified the minimum supply ratio of mandatory rental housing in redevelopment projects, e.g. from 15% or less to 10~15% in Seoul, to lower the profitability of the project.

There was another amendment of the Housing Supply Regulation later in 2017. The main amendment was on the qualification for the 1st rank group among numerous subscribers waiting for the purchase of newly-built housing. In SMR and speculation-ridden areas in non-SMR regions, 2 years of the waiting period after the opening of the subscription account became necessary, which was the extension from the previous 1 year and 6 months respectively.

In the same vein, there was a change in the special supply of housing in 2018 as follows:

① The proportion of housings supplied to newlyweds among the total housing provided doubled from 15% to 30% in national housing and from 10% to 20% in private housing to promote the marriage of the young generation;

② Housings worth more than 900 million won located in speculation ridden areas are excluded from special supply; and

Land owners who sold the land for building public rental housing in urban regeneration projects, etc. are newly included as the beneficiary of special housing supply.

Facing the continuing rise of house prices despite a series of policy packages, the government stepped up the control on the housing transaction in speculation-ridden areas once again in 2020. Firstly, the government designated SMR, Daejon, and Cheong-ju as special areas for speculation prevention to cool down the steep rising house prices not only in SMR but also in major cities in Chungcheong-do provinces, the middle part of Korea.

And secondly, to prevent speculative transactions, the areas near the International Trade and Cooperation Center (in central Gangnam) was designated as the land transaction permission area, or LTPA, which was the first designation of LTPA inside Seoul.

7.4. Conclusion and Future Direction

1) Policy Shift from 1 housing to Multi-housing for 1 household

The Korean government has maintained a '1 housing unit for 1 household' policy for decades. However, considering the structural changes in the housing market, it is time to shift toward a 'multi-housing units for 1 household' policy. For this purpose, the regulations on construction and distribution need to be changed flexibly. In reality, some changes have emerged towards this policy direction in such a way that the scope of rural housing exempted from housing supply regulations has been expanded. Besides, REITs have been promoted by providing tax incentives and financial support to help them to play an important role as a channel for inducing investment as well as managing rental housings.

2) Emphasis on the Improvement and Practical Use of Existing Housing

For decades, as a measure to supply a huge number of housings in a short time, old existing houses tended to be demolished and replaced by high-rise apartment houses on the sites. This type of redevelopment however has adverse side effects accompanied with it such as waste of resources, gentrification, destruction of community, etc. Now is the time to underline the importance of existing housings especially for the improvement of daily life for people on low incomes. To this end, upward remodeling and rebuilding programs have been encouraged along with the construction of long life span housing. Recently, urban regeneration, as well as upward remodeling, have been encouraged after the revisions of the laws. This signifies the changes in the focus of housing supply policy from mass construction and distribution to the combination of construction, structural improvements, and preservation of housing.

Chapter 8

Housing Welfare Policy

8.1. Introduction: Concept and Housing Survey

8.1.1. Concept and Necessities of Housing Welfare

1) Concept

Housing is often considered a universal right. It has always been recognized as comprising a key aspect of everyday life since it is closely associated with security and with health and well-being. Housing welfare can be defined as the general health, happiness, and safety of a person with housing or the status of having a pleasant life through smooth possession of and living in housing. In Korea, housing welfare has been one of the four major pillars in welfare along with education, health care, and child care.[1]

2) Why is Housing Welfare Necessary?

Living in satisfactory housing is often considered to be one of the most important aspects of people's lives. However, housing costs take up a large share of the household budget and represent the largest single expenditure for many individuals and families. Thus, the low-income group in Korea, particularly those in the first and second-lowest income quintile experience difficulty owning their housing and reside in Chonsei or monthly rent housing.

In particular, the root of many social problems can be due to a shortage of adequate housing. Also, housing instability can be a source of social conflict or unrest. Governments are concerned by the increase of people who live on welfare benefits and/or the rise in the number of homeless people due to housing instability. In this situation, the intervention from the government is considered to be crucial and thus the provision and implementation of appropriate services by the government are increasing in Korea along with other countries.

---

1 Housing welfare can also be defined as the status of leading pleasant life based on the smooth possession and utilization of housing.

3) Legal Basis of Housing Welfare in Korea

Housing welfare is proclaimed in the Constitution of Korea. This stipulation manifests the importance of housing welfare in Korean society. Detailed responsibility of the government is identified in the Housing Act. Other related laws and regulations including the Rental Housing Act also stipulate necessary means and procedures for housing welfare.

8.1.2. Housing Survey

In this section, the results of the housing survey will be analyzed to understand the conditions of the housing market and housing welfare services in Korea.

1) Overview

The housing survey is undertaken to enhance the understanding of the residential environment and characteristics of the household. This survey began in 2006 and was conducted every two years until 2016. It has been changed to conduct every year, with 60,000 households since 2017.

The Population and Housing Census is the more accurate survey with a larger sample size conducted every 5 years by Statistics Korea. In contrast, the Housing survey is a sample survey conducted biennially by the Ministry of Land, Infrastructure and Transport (MOLIT).

2) Features of Housing

Housing quality can be measured in various ways. One major element of the quality of housing is the availability of sufficient space in the dwelling. The result of the housing survey shows that the average size of dwellings per person is 27.8 m^2 in 2008, 28.5 m^2 in 2010, 31.7 m^2 in 2012, 33.5 m^2 in 2014, 33.2 m^2 in 2016, 31.7 m^2 in 2018, 32.9 m^2 in 2019, and 33.9 m^2 in 2020. These changes show a substantial improvement of housing conditions and quality in numerical terms has been made.

In the meantime, the number of households living below the minimum residential standard (MRS) has reduced significantly. The number has decreased from 1,840 thousand (10.6%) in 2010 to 1,280 thousand (7.2%) in 2012, 980 thousand (5.3%) in 2014, 1,030 thousand (5.4%) in 2016, 1,110 thousand (5.7%) in 2018, 1,060 thousand (5.3%) in 2019, and further to 990 thousand (4.6%) in 2020. In other words, the number of households living below MRS fell by 850 thousand households or a 46.2% decrease between 2010 and 2020, although there have been ups and downs slightly. This index had shown a 5~6% level since 2014, but dropped below 5% level for the first time in 2020.

Another index meaningful for assessing housing quality is the number of households living in a basement, semi-basement, and rooftop rooms. This number reduced from 0.38 million households (1.9%) in 2018 to 0.27 million households (1.3%) in 2019, and this is the lowest level since 2006. However, the number increased again to 0.33 million households (1.6%) in 2020. Such changes also confirm that there has been meaningful improvement in housing for the quality aspect as well as its quantity.

3) Decrease in Homeownership[2]

The extent of homeownership continuously declined in the first half of the 2010s. In 2010, it was 54.3% but it went down to 53.8% in 2012 and 53.6% in 2014. In particular, the homeownership decreased among the low-income group while homeownership showed an increase in middle and high-income households.

More specifically, change in homeownership varied between different income groups. The homeownership ratio among the low-income group was 46.9% in 2010, 50.4% in 2012, and 47.5% in 2014. However, the homeownership ratio among middle and high-income groups was much higher than that of low-income groups. The home ownership ratio of the middle-income group was 54.0% in 2010, 51.8% in 2012, and 52.2% in 2014, and that of the high-income group was 69.5% in 2010 64.6% in 2012, and 69.5% in 2014. In other words, there

2 This is the ratio of households who are living in their own houses in the total households.

has been a growing disparity between different income groups, leaving the low-income group in the most vulnerable position in the housing.

One of the reasons behind this situation was that the stagnated housing market and declining housing prices in the first half of the 2010s made it more difficult for the low-income group to purchase houses and forced them to stay in Chonsei or monthly rental housing. However, this trend has been reversed in 2016 with the increase of the homeownership ratio to total households. This increase in homeownership ratio is interpreted as the influence of the continuing rise in Chonsei deposits and the recovery of the housing sales market. The recovery of the housing market has changed Chonsei demand into purchase demand resulting in the rise of homeownership from 53.6% in 2014 to 56.8% in 2016, 57.7% in 2017 and 2018, 58.0% in 2019, and 57.9% in 2020.

Figure 24 shows the trend of the homeownership ratio at different income groups.[3] The homeownership ratio of low-income households situated at the lowest, while that of middle-income or high-income households at the upper part. It is worth noting that the homeownership ratio has increased among middle- and high-income levels, whereas that of the low-income level has declined or stagnated. The decline of homeownership in low-income group portrays vividly the aggravating residential condition of these people

3 The homeownership ratio at different income groups has not published since 2018.

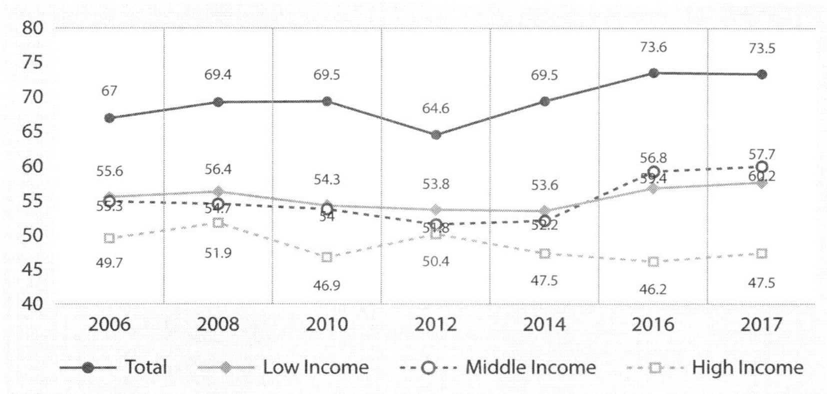

Figure 24 ● Changes in homeownership of each income level
(Source: MOLIT)

The survey results also demonstrated the changes in types of occupancy. In 2019, those living in 'own house' took 58.0%, while 'monthly rental with deposit' took 19.7% and 'Chonsei' took 15.1%. The proportion of monthly rental households had increased significantly until 2016 and slightly stagnated around 60.4% since 2017. Figure 25 shows the reversed proportions of Chonsei and monthly rental among the total households living in rental houses.

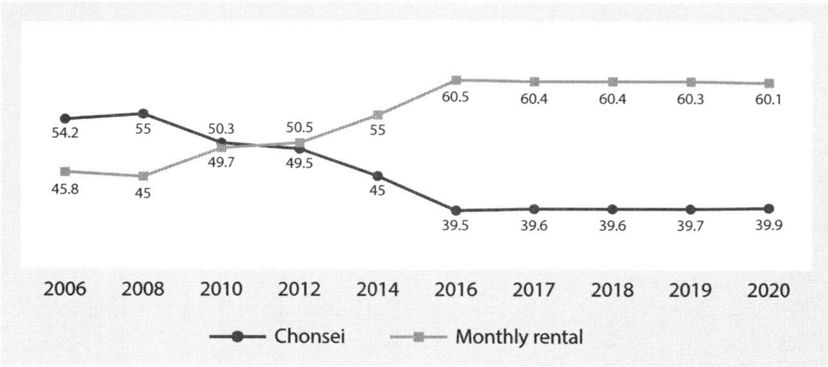

Figure 25 ● Proportions of Chonsei and monthly rental
(Source: MOLIT)

4) Housing Price to Annual Income Ratio (PIR)

Housing cost burden can be assessed with the indices of house price to annual income ratio (PIR) and rent to income ratio (RIR). Firstly, PIR is the index to know the extent to which people's easiness to purchase their own houses. The survey result shows that PIR in SMR has been maintaining a 6.7~6.9 level which is much higher than other regions or other metropolitan cities.

For the nation as a whole, the PIR has changed from 4.3 in 2010 to 5.1 in 2012, 4.7 in 2014, 5.6 in 2016, 5.5 in 2018 and 2020. In the case of SMR, the ratio has been maintained between 6.7 and 6.9 without significant fluctuation. However, the number increased to 8.0 in 2020 reflecting the sharp rise of housing prices in Seoul and vicinity in 2019 and 2020. This result means that ordinary households have to accumulate all of their income for eight years without spending any other to purchase a house located in Seoul.

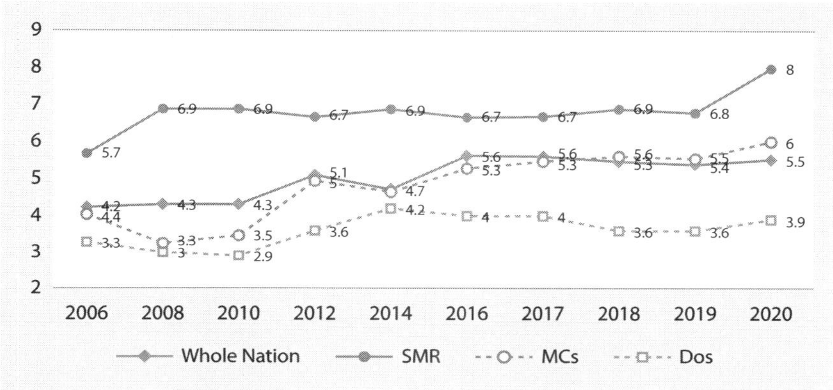

Figure 26 ● Price to income ratio in the whole nation and each region
(Source: MOLIT)

Rent to income ratio (RIR) is to measure to what extent ordinary households spend as a housing expenditure (rent) in their income. In general, RIR is supposed not to exceed 30% to maintain ordinary life spending on necessities. According to the housing survey result, RIR for the whole nation had been lowered from the peak of 20.3% in 2014 to 18.1% in 2016 and 16.1% in 2019, but rose again to 16.6% in 2020. In 2020 RIR in SMR was 18.6%, while that of metropolitan cities was 15.1%, and Dos (provinces) was 12.7%.

It is assessed that the rapid increase of rent in SMR pushed up RIR in the whole nation, which implies that the living condition of the households, living in rental houses in SMR has not improved significantly, albeit the ratio has maintained below 30% level.

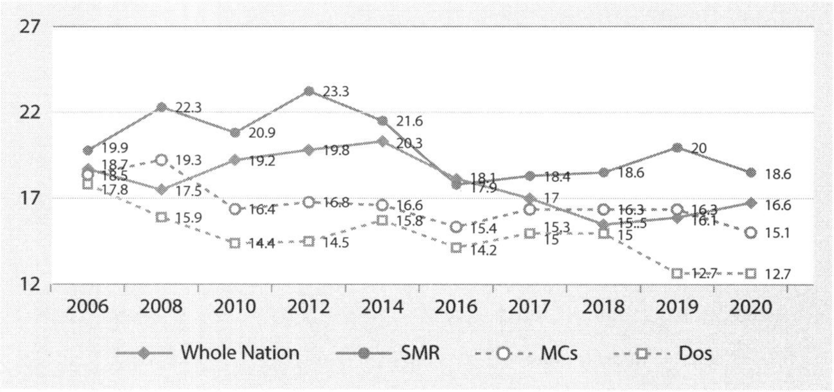

Figure 27 ● Rent to income ratio in the whole nation and each region
(Source: MOLIT)

5) Households Mobility

The average residence period for the whole household has changed from 8.6 years in 2012 to 7.6 years in 2020. In the case of home owners, i.e. the households living in their own houses, the average residence period has changed from 12.5 years in 2012 to 10.6 in 2020, whereas that of tenants has changed from 4.2 in 2012 to 3.2 in 2020. This change shows, firstly, the increased mobility of households in both homeowners and tenants, and secondly, the short period of residency among tenants compared to homeowners representing the housing instability of these people.

The proportion of households who moved within 2 years in the whole nation was 32.2% in 2012, 36.9% in 2016, and then 37.2% in 2020. However, that in SMR was 41.9%. The proportion of home owners who moved within 2 years in the whole nation was 20.3% and that of tenants was 60.9%. This also indicates the unstable residential condition of tenants compared to homeowners, especially in SMR. According to the survey result, the main reason for recent moving was good facility (48.3%), journey-to-work (29.7%), to own home (28.3%), etc.

As a first-time homebuyer, the average period to purchase a house has been gradually diminished from 8.0 years in 2012, 6.7 in 2016, and 7.7 in 2020. On average, around just below 7 years had been maintained since 2014, although the number showed a sharp increase in 2020. This can be partly due to the shift away from early marriage for the young generation in recent years. It can be also because of the low-interest rate and extra financial support for first-time homebuyers. About two-thirds of first-time home-buyers have bought apartment houses since 2014. This means that first-time home-buyers, often represented by relatively young with moderate incomes, prefer an apartment house to a single house which is somewhat difficult to manage.

6) Views on Housing

The proportion of people who provided the positive answer to the question of 'I should have my own house' has recovered since 2016 from the weak trend in the first half of the 2010s. It dropped from 83.7% in 2010 to 72.8% in 2012 and 79.1% in 2014, but recovered to 82.0 % in 2016, 82.5 % in 2018 and 87.7 % in 2020.

This pattern of change may reflect the housing market conditions and the difficulties of tenants living in rental housing with the diminishing number of Chonsei housing and the rising Chonsei deposit. Another thing to note was that the higher the age of the household's head and household income, the higher this ratio was.

The survey also explored the satisfaction level of their housing condition. About the current housing condition, the satisfaction level of people has climbed from 2.92 out of four in 2014 to 2.99 in 2016, to 2.98 in 2018, and then to 3.00 in 2020 based on the assessment of respondents. Satisfaction level on living circumstances has also been enhanced during the period. (Table 60)

Table 60 ● Changes in views on housing

		2014	2016	2017	2018	2019	2020
Satisfaction level on Housing		**2.92**	**2.99**	**2.98**	**2.98**	**3.00**	**3.00**
Regions	SMR	2.88	3.01	2.97	2.96	2.98	2.99
	Metropolitan cities	2.96	2.98	3.00	3.02	3.06	3.02
	Do(Provinces)	2.96	2.98	2.99	2.97	2.99	3.00

		2014	2016	2017	2018	2019	2020
Satisfaction level on living circumstances		**2.86**	**2.93**	**2.97**	**2.94**	**2.94**	**2.97**
Regions	SMR	2.85	2.96	2.98	2.94	2.96	2.98
	Metropolitan cities	2.89	2.91	2.99	2.98	3.00	3.00
	Do(Provinces)	2.85	2.90	2.94	2.92	2.88	2.93

(Source: MOLIT, Housing Survey)

Table 61 shows various indices which indicate the main features of housing stability in Korea. The number of households living under MRS has decreased continuously, while the average size of dwellings per person has been on the rise. The housing environment satisfaction rate showed some fluctuations while the average time to buy their first home has been curtailed. All these figures illustrate the improvement of housing conditions in numbers as well as its quality.

However, a limited change in home occupancy, homeownership rate as well as RIR imply the slow improvement of housing structure and the difficulties that low-income renters may face due to the continuing heavy housing expenditure. Although the indices of these features have improved recently, the government should strive continuously to reach the goal of residential stability of low-income households.

Table 61 ● Main features of housing stability in Korea

Indices			06	08	10	12	14	16	18	19	20
Housing Quality	Households under MRS (%)		16.6	12.7	10.6	7.2	5.3	5.4	5.7	5.3	4.6
	Households in Basement, semi-basement & rooftop		4.0		4.0		2.8	3.1	1.9	1.3	1.6
	Average housing size per person (m^2)		26.2	27.8	28.5	31.7	33.5	33.2	31.7	32.9	33.9
Housing Stability	Home Occupancy (%)		55.6	56.4	54.3	53.8	53.6	56.8	57.7	58.0	57.9
	Home Ownership (%)		61.0	60.9	60.3	58.4	58.0	59.9	61.1	61.2	60.6
	Ratio of Chonsei (Monthly rental) among Lessee households (%)	Nation as a whole	54.2 (45.8)	55.0 (45.0)	50.3 (49.7)	49.5 (50.5)	45.0 (55.0)	39.5 (60.5)	39.6 (60.4)	39.7 (60.3)	-
		SMR	62.1 (37.9)	62.7 (37.3)	57.1 (42.9)	55.9 (44.1)	53.9 (46.1)	46.7 (53.3)	46.3 (53.7)	46.3 (53.7)	-
	Housing Environment Satisfaction (/4)		2.86	2.75	2.84	2.83	2.86	2.93	2.94	2.94	2.97
	Years necessary for first home purchase		8.1	8.3	8.5	8.0	6.9	6.7	7.1	6.9	7.7
Housing Mobility	Average residence period (years)	Whole Households	7.7	7.7	7.9	8.6	7.7	7.7	7.7	7.7	7.6
		Homeowners	11.0	10.8	11.4	12.5	11.2	10.6	10.7	10.7	10.6
		Lessee Households	3.1	3.3	3.4	3.7	3.5	3.6	3.4	3.2	3.2
	Movement ratio (%) (Ratio of households moved within 2 years)		37.5	35.2	35.2	32.2	36.6	36.9	36.4	36.4	37.2
Afforda-bility	PIR of Homeowners (times)		4.2	4.3	4.3	5.1	4.7	5.6	5.5	5.4	5.5
	Lessee Households RIR (%)		18.7	17.5	19.2	19.8	20.3	18.1	15.5	16.1	16.6
Views on Housing	Views on housing ownership I should have my own house (%)		-	-	83.7	(72.8)	79.1	82.0	82.5	84.1	87.7

(Source: MOLIT, Housing Survey)

8.1.3. Housing Welfare Policy

The main target of the housing welfare policy in Korea is those who are on the basic welfare (the lowest income bracket) and those who are just above the lowest income tier (second-lowest income bracket). Also, the households meeting specific criteria such as first home-buyers are included in the target group and eligible for housing welfare policy services.

1) Numbers of the People on Basic Welfare

Table 62 shows the recipients of national basic livelihood assistance and its ratio to the total population. The ratio of benefit recipients to total population had diminished from 2007 to 2014. However, the number has increased since 2015 implying that the economic conditions of the low-income level have been worsened despite the growth of national wealth, which has a significant impact on housing welfare.

Table 62 ● Numbers of the people on basic welfare (000s, %)

	2008	2009	2010	2011	2012	2013	2014	2015	2016	2017	2018	2019	2020
Number	1,530	1,569	1,550	1,469	1,394	1,359	1,329	1,646	1,630	1,582	1,744	1,881	2,134
Ratio	3.2	3.2	3.1	2.9	2.7	2.6	2.6	3.2	3.2	3.1	3.4	3.6	4.1

(Source: Statistics Korea)

2) Measures to Improve Housing Welfare

There are largely two different types of policy measures to enhance housing welfare. One is positive aid and the other is a regulatory approach. Positive aid includes low-price public rental housing and housing subsidy, while the regulatory approach involves control measures on rent or lease period.

In Korea, supplying various types of public rental housing (PRH) has been the core of housing welfare policy and thus other measures were used as supplementary means. PRH has been utilized as a means of tackling both the shortage in the absolute housing stock and the rise of price in the housing market. To resolve the problems caused by an excess demand for housing, the government has expanded low-cost public rental housing. In short, supplying public rental housing was the multifunctional policy measure to address housing market imbalance and to support housing for low-income people.

Housing voucher was also considered as a way of improving housing welfare at the beginning of the 2000s but failed to introduce largely due to budget constraints. Consequently, the Korean government focused on increasing public rental housing, especially Kookmin rental housing, until the first half of the 2010s.

However, in terms of funding, there is a difference between permanent rental housing and national (Kookmin) rental housing. In the case of permanent rental housing, its construction is funded mainly by the government budget (85%) supplemented by tenant rent (15%), and its monthly rent is set at a 30% level of market rent. By contrast, national rental housing is funded by budget (10~40%), tenant (10~30%), and LH (10%), and its monthly rent is set between 50 and 80% level of market rent. Hence permanent public rental housing is more directly contributing to the housing welfare of low-income tenants.

8.2. Current State of Welfare Policy and Future Plan

8.2.1. Policy Circumstances

1) Shortage of Rental Housing

Korea has experienced a persistent shortage of public rental housing due to the growing demand, particularly from low-income tenants suffering from the increasing rental price in the private rental market. Although the Korean government has made much effort, the proportion of public rental housing in Korea is still lagging behind that of advanced countries.[4]

4 Long-term rental housing in the total housing stock in Korea was 5.4%, whereas 11.5% in OECD countries and 9.4% in the EU countries in 2014(MOLIT). Provided the new census result is applied, the ratio of Korea increases to 8.0% in 202019.

Also, Korea has been exhibiting a limitation in expanding the public rental housing stock. The reason for this is that most Korean rental housings have been provided from newly-built housing sites which need a huge amount of money and newly developed land. Furthermore, the lack of available lands in downtown areas has hampered the expansion of rental housing supply in the right places where the demand of low-income people is concentrated.

2) Increasing Housing Expenses for Tenants

On the other hand, the burden of housing expenses for tenants has increased. This is mainly because the private rental market has experienced repetitive Chonsei shortage and the subsequent rise of Chonsei deposit or monthly rent which tends to become larger by applying high monthly rent conversion rate (MRCR)[5] in transferring some amount of Chonsei deposit to monthly rent.

Moreover, low-income households living in private rental housing have become the blind-spot of housing welfare policy. RIR of the rental

5 The MRCR rate is stipulated in the Housing Lease Protection Act (HLPA) to prevent a high conversion rate between Chonsei deposit and monthly rent. The rate is calculated by adding the constant rate stipulated in the HLPA to the key rate of the Bank of Korea. The Korean government changed MRCR in August 2020 from 4% to 2.5% by lowering the constant rate from 3.5% to 2%. However, there are many exceptions in the rental housing market, especially among unregistered private rental housings, and the conversion rate for these cases tend to reach 6%

households at the bottom 20% income bracket was 41.7%, whereas that of the total rental households was 19.2% in 2014. The housing survey conducted by MOLIT showed that the RIR of the randomly selected group of the elderly was 31.0% in 2018 and 29.9% in 2020 illustrating the difficult housing condition of this group. In general, the households which have RIR over 30% are regarded to be at risk of poverty.

8.2.2. Previous Results of Housing Welfare Policy

1) Increase of Rental Housing

The Korean government made a plan to build 1.5 million public housing units in 2008 during the MB government. Among the public rental housings in this plan purchased and leased public rental housings were also included[6] besides the newly-built housing. Table 63 shows the rapidly increasing number of private rental housing and leased rental in the public rental housing compared to permanent, 50-year, and national rental housing.

6 Purchased housings are used for Kookmin or 10-year public rental housing by the LH and local governments.

Table 63 ● Public and private rental housing stock

Year	Total	Private Total	Public Total	Permanent RH	50-year PRH	National RH(30 yrs. Purchased)	Public RH (5,10, Employee)	Happi-ness Housing	Leased RH (3/5 yrs.)
2020	3,270	1,533	1,737	213	112	743	297	89	283
		(46.9%)	(53.1)	(6.5)	(3.4)	(22.7)	(9.1)	(2.7)	(8.7)
2019	3,045	1,385	1,660	209	112	688	322	63	266
		(45.5%)	(54.5)	(6.9)	(3.7)	(22.6)	(10.6)	(2.1)	(8.7)
2018	2,985	1,415	1,570	207	111	684	295	38	235
		(47.4%)	(52.6)	(6.9)	(3.7)	(22.9)	(9.9)	(1.3)	(7.9)
2017	2,444	1,003	1,441	202	109	627	292	16	195
		(41.0%)	(59.0)	(8.3)	(4.5)	(25.7)	(11.9)	(0.7)	(8.0)
2016	2,273	915	1,358	199	108	601	281	2	166
		(40.2%)	(59.8)	(8.8)	(4.8)	(26.4)	(12.4)	(0.1)	(7.3)
2015	1,938	680	1,258	196	108	553	257	1	142
		(35.1%)	(64.9)	(10.1)	(5.6)	(28.5)	(13.3)	(0.0)	(7.4)
2014	1,708	532	1,177	193	106	521	242	-	115
		(31.1)	(68.9)	(11.3%)	(6.2%)	(30.5%)	(14.2%)	-	(6.7%)
2013	1,617	492	1,125	192	103	489	227	-	115
		(30.4)	(69.6)	(11.9%)	(6.4%)	(30.2%)	(14.0%)	-	(7.1%)
2012	1,487	449	1,038	191	102	455	205	-	86
		(30.2)	(69.8)	(12.8%)	(6.8%)	(30.5%)	(13.8%)	-	(5.8%)
2011	1,460	440	1,019	191	101	432	231	-	65
		(30.2)	(69.8)	(13.1%)	(6.9%)	(29.6%)	(15.8%)	-	(4.5%)

(Source: MOLIT)

2) Improvement of Facilities

A plan was set up to renovate the auxiliary or convenience facilities among the ill-managed permanent rental housings that are older than 15 years. For this purpose, a certain amount of budget has been appropriated every year since 2009. 76.5 billion won of the budget was secured in 2012, 33 billion won in 2015, 30 billion won in 2018 and 37 billion won (33.6 million US$) in 2020. This project is called the 'Green Home project' which includes the improvement of facilities in housing sites and the replacement of the heating system.

3) Policy for the Socially Disadvantaged

This policy includes the special supply of housing to the young generation including the newlyweds and university students. 10 to 30% of each housing type is provided to this group. Moreover, the policy also aims to provide housings for the socially disadvantaged persistently.

To this end, the provision of NHUF loans with a low interest rate (2%) has also begun to help the construction of student accommodation for college students. For the aged people, many convenient facilities, such as removal of door threshold, prevention of slipperiness, installation of a height-adjustable washing stand, etc. have been applied to the housing. Also, there was the reform of housing subsidies and the launching of housing vouchers in 2015.

4) Implementation of housing voucher system

(1) Background

Until 2014, a total of 890,000 units of long-term public rental housing and 5 billion US$ loan per year had been provided for the low-income renter households. However, it was not sufficient enough, especially for the households living in monthly rental housings. This is due to, firstly, providing long-term public rental housings to these people needs a huge amount of budget, secondly, a long time is necessary to build, and thirdly, the rigid implementation of NHUF concentrating on the loan for Chonsei rental without the consideration to monthly renters who have no collateral.

The proportion of households living in monthly rental housing was 32% and 29.6% respectively among the first and second low-income bracket households in 2014. RIR of the households in the bottom 20% income bracket and living in private rental housing was 41.7% in that year. This was a heavy burden compared to that of the same income bracket households living in public rental housing that RIR of them was just 25.1%

The Korean government considered introducing the housing voucher program in the early 2000s but failed mainly due to the budget constraint. Housing voucher was available in 28 countries among 34 OECD member countries at that time. By contrast, in Korea, the government provided housing subsidies along with other welfare benefits/subsidies by cash.

However, housing subsidies for the recipients of national basic livelihood assistance had little effect on the living conditions of these people, since they tended to use the money for something else. Therefore it had no direct relationship with dwelling type, rent level, etc., and, consequently, with housing welfare.[7]

In this circumstance, the Korean government concluded that it was necessary to support rent to low-income rental households with a voucher to practically mitigate the burden of housing expenses. For this purpose, the Korean government set up the plan to make a project model to conduct a pilot program in the first half of 2014 and a full-scale project in the second half of 2015.

(2) Structure

The recipients of voucher schemes are the people meeting the criteria of income and asset level. After discussing a series of debates with a budget and predicted expenditures, the government decided to enforce a system in which the households with less than 43% of median income are eligible for receiving a voucher.

The subsidy is given at different rates for different income levels based on standard rent by region. This can be calculated by subtracting

7 In 2013, before the implementation of voucher system, the budget for housing subsidy was 569.2 billion won (450 million US dollars)

the value of income multiplied by the self-burden ratio from standard rent, i.e. *Amount paid = standard rent* − [*income* × *self-burden ratio*].

Local governments pay the amount of housing benefit to the landlord directly to prevent the recipients from using this for other purposes. The important feature of this system is that local governments are sharing the responsibility with the central government hence the cost is shared between the public fund of the central government and the local government budget. In this way, the role of local government has expanded substantially.

Before the introduction of the housing voucher scheme, the public fund from the central government supported 50% of housing subsidies for the housings in Seoul and 80% in local areas. By contrast, in the case of the housing voucher program, 80% of funding comes from the central government budget. Delivery of voucher begins with the submitting of the application form to the local government. Then, the housing welfare agency inspects and certifies the housing where the recipient will reside, and calculates the amount to be paid. And then, the local government deposits the calculated amount of money into the landlord's account.

In 2015, the 'Housing Subsidy Program' began to support low-income rental households. 850 thousand low-income rental households began to receive a voucher to the amount of 110 thousand won as rent subsidy from July 2015. This is the actual beginning of the Housing

Voucher scheme. On the other hand, 120 thousand low-income homeowners are supported with house renovation assistance to the amount of a maximum of 9.5 million won. Table 64 shows the number of housing voucher recipients and the amount paid. The number of recipients has increased from 850 thousand in 2016 to 1.1 million in 2020. The amount paid has also increased during the period.

Table 64 ● Housing voucher recipients and the amount paid (Unit: 000 person/000won)

Classification	2013	2014	2015	2016	2019	2020
Recipients	721	706	800	800	1,040	1,189
Amount paid	80*	90*	108	113	135	153

* The amount paid according to the old housing subsidy system
(Source: MOLIT)

Regarding the qualification for housing voucher recipients. MOLIT announces public notice every year. According to the 2020 notification of MOLIT, 4 member households with the monthly income not exceeding 2,137,128 won are eligible for receiving housing vouchers. And the income level for the qualification is growing with the increase of household members.

Table 65 ● Income levels eligible for a housing voucher

Number of household member	1 member household	2 member household	3 member household
Real Income (won/month)	790,737	1,346,391	1,741,760

Number of household member	4 member household	5 member household	6 member household
Real Income (won/month)	2,137,128	2,532,497	2,927,866

(Source: MOLIT)

5) Expanding the supply of purchased and leased rental housing

From 2004, the Korean government began to purchase or lease existing houses including the houses for multi-households to use as public rental housings. The beneficiaries of these purchased and leased public rental housings are the recipients of national basic livelihood assistance benefit and single-parent family as the most vulnerable group and the households under 50% of average monthly income and disabled people are allocated to the second vulnerable group.

With the increase of housing support to the low-income level, it is necessary to provide rental housing focusing on the target beneficiaries. From this standpoint, a total of 834,862 units of public rental housings were provided during 2015~20. Among these, purchased and leased rental housings accounted for 46.4% (387,420 units)

The government made a plan to supply over 100 thousand units of public rental housings each year, and to diversify the purchasing houses and the targeting groups. In particular, the government decided to increase the supply of purchased rental housing by including studio-type housing and supply preferentially to single-member households, university students, and self-employed entrepreneurs. And the government planned to supply leased rental housing to various classes including young workers and newly-wed couples.

6) Expanding Support for Housing Weak

The Korean government has made efforts to expand support for the housing weak. For the residential stability of non-home owning households, various types of public housing, voucher, low-interest loans are provided.

According to the 2020 housing welfare plan, 210 thousand units of public housings consisting of 141 thousand units of public rental housings, 40 thousand units of private rentals with public support, 29 thousand units of public housing for sale are provided for middle- and low-income households. A housing voucher or subsidy is provided to 1.13 million households with an annual income equal to or smaller than 45% of median income. Also, NHUF provides low-interest loans for purchasing or renting houses for 290,000 households.

Table 66 shows the results of housing supports in previous years and the plan for 2021. As shown here the total number of households receiving government support has been growing. Especially PRH, public housing for sale and housing vouchers have been the main policy tools to increase government support.

Table 66 ● Housing support results and plan (000s)

Supports		2015	2016	2017	2018	2019	2020	2021
Public housing	PRH	124	125	127	148	138	151	145
	Private rental with public support	-	-	-	46	47	40	40
	Public housing for sale	**19**	15	15	19	31	31	35
Housing Voucher(subsidy)		800	804	810	940	1,040	1,130	1,277
NHUF loan	Purchase	85	87	94	100	55	48	69
	Rental	110	106	128	158	230	179	163
Total		**1,138**	**1,137**	**1,174**	**1,411**	**1,541**	**1,638**	**1,729**

(Source: MOLIT)

8.3. Evaluation of Housing Welfare Policy

8.3.1. Outline

The Korean government has built and supplied various types of public rental housing over the last few decades. As a result, the number of households living under minimum residential standards has declined, while conversely, those who are living in PRH have grown substantially. However, Korea is still lacking PRH, whereas the voucher system is at its early stage, and hard to discuss the impact on the housing welfare policy in Korea.

8.3.2. Problems

An enormous amount of financial resources is required to provide housing welfare to the vulnerable people in the housing market. Like many countries, securing stable financial resources for providing housing welfare is the most imminent challenge for the Korean government. Until now, the national budget, NHUF, and LH's development gains have been the main sources to finance housing welfare.

However, with a downturn of house and land sales in the stagnated housing market and a surge of raw land prices in the booming housing market, it has been difficult to secure resources through development gains from LH and ultimately for Korea as a whole.[8] Therefore, it is imperative to find plausible solutions for the lack of financial resources through the measures such as the expansion of government financial support.

Statistics show that the government budget and NHUF investment have expanded again since 2016 with the introduction of voucher in the Park, Geun-hye administration. The government budget and NHUF investment for housing welfare have expanded consistently and this trend is predicted to continue further. The average annual budget for this purpose in each administration was:

8 Debt of LH was 99 trillion won (82 billion US$) in 2015 and 132 trillion won (110 billion US$) in 2020.

- Kim, Dae-Jung (DJ) administration (1998~2002) 185.8 billion won (155 million US$),
- Roh, Moo-Hyun administration (2003~2007) 1,072 billion won (975 million US$)
- Lee, Myoung-Bak (MB) administration (2008~2012) 593billion won (539million US$)
- Park administration (2013~2017) 719billion won(654 million US$) (with the start of Housing voucher)

The size of the budget was expanding in the Roh, Moo-hyun administration due to the full-scale construction of Kookmin PRH and in the Park, Guen-hye administration with the start of a housing voucher.

Unequal distribution of policy benefits among recipients has been another significant problem. People living in permanent rental housing receive larger benefits than people living in any other type of housings, i.e. purchased·leased·national rental housing.

While the recipients of national basic livelihood assistance were 1.6 million people in 2015, the number of permanent rental housing available was less than 200 thousand units. Most of the permanent rental housing was built in the first half of the 1990s and 36,000 households were still on the waiting list in 2015. For this reason, MB administration (2008~2012) decided to build more permanent rental housings. Hence 10 thousand units of permanent housing are being built each year since

2010. However, actual numbers being completed are smaller than what was initially planned and only 13,000 units of permanent PRH were added during 2016~2019.

In essence, households in the same income level should receive similar housing benefits equitably by allocating various supporting measures such as housing subsidies, public rental housing, vouchers, etc. However, government support has been concentrated on the recipients of national basic livelihood assistance, which might have affected the motivation of work and back to the labor market. Therefore, through the fair and considerate distribution of benefits, the self-help effort of those recipients to improve housing levels should be stimulated.

The effect of the old housing subsidy system which was available to the recipients of national basic livelihood assistance before the introduction of housing vouchers was evaluated to be insufficient. The subsidy was ineffective to enhance the housing welfare of low-income people since it was often used for other purposes and duplication of support also existed to those recipients considering the provision of permanent rental housing. Due to these problems, the housing voucher system was introduced in 2015.

The overall picture of the housing market in the first half of the 2010s could be depicted as slowly growing housing transactions and demand, the continuous rise of Chonsei deposits, a weak monthly rent caused by the increase of supply, etc. By contrast, the second half of the 2010s witnessed an entirely different housing market with a steep rise in house price and Chonsei deposit, an exploding housing demand led by the diverting demand from the Chonsei market and speculative demand, and the implementation of a series of policy packages to cope with this boiling market.

From this, practical supporting measures were being requested to help the underprivileged in housing. Housing voucher, one of the supporting measures, has a few conditions to be successful including financial resources, a delivery system, and the adjustment of roles with public rental housing.

8.4. Future Direction and Plan

We can find the direction of housing welfare policy in Korea through the 2nd Long-term Comprehensive Housing Plan between 2013~2022, announced in Dec. 2013. The future direction manifested in the plan is to lessen the dependence on construction-oriented policy and achieve universal housing welfare through the expansion of customized support. The goal of the plan is the provision of housing support to 5.5 million non-home owning households under the 5th income bracket by 2020. The main strategy to achieve the goal is the provision of housing service to 740,000 households annually by the public sector.

Policy measures mobilized for this goal and strategy are:

- Shift to the beneficiary-centered policy measures;
- Expansion of the rental housing supply in downtown areas;
- Strengthening the support for vulnerable customers and
- Improvement of housing welfare delivery system.

Another source to find the direction of housing welfare policy in Kore is the 2nd Long-term Comprehensive Housing Plan Amending Plan (2013~22) announced by the Moon, Jae-in government in June 2018.

This plan aims firstly, the establishment of a housing ladder system for social integration. For this goal, reinforcing the customized housing support according to the phase of life cycle and level of income is pursued. This will be addressed with the package support encompassing customized rental housing and housing support program reflecting the housing demand according to the phases of the life cycle, namely the young, newlywed, middle-aged, and the elderly.

The increase of housing supply for non-home owning people and end-users will be made through the supply of 1 million public housings consisting of 650,000 units of public rental housing for non-home owning people, 200,000 units of public-support rental housing, and 150,000 of public housing for sale.

Table 67 explains the detailed housing support measures according to the phases of the life cycle including customized rental housing, preferential subscription account, low-interest loan, etc.

Table 67 ● Housing support measures (The 2nd Long-term Comprehensive Housing Plan Amending Plan, 2013~22)

Support target	Housing support including PRH	Financial support, etc
The young	Supply of youth housing (300,000 rooms)	• Introduction of the preferential subscription account • Loan customized for Chonsei and monthly rental • Strengthening the housing information delivery and counseling
Newlyweds	• Rental housing specialized for newlyweds (200,000 units) • Newlyweds hope town (70,000 units) • Doubled special housing supply	• Introduction of newlyweds only loan • Housing expense supports for low-income newlyweds
The elderly	• Customized rental housing (50,000 units) • Installation of relief sensor for seniors living alone	• Introduction of annuity type purchased rental housing • Additional provision of maintenance and operation subsidy
Low income, Socially disadvantaged class	• Public support rental housing (410,000 units) • Introduction of an emergency support housing • Expansion of rental housing support for disadvantaged groups including dwellers living in the non-housing structure, juveniles in protection, group home dwellers • Preferential supply of PRH for severely disabled	• Expansion of target and amount of housing subsidy • Emergency housing loan for poor children caring household • Consideration of providing housing subsidy for group home dwellers

The second goal emphasized in this plan is the removal of a blind spot in housing welfare through housing policy. For this goal, the construction of decentralized private cooperation type housing welfare governance will be pursued. In particular, the role of central and local governments will be realigned to provide a livelihood adherence type housing welfare service to residents and to effectively cope with the increasing welfare demand.

The enhancement of accessibility to housing welfare services for the disadvantaged group will also be pursued. Especially, the housing welfare delivery system will be strengthened through the expansion of housing welfare centers, the provision of customized online information such as My-home, the construction of a housing welfare delivery system consolidated with a private network, etc.

Following the above plans, the Comprehensive Housing Plan 2020 materializes policy objectives and strategies as follows:

① Firstly, housing support plan. For the housing stability of non-home owning people, a total of 1.63 million households will be supported through PRH (completion), housing subsidy, financial support including a loan for purchasing, and Chonsei or monthly rent.

② Secondly, as a Housing supply plan, the total number of housings completed in the whole nation will be 457,000 units which are similar to the average level in previous years.

③ Thirdly, as a housing land supply plan, 11.5 km^2 (in this 6.2 km^2 in SMR) of housing land developed by the public sector in the whole nation will get permission to supply.

④ Lastly, as for the housing sector budget, a total of 31.9 (in 2019

27.4) trillion won will be supported by the government budget and NHUF

8.5. Conclusion

The most important policy objectives in housing are to provide appropriate housing support for people including low-income groups and to achieve the stabilization of the housing market. Korea has endeavored to expand the rental housing stock and achieved this goal to some extent. However, the problems in the housing welfare such as a lack of fund resources, a difficulty in offering customized rental housing, the conflicts caused by the concentration of rental houses, etc. have not been solved yet.

Specifically, in terms of funding, Korea has depended on development gains of LH instead of government funds. Due to uniformity in the housing type, it has been difficult to provide customer-tailored rental housing. The concentration of rental housings may contribute to conflicts between different social classes and different income levels. All these issues are casting a shadow on the housing welfare policy in Korea. This means that policy measures need to be revised or combined with new measures such as housing vouchers and private rentals with government support.

In the case of the voucher scheme, thorough preparation and

supplementation of the delivery system is crucial to avoid or reduce unnecessary government expenditure. To provide equitable and sustainable housing supports for those in need, accurate analysis of benefit and cost, as well as a careful implementation, are required.

Chapter 9

Housing Finance and Taxation

9.1. Introduction: Financing, Taxation, and Housing

9.1.1. Overview

In most countries, financing and taxation are the keys to an effective housing policy. Coupled with the globalization of the national economy and the housing market the role of financing and taxation has been growing steadily. More profoundly, these economic traits have been the main pillars of human life. Most transactions of goods and services and the income accruing from these transactions are closely related to a smooth flow of financing and how the government intervenes in this process through taxation.

Financing is necessary to secure funds for economic activity and to make use of income surplus for future economic projects. Tax is a kind of price or fee paid to the lord of a manor or state for services of safety and community maintenance. Both financiers and tax collectors are amongst the oldest types of occupations. As modern society becomes more complex and specialized in economic terms, the role of financing and taxation in the housing market and the national economy has expanded remarkably.

On the other hand, a leap forward in the development of science and technology has accelerated both global financing and the generalization of taxation. The globalization of financing combined with the development of computers and networks has caused the change of finance and banking from mere savings and lending which have continued for a long time into advanced financing including sophisticated structured finance and undertaking global investment and hedging.

Likewise, with the globalized activities of people and businesses, taxations of different countries have become generalized. These changes illustrate that effective financing and taxation measures are becoming more important in enhancing the performance of people and businesses which are intertwined with each other in modern society and economy.

9.1.2. Role of Finance and Taxation in Housing Policy

Most economic policies are based on the mobilization of macroeconomic policy measures consisting of finance, taxation, and fiscal measures along with the specific factors in targeted economic fields. In housing policy, the role of finance and taxation is on the rise, especially in Korea. In the past, the government emphasized the mass supply of housing as an integral part of a thriving economy. Therefore, securing available lands including new towns, construction materials, and skilled labor were of great importance. Restrictions on speculative transactions through higher capital gains tax, LTV, and DTI control were also emphasized to lower the demand for housing.

In the 2010s, the Korean housing market has experienced an excess supply in the first half and then excess demand in the second half, and thus how to maintain a housing demand at a stable and balanced level has become one of the main policy issues for the government. In that respect, tax and finance are regarded as the main policy measures to count on. In the case of fiscal policy, the influence on individuals and the market is indirect and limited. One tricky issue that has arisen is that tax and finance policies have their own goals, i.e. securing a source of government revenue and the equitable distribution of money among individuals and industries in the national economy. This means that there is a limitation in mobilizing tax and financial measures for housing policy.

History demonstrates the swings between excess- and under-mobilization of these policy measures according to the political stance of each government. Here, a question arises as to what kind of policy mix encompassing finance and taxation is desirable for an effective and sound housing market.

9.2. Housing Finance (HF)

9.2.1. Outlines

Housing finance (HF) refers to all borrowing and lending of funds for the acquisition, construction, and use of housing. Housing finance takes a central position in real estate finance. NHUF and private housing funds make up the majority of HF. On the other hand, HF is a general term indicating the flow of money connected to the housing. HF comprises lending (loan), investment finance (investment), and asset liquidation related to housing (securitization).

Before the 1997 financial crisis, the Korean government endeavored to prevent speculation by curbing the inflow of money into the housing market. Even at that time, mortgage loans were the main source of housing finance, but it was linked mainly to small-size housing for people on a low income. The proactive utilization of housing finance to solve various problems in the housing market had not yet been realized.

After the 1997 financial crisis, HF in Korea began to undergo a drastic change. In particular, the integration of the real estate market and financial market has accelerated to match the changes of advanced countries. For the development of real estate finance, securitization is crucial among others. Various real estate finance systems have been introduced sequentially after the 1997 financial crisis such as,

- 1998 asset-backed security (ABS)
- 1999 mortgage-backed security (MBS)
- 2001 real estate investment trust (REITs)
- 2007 'Housing pension' (long-term reverse mortgage loan)
- 2012 'Qualified loan' (long-term fixed-rate mortgage loan)
- 2015 'Anshim loan' (or 'Relief loan' to change from floating to a fixed-rate loan)

Here asset-backed security (ABS) is a security issued based on a pool of underlying assets which are a group of small and illiquid assets producing a flow of income. Mortgage-backed security (MBS) is a bond or other financial obligation secured by a pool of mortgage loans[1]. This is a type of asset-backed security. For this, the mortgages are sold to security issuers such as government agencies or investment banks to make up a package of the loans together and to securitize for the transaction in the securities markets.

---

1 Barron's Dictionary

A real estate investment trust (REIT) is a real estate mutual fund, allowed by income tax laws to avoid corporate income tax.[2] REITs possess various types of real estate including residential and commercial real estate. However, the main part of the property owned by REITs is taken by commercial real estate including offices, shopping centers, warehouses, hotels, and hospitals. A reverse mortgage or a home equity conversion mortgage (HECM) is a type of mortgage designed for elderly homeowners with substantial equity, by which a lender periodically pays a certain amount to the borrower.[3]

HF can be classified in various ways according to the recipients, sources, and structures as follows:

- Supplier finance for the construction or operation of housing vs. consumer finance for the acquisition or renting (Chonsei) of housing;
- Public funds such as NHUF, pension funds, etc. vs. private fund such as bank mortgage loans;
- Public finance systems consisting of primary and secondary financial institutions vs. private finance systems consisting of housing sales under construction and Chonsei.

---

2 ibid

3 ibid

9.2.2. Real Estate Finance System (REFS)

REFS is a system in which decisions on real estate finance are made through the transaction and interaction among many economic players (Han & Cho, 2008). Figure 28 shows the structure of REFS and the roles and interactions of participating players.

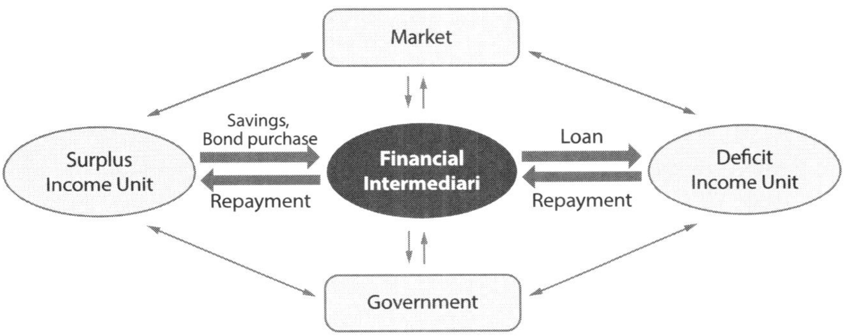

Figure 28 ● Structure of real estate finance system

1) Structure of REFS

There are five main players in the REFS, namely surplus income units, deficit income units, financial intermediaries, market, and the government. Among these, the surplus and deficit income units and financial intermediaries are directly related to the flow of money, whereas the market and government provide the infrastructure and environment for the smooth flow of money. Here, the market consists of the real estate (RE) space market and RE asset market, while the government is comprised of financial regulatory agencies and housing/land authorities.

2) Role of REFS

The decision makings of individual players and the REFS interact with each other. The REFS promotes or restrains an individual's decision-making. Conversely a collection of individual decisions determines the direction and characteristics of REFS. This means that individual financial decision-making and the REFS as a whole have a mutually interactive relationship.

In REFS, a market function plays a pivotal role. Main financial instruments consisted of equities, bonds, and derivatives are transacted and exchanged in the market. These transactions are the most vibrant in the USA. The role of the market encompasses price determination, competition among and replacement of market participants, and the sanctioning products below market norms and standards. A company whose products fail to reach the criteria of consumers will face a sales drop-off and subsequent removal from the market.

3) REFS' Components and Their Roles

① Surplus income units i.e. savers or depositors determine the necessity of investment and object assets, direct or indirect investment, and the maximization of risk-adjusted profit.

② Deficient income units, usually industry, determine the real estate acquisition demand, funding, financial instruments, and the minimization of financing cost.

③ RE financial market determines loans, the transaction of indirect investment vehicles, and their prices.

④ Public and private financial intermediaries, especially banks, determine financial instrument development, intermediation, and risk management.

⑤ Government determines housing welfare, supervision, and market formulation.

4) Classification of Real Estate Financial Market

The RE financial market can be firstly classified into a money market and a capital market. A money market deals with short-term securities with a maturity of one year or less. By contrast, the capital market deals with long-term securities with a maturity over one year, which comprises a stock market (equity market) and a bond market. Real estate finance is performed mainly in the capital market since real estate tends to necessitate long periods to construct, make transactions, maintain and operate.

Secondly, the RE financial market can be further classified into the public market and private market. In the public market, the general public seeking a financial transaction can participate. The representative public market is the stock exchange which is strictly ruled by the Financial Services Commission (FSC), Financial Supervisory Service (FSS), and other oversight institutions to protect innocent investors. In the private market, only those having specific interests participate, and the private equity fund (PEF) market (or private investment companies) is a part of this market. Unlike the public market, the government's role in protecting investors is weak and the regulations on transactions and investments are substantially relaxed.

Another important classification is the primary and secondary financial market. The primary market is for the provision of loans and the first issuance of related security. The secondary market is a market where these securities are traded. Having a sound secondary market is crucial for the development of the primary market and the financial system as a whole, through which funds can be supplied consistently. With the secondary market, the salability of securities (liquidity risk) and consequently the funding cost or interest rate can be markedly lowered. This is essential for the vitalization of the primary market. More importantly, this market enables small investors to participate in the financial market and emerge as one of the main financial players.

5) Real Estate Financial Market and Financial Instruments

Financial instruments are traded at the optimum price between suppliers and buyers in the market. Securities are traded through a specific stack exchange (NYSE, KRX, KOSPI) or an electronic stock exchange (NASDAQ, KOSDAQ).

Residential and commercial mortgages, securities backed by these mortgages, equities of REITs, real estate funds are the main RE financial instruments. Purchasing a real estate financial instrument means investing in real estate for individual investors, i.e. an indirect investment on RE. This eloquently shows the diversifying investment methods or channels. Investment on RE can be classified into public investment and private investment according to whether the transaction is made through an open market or not. The main investment objects are equities, bonds, and derivatives.

9.2.3. Real Estate Finance in Korea

1) Structure

RE financing consists of two finance systems, i.e. the public finance system and the private finance system. In the public finance system, public institutions are playing a central role in various financial decisions and transactions. By contrast, the private finance system is operated without the participation of public institutions in financial activities.

The public finance system is once again classified into two kinds, transactions and investments based on public funds and those based on private funds. The NHUF and the farming and fishing village housing renovation fund (FHRF) are included in the public fund, while various loans and investments made through direct contact between sellers, dealers, and consumers are based on private funds. Chonsei and the housing sale under construction (HSUC) can be included in a broader term of the private fund.

Figure 29 shows the overall structure of RE finance in Korea encompassing public and private finance systems.

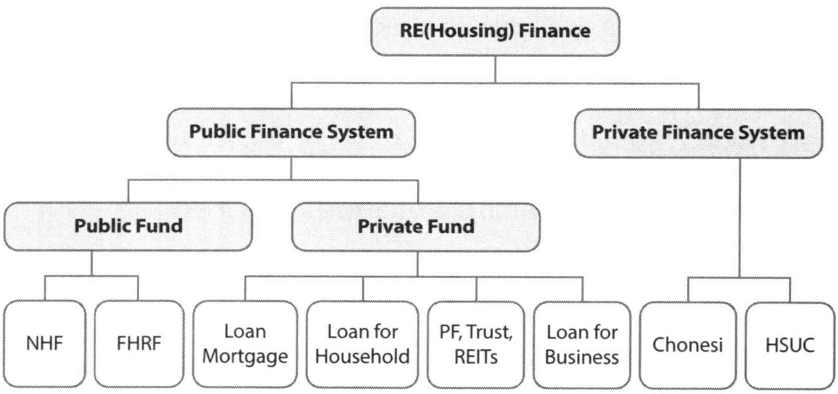

Figure 29 ● Structure of RE finance in Korea

2) Size of the housing finance market and its change

(1) Housing Mortgage Loan

At the end of 2020, the bank loan balance was 1,893.7 trillion won (1,722 billion US$). This is a 204.1 trillion won increase year-on-year. In the total increased amount, household loans take 43.9% (89.7 trillion), while corporate loans take 56.1% (114.4 trillion). In the case of housing mortgage loans at the end of 2020, the balance was 910.6 trillion won, showing 67.7 trillion won up year-on-year, and this increase was 75.5% of the growth in whole household loans. The weighted average interest rate of housing mortgage loans and household loans were 2.67% and 2.77% respectively in 2020.[4] The proportion of fixed-rate mortgage loans has been rising by the government policy from 3.1% in 2011 to 14.2% in 2012, 23.6% in 2014 and 39.1% in 2016, 29.9% in 2018, and 30.6% in 2020.

In housing mortgage loans, the private sector dominated by banks accounts for an 80~90% proportion, while the public sector was at a 10~20% level. Before the 1997 financial crisis, the NHUF represented a majority share of housing finance contrary to the current status illustrating a drastic change in the Korean financial market after the financial crisis.

(2) Sources of Fund

- National housing and urban fund: NHUF created in 1981 has been the core of public housing finance. The NHUF is funded by government contributions, national housing bonds, lottery funds,

4 Bank of Korea

deposited money from the financial market, NHUF bonds, and housing subscription savings. Lending is made in the form of loans to local governments, LH, housebuilders, and consumers. The main objectives or goals of the NHUF are to provide support for the building of affordable housings and for purchasing capacity of low-income households.

- Local banks: the sources of a local bank's lending are the bank's capital, savings and deposit received, and housing subscription installments. Lending is made in the form of a business loan consisting of a working capital loan and corporate facility loan and housing loan funded by private housing fund and other sources.

9.2.4. Operation of NHUF and Others

As of 2020, the total amount collected in the NHUF was 100.3 trillion won (91.2 billion US$). Out of this amount, 26.7 trillion won was for investments and loans such as housing construction, acquisition, and the Chonsei fund and the remaining 73.6 trillion won was allocated for repayment of the principal and interest, etc.

This table shows that housing subscription savings have been the biggest and most consistent source of funds recently, while loans to consumers and rental housing construction were the two most utilized aspects of the fund. The changes in main project expenditure in the

2010s reflect the bouncing of the housing market in which construction activities and buyer purchases recovered.

Table 68 ● Operation results of NHUF (trillion won, %)

Classification		2012	2015	2016	2017	2018	2019	2020
Fund Raising	· Housing subscription savings	11.3	21.9	19.1	18.3	17.1	16.2	21.2
	· National housing bond	9.7	16.2	15.9	14.3	15.1	15.4	18.7
	· General budget contribution	0.06	n.a.	n.a.	n.a.	n.a.	n.a.	2.4
	· Lottery fund contribution	0.5	0.6	0.6	0.6	0.6	0.6	0.6
	· Beginning balance	10.5	24.2	13.1	13.3	11.9	15.9	30.5
	· P & I repayment, etc.	13.3	17.1	18.7	20.1	24.6	26.5	26.9
Total		45.4	80.0	67.4	66.6	69.3	74.6	100.3
Use	· Total expenditure (Main projects)	19.3	20.6	21.1	23.6	23.4	28.7	26.7
	- Rental housing	3.6	6.5	6.5	7.7	13.1	15.6	15.1
	- Sales housing	4.9	0.6	0.5	0.5	0.3	0.2	0.1
	- Loans to consumers	7.4	10.8	11.3	12.7	8.8	9.4	9.9
	- Other uses	3.4	2.7	2.8	2.7	1.2	3.5	1.6
	· Debt repayment etc.	15.0	23.1	29.7	30.1	37.0	33.6	40.4
	· Extra money	11.0	36.3	16.6	12.9	8.9	12.3	33.2

(Source: MOLIT, NHUF Portal)

On the other hand, the trend of debt repayment has been accelerated contrary to the shrinking or stagnating expenditures on main projects such as the loans to sales housing and consumers. This result manifests that the supply of public rental housing and the support for consumers to purchase a house or get Chonsei rental have become two key tasks to be tackled by the NHUF reflecting the changing market situation in Korea.

Table 69 shows the financial status of the NHUF. The total asset, debt, and net assets have increased steadily. In 9 years between 2012 and 2020, the total asset has increased by 109.5%, loan amount by 55.6%, and net asset by 128.9%. Net assets of the NHUF reached 27.2 trillion won in 2020.

Table 69 ● Financial status of NHUF (billion won)

Classification	2012	2013	2014	2015	2016	2017	2018	2019	2020
Total Asset (Loan amount)	95,178 (79,529)	104,036 (81,213)	117,381 (83,628)	136,221 (85,440)	148,870 (87,644)	163,346 (95,995)	171,314 (106,431)	182,189 (117,163)	199,418 (123,779)
Debt	83,292	92,594	102,312	120,899	132,418	143,384	150,504	158,157	172,209
Net Asset	11,886	11,442	15,067	15,322	16,452	19,962	20,810	24,032	27,209

(Source: MOLIT, NHUF Portal)

9.2.5. Real estate indirect investment vehicles

1) Outlines of Real Estate Investment Trust (REIT)

(1) Concept of REIT

REIT is a company or investment trust which collects funds from the general public and makes a profit by investing the fund into various real estates or providing finance. REIT is an indirect investment vehicle, a sort of mutual fund investing in real estate. Investors can invest in commercial buildings, ABS, MBS, etc. without professional knowledge and a workforce. Equity of REIT is a product of real estate securitization and has the trait of liquidity and fluidity. Therefore, the REIT investor can liquidify his or her equity at the most advantageous time.

(2) Basic Structure

REIT in Korea is similar to the corporate type investment trust in the USA. This is a kind of modified type from the US corporate type REIT taking into account the domestic financial and real estate market conditions. REIT is a real estate company with a special purpose whose assets are managed by the general meeting of stockholders (GMS) and the board of directors (BOD). Peripheral management works are entrusted to subsidiaries or outsourced. In short, the original form of Korean REIT is a permanent enterprise. A paper company type REIT was introduced several years later.

Over 90% of asset operation profits should be paid to shareholders as a dividend, and in so doing REIT is regarded as an investment conduit. Shares of REIT are going for an IPO and traded in the stock market to secure liquidity. A REIT has internal organizations comprising of GMS, BOD, auditor, asset management specialists, and external organizations such as facility management, investment consultants, etc.

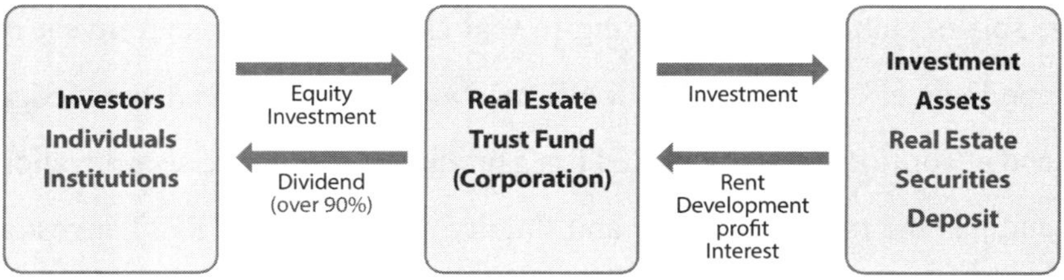

Figure 30 ● Brief structure of REITs

Figure 30 shows the brief structure of REITs. Individual and institutional investors put money in and get the shares of REITs. REITs invest in real estate, RE-related securities, and deposits in financial intermediaries and get returns from the investment in the forms of rent, development profit, and interest. If REITs earns a certain amount of profits by subtracting expenses from income then it will pay back over 90% of profits to investors as a dividend.

2) Current Status of REITs in Korea

At the end of 2020, a total of 282 (128 in 2015) REITs were operating and the total asset size was 61.3 (18.3) trillion Won or 217.4 (142.7) billion Won on average. There are three kinds of REITs in Korea.

- Corporate restructuring REITs are aiming to deal with the real estates for sale to improve the financial status of failed companies. To expedite the normalization or liquidation of failed companies, some requirements are relaxed compared to the following types of REITs.

- Entrusted management REITs are paper company type REITs having no internal organization and these REITs are managed by asset management companies (AMC).
- Self-management REITs are corporate-type REITs that have internal and external organizations and are managed by their internal organization.

Table 70 ● Current status of REITs in Korea (end of 2020)

Classification	Number of REITs	Asset size (in trillion won)	Proportion (%)
CR-REITs	26	3.8	6.2
Entrusted management REITs	252	57.0	92.9
Self-management REITs	4	0.5	0.9
Total	**282**	**61.3**	**100.0**
Listed REITs	13	5.8	9.4

(Source: MOLIT)

Among the property types, the investment in housing made up 59.2% of the total investment of REITs, and the investment in office building followed.

Table 71 ● Property types invested by REITs in Korea (as of the end of 2020)

(trillion won)

	Office	Retail	Housing	Logistics	Hotel	Others	Total
Numbers	64	36	141	22	5	14	282
Asset size	14.7	7.5	36.3	0.9	0.4	1.5	61.3
Ratio (%)	24.0	12.2	59.2	1.5	0.7	2.4	100.0

(Source: MOLIT)

For investors, the return or yield from the investment in REITs is more important than anything else. Regarding this MOLIT reported in 2021 that the average annual yield of REITs investment in 2020 was 8.33%, which was much higher than other financial tools such as 3-year corporate bond (2.13%) and savings bank interest (1.03%). Among the property types, the office was the highest yielding investment object (9.27%), overwhelming retail building (8.23%), and others.

3) Future Development

Since the onset of the system at the beginning of the 2000s, REITs have shown steady development. However, in terms of the extent to which REITs play a role in the real estate market and the national economy, the performance of Korean REITs can be said to be meager when it is compared with those of Japan and Singapore which were introduced in each country at a similar time.

For a stable development of Korean REITs, 1) to secure suitable properties, 2) to improve the real estate management capabilities, 3) to broaden their working boundaries, and 4) to make the management of REITs transparent further have been requested. Besides, tax incentives, especially the reduction of corporation tax for self-management REITs, and the deregulation with the listing of REITs have been pointed out as imperative to enhance the profitability of and to encourage individual investors to participate in REITs. The following are the policy efforts of the Korean government to make REITs a formidable policy measure to alleviate problems in the housing market and more broadly the real estate market.

(1) Policy Issue 1 - Increasing Rental Housing through REITs

① Outlines

This policy was introduced in 2015 to utilize REITs to solve the current housing problems in Korea. By allowing REITs to purchase and manage rental housings, it was anticipated that the supply of rental housing for people on low-income could be invigorated with the expected growth of real estate investment and transactions. For this purpose, the LH and Korea Construction Guarantee were called on to play an important role, i.e. the AMC of paper company type REITs. Tax incentives along with compensation for losses coming from the operation of rental housing were to be given to the activities of rental housing REITs.

The main reason for the introduction of this type of REITs was that 1) with the shortage of PRH, and difficulties in increasing its supply, the utilization of the private fund could be a plausible alternative to count on, and by doing this, 2) the reinvigoration of the real estate market was expected. In short, by introducing rental housing REITs, the government tried to increase private rental housing supplementing the shortage of PRH, stimulate real estate transactions, and help the poorer households suffering from both the burden of mortgage debt repayments and house price drops.

② Methods

The rental housing REITs financed by public funds such as the NHUF and the National Pension Fund and the private funds equipped with the credit reinforcement of LH are set up. The rental housing REITs purchase housing in the market and provide their houses as PRH for people on lower incomes. If there is a homeowner who is suffering from mortgage loan debt, he or she can live in the house after selling the house itself or the equity of the house to the REITs and by leasing back the house from the REITs.[5]

5 The incentives including the exemption of acquisition tax and the application of lowest rate of property tax (0.1%) will be given and these incentives are expected to secure profitability of REITs.

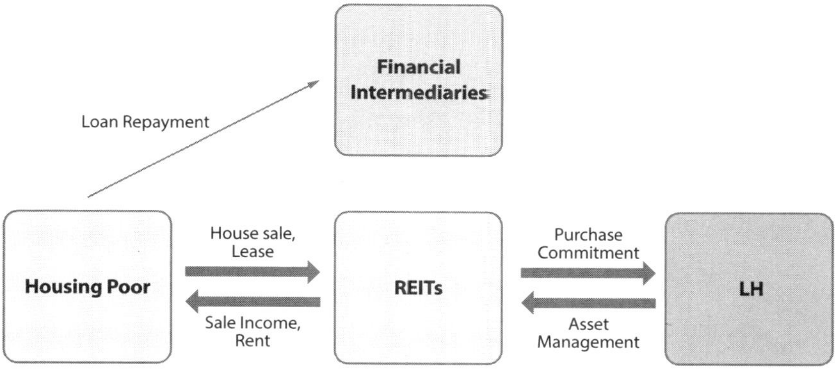

Figure 31 ● The business structure of rental housing REITs
(Source: MOLIT)

With a growing interest in the role of institutionalized private rental housing, the rental housing REITs were expected to play a significant role in the stabilization of the housing market and the invigoration of the real estate industry. Aided by the policy effort, housing REITs has become take the largest part in the total REITs in terms of both numbers and the amount of asset.

(2) Policy Issue 2 - Increasing the Listed REITs

The Korean government realized that the development of REITs is unlikely without the vibrant participation of individual investors in the financial market. To this end, public offerings of REITs need to be accelerated through deregulation and incentives hence a set of policy initiatives were announced in February 2016. To encourage the participation of individual investors in REITs, the Korean government pursued three policy goals:

- The first goal was the revitalization of public offerings of REITs. For this purpose, financial assistance was to be provided through the participation of NHUF and tax incentives for individual investors. To promote the activities of anchor-REITs led by big investors the stock ownership limit was relaxed from 40% to 50% and the voting right of stock ownership was expanded;
- The second goal was that the regulations of entry, funding, asset investment, and management were eased and the profitability of asset management companies (AMC) was expanded through the deregulation of AMC investment on REITs from 10% to 30%;
- Lastly all the information of REITs management and data for investment became widely notified and publicized for the protection of investors and promotion of investment.

Through the enactment of these policy initiatives, the Korean government expected a more active role for listed REITs in stabilizing the housing market and invigorating the real estate industry. Further deregulation was made in the latter half of 2016 in such a way that tax incentive was given to the investment made through individual savings account (ISA) and that the turnover criteria for the listing of REITs were lowered from 10 billion won to 7 billion won.

Another policy package for the invigoration of listed REITs was announced in Sep. 2019. The main initiatives included in this package are:

- Firstly, a priority in developing public lands is given to the listed REITs in developing multi-purpose development of station building or area adjacent to the station, commercial sites in new towns, etc.;
- Secondly, tax incentives are provided. In particular, the dividend tax for investors to the listed REITs is lowered and the property tax and acquisition tax are reduced for the properties operated by the listed REITs;
- Thirdly, for the protection of investors, the REITs performance index will be developed and noticed to investors. And anchor REITs initiated by public funds will be made to encourage private investors to the listed REITs;
- And lastly, as a deregulation measure, the increase of floor to area ratio (FAR) or easement of location regulation for the listed REITs will be made to support the profitability of REITs.

All in all, including these kinds of efforts, the Korean government is continuing efforts to promote the listed REITs substantially.

9.3. Housing Taxation and Issues

9.3.1. Taxes in General

1) Taxes Related to Real Estate - Possession and Transaction

Real estate especially housing is the main source of tax revenue in most countries. The fixity of real estate in a specific location provides the ground for the government, in particular local government, to assess the tax bearing capacity of the owner or user. In particular, the government levies taxes on the possession and transaction of real estate as the most typical taxations.

- Taxation on the possession of real estate: Government finds the tax-bearing capacity of people with the possession of the real estate and levies a tax. In most countries, this is the basic taxation and becomes the main financial source of local governments. Property tax is the most typical one.
- Taxation on the transaction of real estate: The government levies taxes on the profits from real estate transactions. Capital gains tax in general and special surtax on corporation tax which is levied on corporations' capital gains are the representative ones. Acquisition tax is one of the main financial sources of local governments and this is another type of taxation on the transaction.

Besides these taxes, another type of taxation i.e. indirect taxation is levied in Korea. Farmland tax and the surtaxes on the national tax including education tax and special taxes for rural areas are representative indirect taxation on real estate

2) Housing-related Taxes

Housing-related taxes can be divided into three groups according to the stages of housing-related activity, i.e. construction, registration, and transaction. At the stage of housing construction, four types of taxes are levied:

- Firstly, taxes are levied on the acquisition of housing land. Acquisition tax, registration tax, local education tax, and stamp tax are included in this type of taxes;
- Secondly, taxes are levied on those who have housing land. Local education tax, special case property tax (a kind of urban planning tax), common facilities tax, corporation tax are included in this type;
- Regarding the building permission, license tax and other charges such as national housing bond, urban railway bond, and farmland diversion charges are levied, and concerning construction work, value-added tax and office tax, as well as urban railway bond, are levied;
- And finally, acquisition tax, registration tax, education tax, special taxes for rural areas, and development charges are levied at the

stage of completion and registration of housing.

Some taxes are levied on the transfer of property rights and possession. Corporation tax, a special surtax on corporation tax, value-added tax, property tax, local education tax, special case property tax, and common facilities tax are included in this category, and acquisition tax and registration tax are also levied. And at the possession stage, acquisition tax and registration tax are levied. Table 72 shows all the housing-related taxes in Korea. Here it is found that some taxes such as acquisition tax and registration tax are levied multiple times according to the stage of housing-related activities.

Table 72 ● Housing-related taxes in Korea

Taxes	Housing Construction				Completion and Registration	Transfer of Property right	Possession
	Acquisition of Land	Possession of Land	Building Permission	Construction Work			
Acquisition Tax	●				●	●1)	
Registration Tax	●				●	●1)	
Property Tax							●
Comprehensive Property Tax							●
Local Education tax	●	●			●	●	
Stamp Tax	●						
Special Case Property Tax		●				●	
Common Facility Tax		●				●	

Taxes	Housing Construction				Completion and Registration	Transfer of Property right	Possession
	Acquisition of Land	Possession of Land	Building Permission	Construction Work			
Corporate tax		●				●	
License tax			●				
Value Added Tax				●		●	
Office Tax				●			
Special Taxes for Rural Areas					●		
Special Surtax on Corporation Tax						●	
National Housing Bond			●				
Urban Railway Bond			●	●			
Charges on Farm Land Diversion			●				
Development Charges					●		

1) Taxes paid by the purchaser of newly-built housing

9.3.2. Changes in the Contents of Housing Taxation

1) Acquisition Tax

Acquisition tax has been regarded as the most important taxation measure for the revenues of local governments as well as for managing housing demand in the market. Until 2004, a 5% single tax rate was levied based on the current real estate price. The rate was lowered from 5% to 4% in 2005 and again to 2% in 2006. After that, a series of complicated changes continued until 2013.

From 2014, the tax rate for housings below 600 million Won was 1%, 600~900 million won is 2% and the house exceeding 900 million Won was 3%. Table 73 shows the acquisition tax and surtaxes and their rates before the overhaul of the acquisition tax system in 2020.

Table 73 ● Acquisition tax and surtaxes and their rates during 2014-2020

Price (billion Won)	Size	Acquisition Tax	Farming and Fishing Village Special Tax	Local education Tax	Total
Below 0.6	~ 85 m^2	1%	Tax free	0.1%	1.1%
	Over 85 m^2	1%	0.2%	0.1%	1.3%
0.6~0.9	~ 85 m^2	2%	Tax free	0.2%	2.2%
	Over 85 m^2	2%	0.2%	0.2%	2.4%
Over 0.9	~ 85 m^2	3%	Tax free	0.3%	3.3%
	Over 85 m^2	3%	0.2%	0.3%	3.5%

There was a big change in the acquisition tax rate in 2020 to quell down the continuing housing speculation leading to the housing price hike. The Korean government raised sharply the acquisition tax rate imposing on multi-homeowners in July 2020 to prevent speculation. 8% of the acquisition tax rate applies to individuals who own 2 houses, while 12% of the tax rate applies to those who have 3 and more houses and corporations.

Table 74 ● Changes in acquisition tax rates in 2020

<table>
<tr><th colspan="3">Before</th><th colspan="3">After</th></tr>
<tr><td rowspan="4">Individuals</td><td>1 house</td><td rowspan="3">1~3% of house price</td><td rowspan="4">Individuals</td><td>1 house</td><td>1~3%</td></tr>
<tr><td>2 houses</td><td>2 houses</td><td>8%</td></tr>
<tr><td>3 houses</td><td>3 houses</td><td rowspan="3">12%</td></tr>
<tr><td>more than 4</td><td>4%</td><td>more than 4</td></tr>
<tr><td colspan="2">Corporations</td><td>1~3%</td><td colspan="2">Corporates</td></tr>
</table>

2) Capital Gains Tax

Capital gains tax (CGT) was levied on the capital gains by transacting properties such as land and house with the rate from 6 to 38% until 2017. In the case of housing worth 900 million won or less, the capital gain tax was exempted when an owner transfers after possessing more than two years. When the house was worth more than 900 million Won, the capital gains tax was levied on the amount exceeding 900 million won. Higher capital gains tax was levied on multi-house owners based on the law enacted in 2007 to control and discourage speculative investments in the housing market. However, it was abolished at the end of 2013 to boost the housing market and then reintroduced in 2019.

Facing the continuing rise of house prices and the increasing housing speculation, the Korean government raised the CGT tax rate significantly in 2018 for the multi-house owners and short-term owners. Additional 10% and 20% were decided to be levied for these cases on top of regular tax rates.

Capital gains tax has been raised once again in 2020. The tax rate applying to the capital gains obtained by corporations from the transactions of houses was raised substantially. Formerly, it was normal corporate tax rate (10~25%) + 10%, but raised to corporate tax rate + 20%. This was announced in 2020 and regarded as a strong measure to prevent speculation by corporations.

Also, it was announced that the heavy tax rate on the capital gains from the short-term transaction and that of multi-homeowners was increased. A heavy tax rate is decided by adding extra rates on the basic rate (5~42%). This heavy tax rate was raised in case of the capital gains accrued from the selling of the purchased house within 2 years. If the selling is made within 1 year, then the tax rate will increase to 70% from formerly 40%. If the selling is made within 1~2 years formerly it was basic rate but it was raised to 40% in 2019 and again 60% in 2020. The heavy tax rate imposed on the multi-homeowners in speculation areas also increased from basic rate + 10% (for 2 houses) or 20% (for 3 houses) to basic rate + 20% or 30% from July 2020. Table 75 shows the current capital gains tax system and rates after a series of revisions until 2020.

Table 75 ● The current capital gains tax system and rates

Classification	Tax Base	Tax Rate	Amount deducted progressively	2 houses owner	3 houses owner
Ownership over two years (Basic rate)	Below 46 million won	15%	1.08 million Won	25%	35%
	46~88 million won	24%	5.22 million Won	34%	44%
	88~150 million won	35%	14.9 million Won	45%	55%
	150~300 million won	38%	19.4 million Won	48%	58%
	300~500 million won	40%	25.4 million Won	50%	60%
	Over 500 million won	42%	35.4 million Won	52%	62%
Short-term Ownership	**Land**	**Housing**	**Ownership of a lot**	**Speculative readjustment area**	**Right of residence**
Shorter than 1 year	50%	70%	50%	Basic rate + 20%(2 houses) or 30%(3 houses)	40%
Shorter than 2 years	40%	60%	40%		40%

3) Property Tax

Property tax rate was lowered from 0.15~0.5% to 0.1~0.4% in 2009, and thereafter, this rate has been maintained. Many scholars have asserted that the property tax rate needs to be raised, while the acquisition tax rate should be cut in order to achieve the goal of fair taxation and to prevent speculative investment. However, considering the potential impact on the economy and household from the tax rate change, the Korean government has maintained the current tax rate without a significant change.

4) Comprehensive Property Tax

Comprehensive Property Tax (CPT), which has a feature of the strengthened progressive tax system, was introduced in 2005 to make a more balanced tax burden among households with different incomes and to prevent speculation on real estate including housing. To levy this tax, prices of the real estate possessed by a household are summed up. The comprehensive property tax is levied based on the condition that it exceeds 600 million Won. The tax rate was 1~3% during the Roh, Moo-hyeon administration.

The tax amount to be paid can be calculated as follows:

Amount of CPT = (aggregated housing prices owned by the household- 600 million won) × 80% × tax rate

Here housing prices are appraised and notified by the government every year and 80% is the fair market value ratio to relieve the impact of tax increase.[6]

However, this tax was criticized for being excessively heavy or punitive for house owners with 600 million won or more. Therefore, a big change was made in 2008 during the MB administration. The main modifications were that the tax was upon each person rather than the household unit to lower the tax base and 300 million won of basic

6 In 2018 the government decided to raise this fair market value ratio by 5% every year to reach 85% in 2019 and finally 100% in 2022.

deduction applied to each house owner. The tax rate also was lowered to 0.5~2%.

Another reversal has occurred in the late 2010s. With the rise of house prices and the increase of speculation, the Korean government has strengthened the criteria and increased tax rate continuously, especially 3 years in a row from 2018. With the change in 2019, the tax rate was raised to 0.6~3.0% in general and 0.8~4.0% for the people owning 3 houses or those owning 2 houses in speculation areas. Besides, in 2020, in the case of a corporation, the unit rate was raised to 3.0% in general and 4% for the corporations owning 3 houses or those owning 2 houses in speculation areas.

The main feature of this revision was to raise tax rates for and to apply progressive taxation to multi-homeowners to prevent the wealthy and corporations from speculative investment in housing.

Table 76 is showing the comprehensive property tax rate revised until 2020. Tax rates have increased in general and for multi-homeowners in special. Here, the cap of increased tax amount is the limitation of levied tax increase compared to the tax amount levied in the previous year. This is to prevent harsh taxation for taxpayers. In short, in the late 2010s, a tax burden for expensive house owners and especially multi-house owners have increased significantly for the prevention of speculative investment and thus for the stabilization of the boiling housing market.

Table 76 ● Comprehensive Property Tax rate (Revised in Dec. 2019 and Jul. 2020)

Tax base	Past	General	3 house owners & 2 house owners in speculation adjustment areas
Smaller than 300 million won	0.5%	0.6%	1.2%
300~600million won	0.7%	0.8%	1.6%
600~1200 million won	1.0%	1.2%	2.2%
1.2~5.0 billion won	1.4%	1.6%	3.6%
5.0~9.4 billion won	2.0%	2.2%	5.0%
More than 9.4 billion won	2.7%	3.0%	6.0%
Cap of increased tax amount	150%	150%	300%

5) Local Government Finance and Real Estate Taxes

Figure 32 shows the different tax components composing local government finance in 2015 and 2020. Acquisition tax, local income tax, and property tax took a big share in the local government finance. This graph verifies that the taxation on real estate is the most important financial source for local governments.

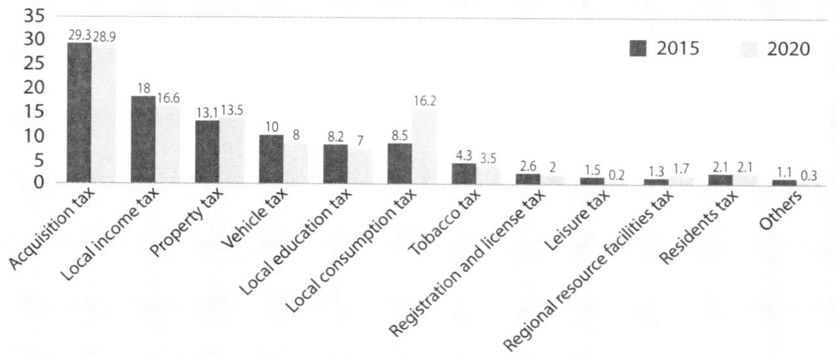

Figure 32 ● Taxation on real estate
(Source: Statistical Yearbook of Local Tax 2016 and 2020, Ministry of Interior and Safety)

9.3.3. Future direction for the Stabilization of Housing Market

Substantial care has to be given in changing or modifying tax rate and the structure of housing policy since it can cause a severe social and political confrontation as well as a big burden for ordinary households. However, a customized adjustment system is necessary to stabilize or vitalize the real estate market, for example, for REITs, tax deduction or postponement of capital gains tax. This is because, in reality, taxation is the most influential policy measure for the Korean government to stabilize and control the housing market where massive housing supply style measures are no longer effective. However, a kind of balanced policy mix including the increase of housing supply in urban areas and balanced regional development is required.

Chapter 10

Housing and Urban Renewal

10.1 Introduction

10.1.1. Concepts and backgrounds

Housing and urban renewal programs are closely related to housing problems and policy. In urban areas, most of the newly built houses are supplied in the housing reconstruction or urban redevelopment sites. Moreover, these programs contribute to the improvement of the life quality of the residents living in old houses and derelict areas.

First of all, various concepts related to housing and urban renewal need to be clarified. Housing renewal is stipulated as the activities to improve the urban environment and to elevate the quality of residential life by efficiently improving dilapidated and low-quality structures in the Act on the Maintenance and Improvement of Urban Areas and Dwelling Conditions for Residents [MIUDCA]. Usually, housing renewal is executed as a part of or in linkage with urban renewal.

On the other hand, a dilapidated and substandard building is defined in the MIUDCA as follows:

① A building having the possibility of collapse or safety accident due to damages or the partial destruction

② A building without a seismic performance and having structural defects

③ And a building having an inferior residential environment or incurring high costs for reconstruction or harming city appearances.

As was discussed previously (1.3.2), dilapidated and sub-standard structures are classified into four types based on the characteristics of these structures and areas. Among these, sub-standard housing has the features of an insecure structure, unsanitary environment, and poor appearance. By contrast, the blighted area, slum, and squatter tend to be filled with sub-standard housings due to specific reasons. Figure 33 shows the areas filled with substandard housings. The upper one is the Guryong village in Gangnam district, a representative squatter remaining, and the lower one is the Baeksa village, a representative blighted area located in the northern part of Seoul.

Figure 33 ● Substandard housings in Seoul

10.1.2 Necessities of housing management and rearrangement

1) Current situation

To relieve the problem of housing shortages, a continuous supply of housing is important. However, newly constructed housings are not enough in number to fulfill housing demand. Therefore, for the residential stability of people, how to use already built housings emerges as an important issue

In 2020, apartment houses took 62.9% of the total housing stock and single-family houses took 21.0%. And the households living in apartment houses were 10.8 million and this was 51.5% of the total households.[1] One problem is that there are growing conflicts with the management of both apartment housing sites and areas filled with single-family housings. This means that an appropriate solution for management is necessary for these areas.

The situation of dilapidated housings in Korea can be figured out with the following tables. Table 77 shows that housings with the age between 20 and 30 years take 29.7%, while those older than 30 years take 19.4% in 2020. This means that almost half of the total housings are older than 20 years.

Table 77 ● Stock of dilapidated housing by type in 2020 (000units, %)

Age of housing	Total	Single	Apartments	Row house·Multi-family	Non-residential structure
Total	**18,526**	**3,898**	**11,662**	**2,752**	**214**
	(100.0)	**(100.0)**	**(100.0)**	**(100.0)**	**(100.0)**
20~less than 30 yrs.	5,504	864	3,854	720	66
	(29.7)	(22.2)	(33.0)	(26.2)	(30.8)

1 Apartment houses have increased dramatically during the last 50 years at the expense of single-family housings. The proportion of apartment houses has increased from 0.8%('70) → 49%('10) → 62.9%('20), while that of single-family houses has declined from 95%('70) → 27.3%('10) → 21.0%('20).

Age of housing	Total	Single	Apartments	Row house· Multi-family	Non-residential structure
More than 30 yrs.	3,597	2,006	1,120	396	74
	(19.4)	(51.5)	(9.5)	(14.4)	(34.6)

(Source: Statistics Korea [KOSIS])

It is found that the proportion of housings with the age of 30 years and older is much higher in case of single-family housings compared to apartment houses. This fact coincides with the increasing request for redevelopment or regeneration in those areas filled with single-family housings. The distribution of dilapidated housings at the province level (Shi or Do) is exhibited in Table 78.

Table 78 ● Dilapidated housings by Shi/Do in 2020 (000units, %)

Shi/Do	Total	Housings of 20~30 years old		Housings older than 30 years	
			ratio		ratio
Whole nation	**18,526**	**5,504**	**29.7**	**3,597**	**19.4**
Seoul	3.015	836	27.7	588	19.5
Busan	1,276	372	29.2	307	24.1
Daegu	810	286	35.3	152	18.8
Incheon	1,033	327	31.7	194	18.8
Gwangju	538	195	36.2	95	17.7
Daejeon	497	192	38.6	95	19.1
Ulsan	395	140	35.4	59	14.9
Sejong	137	10	7.3	9	6.6

Shi/Do	Total	Housings of 20~30 years old		Housings older than 30 years	
			ratio		ratio
Gyeonggi	4,495	1,264	28.1	465	10.3
Gangwon	644	201	31.2	159	24.7
Chungbuk	640	200	31.3	143	22.3
Chungnam	865	256	29.6	180	20.8
Jeonbuk	741	252	34.0	200	27.0
Jeonnam	802	219	27.3	285	35.5
Gyeongbuk	1,094	332	30.3	315	28.8
Gyeongnam	1,297	371	28.6	294	22.7
Jeju	246	52	21.1	54	22.0

(Source: KOSIS)

Here, Shi is a metropolitan city, and Do is a province. There is a sharp divide between metropolitan cities and provinces. The proportion of housings with the age of 20 to 30 years is higher in metropolitan cities, while that of housings older than 30 years is much higher in provinces. This implies that the necessity of renewal projects is more pressing in medium and small cities in the provinces than bigger metropolitan cities. Seoul and Busan have more old houses than other metropolitan cities, while Jeonnam and Gyeongbuk provinces stand out among provinces.

The renewal of dilapidated single- and multi-family housings, especially apartment houses massively built since the late 1980s has become a matter of policy concern. Here, the term 'renewal' includes redevelopment, reconstruction, a new town in town, etc. in Korea.

Conflicts that occurred surrounding urban or housing renewals have become a big social problem. There has been a sharp contrast between a private project measuring profitability and a public project emphasizing publicity. The problem is that each urban renewal project bears both aspects.

Another problem was that, in a stagnated market, the possibility of selling as well as the price of newly-built housings was declining and the completion of the project became more difficult. Subsequently, the difficulty of liquidation due to sunk costs worsened the hardship of low-income homeowner association members.

2) Housing and urban renewal and housing supply

Housing redevelopment reached its peak in 2008 with the demolition of 111,000 units in 231 sites and the construction of 254,000 units on the sites. However, it dropped in 2012 with 20,000 units in 80 sites demolished and 58,000 units constructed on the sites.

Urban renewal associations, etc. had requested government supports to reduce the sunk costs spent for the projects, but private projects were ineligible for the supports. However, after a long discussion, the government decided to amend the MIUDCA to enable local governments to support a part of sunk costs in 2015. All in all, housing and urban renewal is a hard task and necessitates an exploration of its reality, challenge, and future directions.

Figures 34 and 35 show the trend of housing reconstruction. Figure 34 indicates the number of housings permitted for reconstruction. The number of housing units included in the reconstruction projects rose sharply during 2015 and 2017. By contrast, as shown in Figure 35, the number of housings completed reached its peak during 2018 and 2020. This implies that there exists a 2 or 3 years' time gap between reconstruction permission and completion and that the volume of housings that will be supplied in the market through reconstruction projects will be diminished at the beginning of 2020s considering a small number of reconstruction permissions at the end of 2010s.

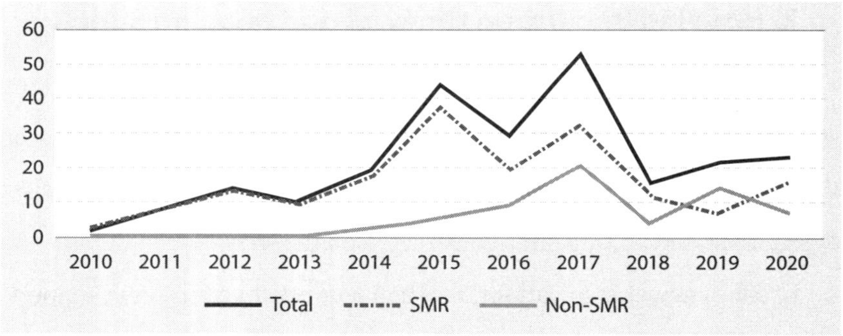

Figure 34 ● Housing numbers permitted for reconstruction (000s)
(Source: MOLIT)

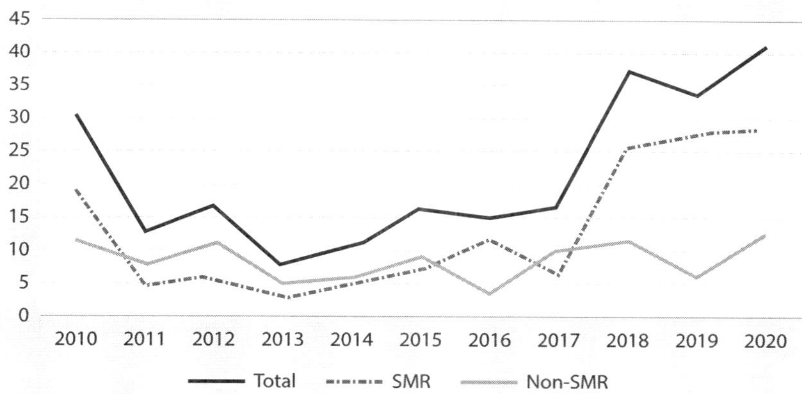

Figure 35 ● Housing numbers completed through reconstruction (000s)
(Source: MOLIT)

Figure 36 shows the historical changes in the numbers of housing units built through redevelopment projects and residential environment improvement projects or REI projects. As seen here, redevelopment projects are on the decline, which has become one of the main reasons for a declining housing supply in Seoul and major cities. Redevelopment projects showed a sudden increase in 2020. However, it remains to be seen whether this rise will continue. By contrast, REI projects increased in 2017 but submerged once again since 2018. These changes also provide a basis for the prediction of a shortage of housing supply in major cities including Seoul at the beginning of the 2020s.

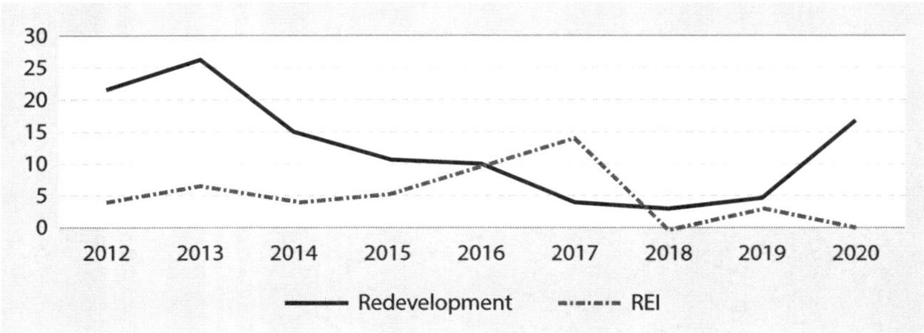

Figure 36 ● Housing numbers completed through redevelopment and REI projects (000s)
(Sorce: MOLIT)

10.2. Housing and Urban Renewal System

10. 2. 1. Types of renewal projects

1) The necessity of Diverse Renewal Projects

Housing and urban renewal aim to restore city functions, rearrange infrastructure, and improve and construct structures including housings. To achieve these goals section 2 of the MIUDCA delineates 6 types of renewal projects in detail, namely residential environment improvement project (REI), housing redevelopment project, housing reconstruction project, urban environment rearrangement project, residential environment management project, and block-unit housing rearrangement project. The reason why various renewal methods are necessary for housing and urban renewal is that the composition and shape of old and derelict areas vary according to the historical background and current situation of each city. The Korean government institutionalized 6 renewal methods based on whether the targeted area is residential or commercial, whether the infrastructure is good or bad, whether poor housings are concentrated or not, whether the size of the area is big or small, etc.

2) Conditions and Contents of Renewal Projects

Figure 37 ● Residential environment improvement project area

The first one is the residential environment improvement project. As seen in Figure 37, this project is necessary for areas where lots of low-income urban residents are living collectively and infrastructure for rearrangement is extremely poor or dilapidated and low-quality structures are highly concentrated. In short, this project is implemented to improve the area where conditions for a living are unbearable. The government mobilizes various supporting measures for the residents such as the rebuilding of community facilities, the expansion of bystreets, the provision of low-interest loans for house renewals, the legalization of no permit buildings, etc.

Figure 38 ● Housing redevelopment project area

The second project to improve residential environments is the housing redevelopment project. As seen in Figure 38, the living condition of this area is a little better than the first one. However, in this area, the infrastructure for rearrangement is also poor, and dilapidated and low-quality structures are concentrated.

The third project to improve the residential condition is the housing reconstruction project. As seen in Figure 39, the infrastructure for rearrangement in this area is good but dilapidated and low-quality structures are concentrated.

Figure 39 ● Housing reconstruction project area

Next, the urban environment rearrangement project is for the improvement of urban environments in commercial areas, industrial areas, etc., not residential areas. This project was introduced, especially to revitalize commercial zones and to make these zones work as the center or secondary center of a city.

Figure 40 ● Urban environment rearrangement project area

Another project to improve the living circumstance of an urban area is the residential environment management project. For a better living environment, this project enlarges infrastructure and joint-use facilities in an area where low-height single-family and multi-household houses, etc. are concentrated. Figure 41 shows an area before and after implementing this project

Figure 41 ● Residential environment management project area

The last project is the block-unit housing rearrangement project. This project was introduced to improve the residential environment of an area by implementing a small-scale renewal project while maintaining the existing block as seen in the concept design below.

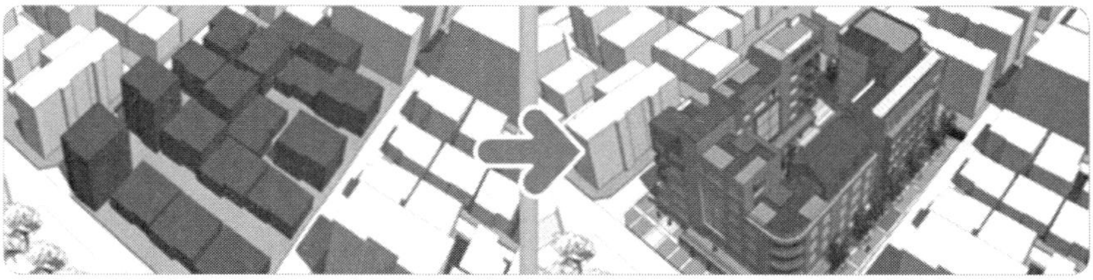

Figure 42 ● Concept design of block-unit housing rearrangement project

To solve the problem of overall demolition and to introduce on-site improvement and rearrangement, the block-unit housing rearrangement project, residential environment management project, etc. were newly introduced in 2012. Basically, at the beginning of the 2010s, there has been increasing recognition of the importance of suburbs compared to green field new towns and on the necessity of urban rearrangement and regeneration rather than physical redevelopment.

In particular, regarding urban regeneration, the government conceptualized its system and conducted pilot projects in Changwon and Jeonju. Based on these, the Special Act on Promotion of and Support for Urban Regeneration was legislated and came into effect in 2013 and after that, the designation and implementation of leading areas have followed.

10.2.2. Changes in Housing and Urban Renewal System - Regulation and Deregulation

The regulations on the housing and urban renewal projects have been influenced by the housing market situation. In the booming market, the government tightened regulations on these projects to prevent speculative investments in the designated or predicted renewal areas, and vice versa. The main reason for this swinging regulation is that only through these renewal projects new houses can be supplied in the fully developed and packed metropolitan cities, and thus that people tend to concentrate on these projects as a real or speculative demand.

On this basis, various deregulations on housing and urban renewal were carried out in the depressed housing market. For example, in 2014, the government introduced diverse measures such as:

- shortening the period needed for reconstruction to maximum of 30 years from 40 years;
- allowing the reconstruction in the case of inconveniences for living including noise between floors;
- lowering the obligatory building ratio of rental housings by 5%p

In 2015, the MIUDCA was amended to introduce the sunk cost support for renewal associations by local governments, to relax the consent ratio of residents in each block for the authorization of association from 2/3 to 1/2 and to allow the cash payment by developers to local authorities instead of donating land for the construction of infrastructure, etc.

Conversely, regulations on renewal projects were tightened in the bullish times such as the later 2010s. For example, in 2017, regulations on reconstruction were strengthened by:

- limiting the number of housings supplied to multi-home owning members of the renewal associations from 3 to 2 houses;
- making the excess rebuilding gains retrieval system to come into effect from 2018;

- extending the residence requirement from 2 years to 3 years in the project sites to become a new member of the renewal associations;
- introducing the lower limit, at least 5% of the total, to build obligatory rental housings in redevelopment sites

10.2.3. Renewal Procedure

1) Basic Policy and Master Plan

For renewal projects, the basic policy and master plan should be established in advance. Firstly, the basic policy for urban and housing environment rearrangement projects should be established, and this system was introduced in 2012.

MOLIT is in charge of establishing a basic policy every 10 years, and reviews and modifies this plan every 5 years. This plan contains various issues including the direction of national policy and master plan for urban and housing environment rearrangement, the investigation of dilapidated and low-quality housing sites, and the establishment of an improvement plan and financial support plan for the improvement of urban and housing environment.

Based on the basic policy the urban and housing environment rearrangement master plan is established by the mayors of special city and metropolitan cities and the governors of provinces, which is set up every 10 years. In non-metropolitan cities, only the cities designated by governors set up this plan.

2) Procedure for the Designation of Rearrangement Zone

First of all, the head of shi/gun establishes the rearrangement plan for the areas fulfilling stipulated conditions. After that, there follow notification to residents, hearings, and public inspections within 30days and the listening to the local assembly within 60days. After completing the procedures, the head of shi/gun (local authorities) requests for the designation of rearrangement zone to the governor of the province. This plan is put on the deliberation of the Regional Urban Planning Committee and then a rearrangement zone is designated by the governor. After the designation, the processes of notification on the official gazette, report to MOLIT, and public reading follow one after another. With the designation of rearrangement zone, the district unit plan and urban design district are deemed to be decided and designated for a faster process.

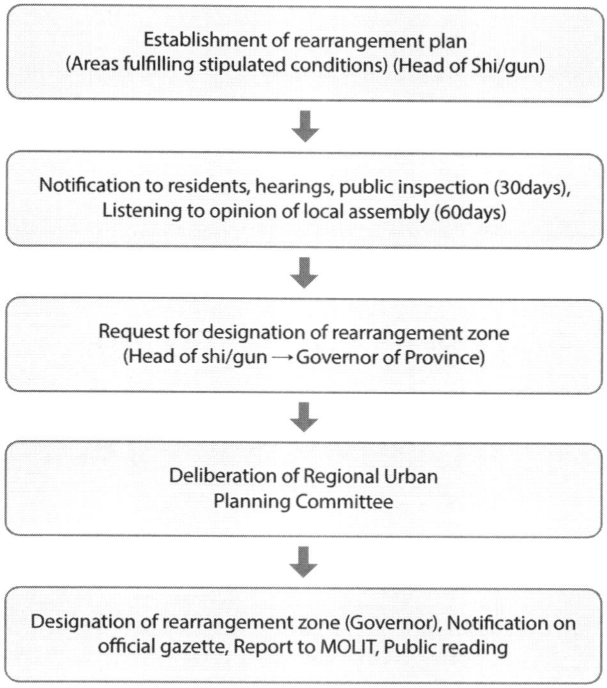

*With the designation of rearrangement zone, District Unit Plan (urban design) & urban design district deemed to be decided & notified

Figure 43 ● Procedure for the designation of rearrangement zone

The conditions and criteria for the designation of rearrangement zones are specified in the ordinance of a metropolitan city/province. In the case of residential environment improvement projects (REI), eased conditions apply compared to ordinary redevelopment projects. In designating a residential environment improvement project, the density of housing units, the ratio of dilapidated and low-quality housing, the ratio of lot circumference bordered to the road, and the proportion of excessive small lots are examined. In contrast, in designating housing redevelopment projects, the minimum size of the project area, the ratio of dilapidated and low-quality housing, the ratio of lot circumference bordered to the road, the ratio of excessive small lots, and the density of housing units are examined. Compared to Gyeonggi Do tighter criteria for the projects apply in Seoul

10.3. The Current Housing Renewal Policy

Massive demolition type redevelopments have brought about an increased burden not only for residents but also for developers and local governments, and thus the improvement of existing housing sites began to be emphasized and is being conducted in parallel with redevelopments. Accordingly, MIUDCA was amended to introduce the block-unit housing rearrangement project and residential environment management project in 2012. Also, the Special Act on Promotion of and Support for Urban Regeneration was enacted to vitalize the community and expand economic bases in 2013.

Concerning these changes, it can be said that diversification of systems is desirable to face the changing circumstances, but a kind of role sharing between systems or between projects is necessary. At the same time, an effort to balance the cost and benefit or economic feasibility of projects is needed by utilizing e.g. an increase of floor-to-area ratio, financial support for infrastructure, etc. The Moon, Jae-in government announced the 'Urban Regeneration New Deal' policy in 2017 highlighting the importance of regeneration.

10.4. Urban regeneration and Community

10.4.1. Background

There is a need to vitalize urban regeneration for the comprehensive restoration of functions including economy, environment, etc., especially in declining cities ailing deteriorated old towns, and falling industry. Urban regeneration has become an issue of concern in Korea for over 10 years since the beginning of the 2010s. However, its concept and scope have been diverse according to different perspectives. Urban regeneration can include the concept of redevelopment or renewal but has the meaning of 'economic rehabilitation' (Turkington and Watson, 2014).

Even in regards to the background and ways of achievement, the views of scholars and policy makers are different from each other. Foreign countries tend to have been focusing on the solution for inner-city problems, such as the restoration of city functions, etc. By contrast,

Korean people and policy makers regarded this as an alternative to large-scale redevelopment projects. With this background, the Special Act on Promotion of and Support for Urban Regeneration (SAPSUR) was enacted in 2013.

10.4.2. Definition, Planning System, and Supporting Measures

The SAPSUR defined urban regeneration as '… targeting the declining cities due to decrease of population, industrial change, urban sprawl, etc. and through the strengthening of regional capacity, introduction or creation of new function, and utilization of regional resources and aims to vitalize the city economically, socially, physically and environmentally'

The act introduced the urban regeneration planning system. As a national plan, the National Urban Regeneration Basic Policy is set up and, based on the national plan, local governments, reflecting the opinion of residents establish regional plans, set up the Urban Regeneration Strategic Plan (URSP) as a basic design, and the Urban Regeneration Invigoration Plan (URIP) as an implementation plan. URSP designates a strategic target area named the Urban Regeneration Invigoration Area (URIA). The URIP on a URIA is a detailed action plan made by the head of the local government.

Subsidies and loans are provided for urban regeneration projects.

The central government provides direct support such as local authorities' planning expenses, basic infrastructure for living, house repairing costs, etc., and indirect supporting projects including the setting up of community enterprises. All the national supports included in local governments' URIP are examined at the Urban Regeneration Strategy Committee established in the central government and provided in the form of a support package with the collaboration of concerned ministries. As another supporting measure, building regulations such as floor area ratio (FAR), building coverage ratio (BCR), a height limit, etc. can be relaxed for regeneration projects.

10.4.3. Urban Regeneration New Deal Projects

Urban Regeneration New Deal projects were announced in 2017 with the inauguration of the Moon, Jae-in government. The government expanded urban regeneration projects to serve as an impetus for economic revitalization and job creation. For this purpose, the construction of small-scale convenience facilities such as community libraries, parking lots, etc. replaced the position of the massive demolition and rearrangement. These projects are planned and implemented under the leading role of the locals and the support from the government.

For effective implementation of the planned projects, urban regeneration projects were more diversified from 2 types to 5 types according to the size and characteristics of project areas. 5 project types are:

① Save our village type, ② Residential rearrangement support type, ③ General community type, ④ City center type, and ⑤ Economic base type in the order of size and characteristics.

A substantial part, about 70%, of the power of project area designation authority was decided to be decentralized. This was for a tailored regeneration filled with specialized projects linking residents' capability and regional resources. For the success of these projects, so-called a warm regeneration was sought for with the regeneration projects containing a win-win strategy in and between communities. In the meantime, the real estate market was to be carefully managed by taking measures to prevent a market disturbance or speculation.

The criteria for the selection of New Deal projects are:

- The urgency and necessity of the project such as the extent of decline and the intention of residents' participation,
- The feasibility of the project including budget, securing of land, etc.,
- The effects of the project such as the improvement of life quality, job creation, etc. and
- The prevention of gentrification, the management of the real estate market, green building construction, the vitalization of social economy, etc.

The Korean government made a plan to invest a huge amount of public funds into the urban regeneration new deal projects (URND). The investment was planned to include 2 trillion won of annual government expenditure, 5 trillion won from NHUF fund, and 3 trillion won of public corporations' investment.

10.5. Future Direction

Urban housing rearrangement has long been implemented in such a way that numbers of dilapidated single housings are demolished and large-scale apartment houses are built on the site. This method has been successful in supplying housings massively in a short time, but accompanied many problems and received a lot of criticism. The main problems indicated were:

- The stoppage of reconstruction projects due to the stagnation of the real estate market which leads to the damages of residents,
- The residential instability of low-income households including renters with the low resettlement level, merely 20%, after the completion,
- The change or destruction of communities resulting in the severance of neighborhood relationships, and
- Construction of monolithic apartments harmful for the traditional culture and landscapes.

Consequently, besides the overall demolition method, a local improvement and rearrangement method was requested and introduced. On this basis, the residential environment management project, block-unit housing rearrangement project were newly introduced in 2012. It is expected that in parallel with the vitalization of urban regeneration, various kinds of housing rearrangement methods are likely possible.

However, there are some questions to be considered and answered in Korea as follows:

- What is the representative housing type and culture in this era?
- How to develop a relevant housing rearrangement method inflicting no harm to the residential stability of low-income residents?
- What are the criteria and strategies in assessing and classifying areas to be preserved or developed?

PART III

Future Direction of Housing Policy in Korea

Chapter 11

Housing Market at Present: Challenge and Response

11.1. Market Context

11.1.1. Continued fluctuation of the housing market

The main feature of the housing market in Korea until the end of the 2010s can be summarized with a sharp contrast between before and after the mid-2010s. In the former period, there was a consistent decline in housing price in SMR due to excess supply and a slow rise of housing price in the non-SMR housing market. By contrast, in the latter period, there was an upsurge in housing prices in SMR and other major metropolitan cities mainly due to the shortage of housing supply, especially in downtown areas. Indeed, the housing market began to show recovery with the increase of transactions from 2014 and faced a more flourishing stage in 2015 and 2016 with continuous policy interventions and government efforts.

In general, approximately 1 million houses are traded in a year in Korea. However, until 2013, the number of transactions declined from 1,082 thousand units in 2006 to 870 thousand in 2009 and 735 thousand in 2012, but the number went back to 1,005 thousand units in 2014, 1,163 thousand in 2015, and 1,053 thousand in 2016. The number declined slightly during the period between 2017 and 2019 but bounced back to 1,279 thousand units in 2020. Many kinds of literature discussed that demand restraint policy and excess housing supply, as well as the global economic crisis in the late 2000s, were major driving forces for the stagnated market in the first half of the 2010s. Especially, housing supply has steadily increased or at least maintained notwithstanding the decreasing long-term housing demand. However, this trend has been reversed in the second half of the 2010s with the combination of galloping housing demand and limited housing supply in Seoul owing to the strict regulations on reconstruction and redevelopment for about 10 years.

The following figure shows the converging trend of the housing price index between the nation as a whole and the Seoul metropolitan region (SMR). Here, it is found that housing price indices in SMR and

Seoul were rising more rapidly in the booming period, i.e. during the periods from 2005 to 2008 and from 2017 to 2020. This exhibits that the housing market in SMR and Seoul are more volatile than non-SMR housing markets and that how to manage these markets is the key to the stabilization of the housing market in the whole nation.

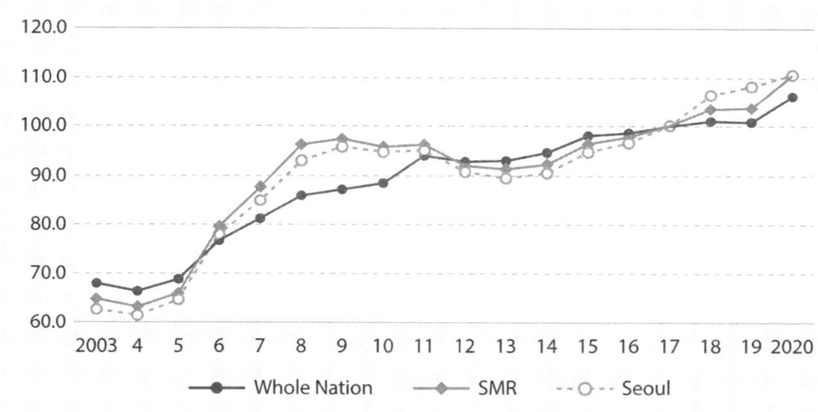

Figure 44 ● Housing price index in the nation as a whole, SMR and Seoul
(Source: Korea Appraisal Board (KAB))

For a long time, various policies and regulations have been implemented under the principle of 'one housing unit for one household' such as the imposition of heavy capital gains tax on multi-home owners (this was abolished in 2014, but reintroduced in 2019), incentives for non-homeowning households in subscribing a new housing and in levying acquisition tax and capital gains tax. These antiquated policy measures did not keep up with a fast-changing shift in the housing market and were not successful to create stable demand in the market.

This has resulted in a rattling market periodically following the infiltration or retreat of the speculative demand seeking for capital gain. The high-risk, high-return style housing industry also has been another obstacle to achieving the stability of the housing market and this justifies the government's intervention to make a more predictable and consistent housing supply in the housing market.

Figure 45 demonstrates the fluctuation of the housing market over the last decade through the trend of building permits in SMR and non-SMR. During the 15 years between 2005 and 2020, the number of building permits issued in SMR has shown a more volatile movement compared to that in non-SMR except for the period during and after the global financial crisis, between 2008 and 2011. Also, even in the depressed housing market, the number of permits issued in SMR maintained a substantial level exhibiting a stable housing demand in the region.

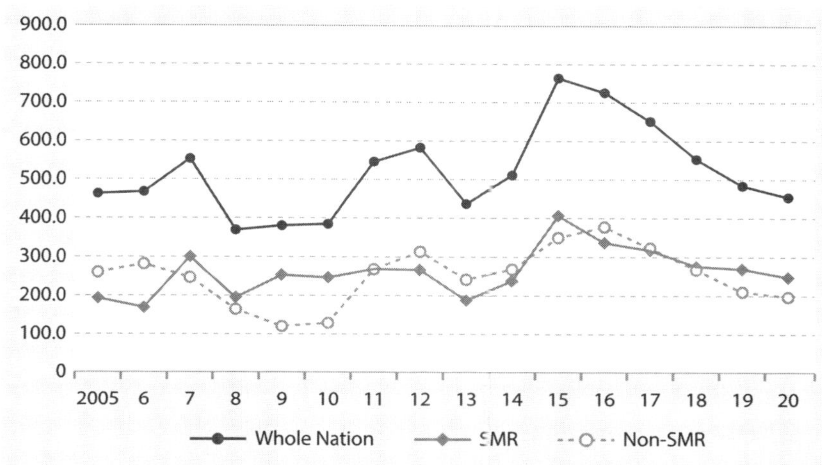

Figure 45 ● Building permits issued in SMR and Non-SMR
(Source: MOLIT)

Many regulations or deregulations and public housing supply control measures have been mobilized by the government to maintain the stability of housing demand and supply, and consequently the housing market. However, it seems to be still insufficient. The aforementioned efforts to maintain a stable and appropriate housing demand and supply are further requested in the changing market circumstances.

11.1.2. Growing Demand for Rental Housing and Housing Welfare Policy

In the Korean housing market, there has been a growing demand for rental housing, especially for long-term public rental housing, whereas its supply is relatively stagnant.[1] As discussed above, the low-income people living in private rental housing are suffering more with a high RIR than those living in PRH. This disparity eloquently illustrates the trouble of low-income households living elsewhere out of PRH. However, the increase of long-term PRH usually takes a long time to build and costs a huge amount of money. Besides, building rental housings in downtown areas where PRH demand is concentrated is far more difficult due to the lack of available land.

The housing expense burden for individual renters has been continuously increased especially due to the repeated Chonsei price surge and the assistance of the government for the low-income households in the private rental market has been negligible. Although the housing voucher scheme has been implemented since 2015, it is too early to evaluate the performance of the voucher system.

In this circumstance, New Stay or public support private rental housings and Happiness Housing projects are a positive signal for the Korean government to expand rental housing and housing welfare policy. In this regard, the government should consider how to increase new PRHs in the right place and how the government can work with private rental housing more effectively since these can be alternative options to provide actual housing welfare services for low-income renters.

1 Long-term rental housing in the total housing stock was 5.4% in 2014 and 8.0% in 2020.

11.1.3. Growing Interest in Housing Quality

In fast-changing countries like Korea, having pleasant and decent housing has become a very important element in people's lives over the recent decades. In particular, the demand to live in good environments such as noise-free neighbors and clean indoor air quality has increased significantly. Residents living in newly developed housing sites request well-equipped facilities for a convenient commute and better education.

Also, some apartment houses built from the end of the 1980s have been deteriorating in need of refurbishment, repairing, and sometimes redevelopment. The ratio of houses over 30 years to total houses was 9.7% (1.35 million) in 2010. This has changed to 16.3% (2.67 million) in 2015 and 19.4% (3.60 million) in 2020. Thus, there have been expectations for upgrading the housing environment among the residents living in old dilapidating housings. However, the limitations of expanding the floor spaces and/or the projected increasing price of the house after the refurbishment have been major barriers to renovate many sites. Some places including Seoul have indeed withdrawn their plan to renovate their community and dwellings. All in all, the supply of decent housing and the renovation of dilapidated housing have become challenging policy issues.

11.2. Recent Policy Responses

11.2.1. Overview

Due to the fast-changing market context, the Korean government has implemented diverse policy measures included in a series of policy packages. While the Comprehensive Housing Plan has been announced and initiated every year, special policy packages have been intermittently injected to stabilize the housing market. The main directions of housing policy presented in these plans and policies are as follows:

- Firstly, the normalization of the housing market has been emphasized. To stabilize the housing market and to maintain housing price below the inflation rate, a consistent and solid housing supply and demand are emphasized;
- Secondly, the achievement of universal housing welfare is pursued. The government tries to expand the scope of housing support by including those who live in rental housing and having below-median income;
- And lastly, the government also aims to enhance housing space and quality as one of their important goals. Many measures, such as the prevention of atopic dermatitis and indoor dewfall and the revitalization of housing remodeling have been pursued to achieve this goal.

11.2.2. Materializing Plans

1) Normalization of Housing Market

For the stability of the housing market, housing supply and demand should be managed meticulously not to bring about a state of excess supply or excess demand. Housing supply needs to be managed through the flexible adjustment of public housing supply and inducement of voluntary increase or decrease of private housing supply. The appropriate level of housing demand can be maintained through means of financing, modification of the housing subscription system, reduction or increase of acquisition and transaction tax, financial support for first home-buyers and homeowners changing houses.

As one of the ways to achieve residential stabilization, the rental housing business needs to be promoted, and the public role here should be strengthened. In this respect, a variety of policy measures such as the vitalization of specialized lease management companies and REITs and the introduction of quasi-public rental housing should be mobilized.

For the actively growing market which reappeared in the mid-2010s, housing supply needs to be expanded through the increased supply of housing land developed by the public sector and the deregulation on land use and house building. At the same time, strong measures to rein in the housing speculation should be mobilized which include the extension of the resale period, stricter subscription standards, and the increase of tax burden.

In the stagnating housing market and housing prices, government support is necessary for homeowners whose housing is valued less than their mortgage (so-called the 'house poor') and renters whose landlords are unable to refund their deposit even after selling the rental houses (the 'rent poor'). Such a supporting scheme has become one of the important policy measures for market stability. For this, measures such as selling home-owner's equity, providing Chonsei with a lower deposit, and a loan for a Chonsei tenant can be considered.

2) Achievement of Universal Housing Welfare

This is another important policy goal that should be addressed through the followings:

① 130,000 units of public housing will be supplied every year. To achieve this goal successfully, the policy direction should move from the construction of new rental housing to the making use of purchased or leased public rental housing in different types and from suburban areas to downtown areas in the location.

② Expanding the housing welfare supports for consumers is another important policy goal. For this purpose, the introduction of housing vouchers, and the expansion of NHUF loans are undertaken in addition to the supply of public rental housing continuously.

③ Customized supports fitting for consumers' life cycle are

emphasized. In particular, the need for college students, newly-wed couples, single-person households, and old-age households should be considered and appropriate services should be provided.

To achieve the goal of universal housing welfare, the support for the low-income people, living in private rental housings should be emphasized. To this end, the government should encourage private developers to supply more affordable private rental housings through taxation and financial assistance. The successful launching of Happiness Housing implies the importance of flexible and diversified policy schemes for the stability of the housing market.

3) Enhancement of Housing Quality and Environment.

To this end, vitalizing the redevelopment of outdated residential areas is essential. Specifically, expansion of public support and refurbishment of houses instead of the demolition of whole houses can be a more feasible option. As an alternative, upward remodeling is attracting the interest of the residents living in old apartment houses. From a wider perspective, the demands for housing renovation need to be adjusted and coordinated with urban regeneration. Increasing the supply of healthful houses should be also continuously encouraged.

11.3. Conclusions

Recently, the housing market in Korea has experienced another cyclical change showing a stark contrast between a long-running slump until the mid-2010s and a sudden boom thereafter. In the first half of the 2010s, with sufficient housing stock exceeding 100% in the housing supply ratio, the structure of the market changed from seller's market to buyer's market. In this circumstance, a new approach was necessary for the stabilized housing market. The main focus should have been put on moving from mass production with fewer options to small productions with various and wider options for customers to meet their different demands. In the latter half of the 2010s, facing another seller's market, the opposite approach characterized by the mass production and supply of housing had to be resummoned.

Only the policy being implemented at the right time and situation can bring the most effective and expected result. In the stagnating housing market, policy measures which can stimulate demand are important. For this purpose, powerful and active implementation of deregulation, tax cut, changes in fiscal expenditure, investment through indirect investment vehicles, etc. are required. On the contrary, in the expanding market, flexible and meticulous policy measures to adjust the momentum of the market as well as to prevent the appearance of the bubble are required.

Overall, to achieve the targeted policy goal it is necessary to integrate and harmonize diversified policy measures (policy mix). This seems particularly relevant for the countries experiencing fluctuating housing markets like Korea.

Chapter 12

Future Direction for Housing Policy

12.1. Expansion of Supply

12.1.1. Housing Supply Ratio in 2020

Even though the housing supply ratio is reached 103.6% in 2020, newly-built housings should be supplied in the market continuously. The main reason for this is that, firstly, there remain excess demands in main metropolitan cities, especially in Seoul and its neighboring cities, and secondly, the demand for good quality housing among homeowners has been increasing.

The central government made a plan to supply 5 million units of housing between 2010 and 2020. During this period, an average of 500 thousand housing units was to be provided every year. Following this plan, the 2nd Long-term Comprehensive Housing Plan Amending Plan (2013~22) was set up. According to this plan, the housing supply ratio will be reached to 106.5%, the number of housings per 1,000 people will be 422 units and the stock of long-term public rental housings will be expanded to 1.9 million in 2022. These kinds of efforts need to be maintained well into the 2020s and 2030s to meet the continuing demand for newly built housing caused by growing nuclear households and deteriorating houses built massively in the 1980s and 1990s.

12.1.2. Provision of Low-rise, Low- and Medium-density Housing

Currently, out of the total newly-built housings, apartments take more than 60%. Single-family houses account for 10%,[1] but this ratio is expected to rise with the growing number of people who want to live in the countryside. The density (floor area ratio) of apartments was to be adjusted downward to 200% on average for every city. However, facing the galloping housing prices in the latter half of the 2010s, the Korean

1 In 2015, building permission for apartments took 69.9 %, while that of single family houses was 11.5%. These ratios have changed to 76.9% and 10.9% respectively in 2020.

government changed the policy to allow high-density development in downtown areas of major metropolitan cities.

12.1.3. Stable Land Supply

According to the government plan, 40% of the newly required developable land is from the existing urban management tools such as redevelopment, reconstruction, and utilization of unused land whereas the remaining 60% of the land to be obtained through new town developments.[2] The government estimated that the total area of housing land developed by the public sector will reach 12.0 km^2(9.9~14.1 km^2) during 2020~2025. This land, combined with the privately developed land, is used for building 361.2 thousand units of housing per year.

To prevent a disordered development and inefficient utilization of land, it is required that the future developable land will be designated in advance and the government will encourage the planned development. In this way, farmland and green zones near cities can be utilized through a selective and phased development with a long-term plan to create developable land.

---

2 However, with the increasing demand for housing in down town areas, the proportion of the land in new towns is expected to be declined.

12.2. Expansion of Rental Housing Supply

1) Expansion and Diversification of Rental Housing Supply

Until now, rental housing such as permanent rental housing and national rental housing was homogeneously supplied. To support homeownership and bring residential stability for non-homeowners, the government plans to supply various types of housing to provide affordable housings to different income groups as per their demands.

Rental housing types will be divided into various categories such as permanent rental housing, national rental housing, installments payment type rental housing, long term rental housing on a deposit basis (Chonsei type), 10-year rental housing, Happiness Housing, and New Stay or later public support private rental housing. Moreover, middle- and small-sized housing units will be supplied to non-home owners at reasonable prices.

On the other hand, to expand the supply of rental housing for middle-income households, the government plans to promote private rental housing in such a way that:

① Increase business profit through providing tax and financial support,

② Provide preferential developable land, and

③ Allow investment in rental businesses by small investors through

Asset-Backed Securities (ABS) or Real Estate Investment Trust (REIT) system.[3]

2) Housing Welfare for the Underprivileged

The central government plans to make efforts to improve housing welfare for different income class groups. Selective support measures will be prepared taking into consideration asset ownership levels and housing standards under the policy targets. The policy targets will be classified into the low-income class, low- to middle-income class, and middle-income class and various measures will be taken to satisfy the minimum standards.

The different programs of rental housing for the low-income class such as permanent rental housing, public rental housing, and national rental housing will be streamlined and it will be ensured that housing supply is continuously made to accommodate 20% of the total households.

New measures are in the pipeline. For instance, the bottom-pillar of public rental housing can be modified as rental housing equipped with facilities for the old and the disabled. The aged and disabled residents can now apply for improvement of public housing at lower interest rates or newly built public housing.

3 Based on this long-term plan, the New Stay housing, later public support private rental housing, is being implemented as a main policy initiative.

The policy makers will essentially develop the indicators of housing welfare and minimum residential standards to provide welfare services to the residents. The housing welfare indicator will include dwelling indicators (e.g. density, equipment, facility), environment indicators (e.g. green space ratio, etc.), and culture indicators (e.g. existence of cultural facility). Local governments will be required to set up the minimum recommendation standard and to plan funding, the application process, and methods for meeting those standards.

The government also plans to reinforce the legal element for resident's housing improvement which was introduced in 2004 so that every resident can live above certain residential standards regardless of his/her region, class, and employment. Also, tax and financial benefits will be granted for providing housing support to the underprivileged, and the housing voucher system introduced in 2015 will be improved by complementing shortfalls in implementing the system.

12.3. Efficient Preservation and Management of Housing Stock

Since the proportion of apartments is significantly high in Korea, it is also important to have an effective management system of apartment housing stock. The automated management system will play a significant role in reducing apartment maintenance costs. The repair guarantee period and defect guarantee period need to be adjusted taking into consideration the facility and material life cycle.

Moreover, the houses that applying multi-family housing management system will be increased and the support for remodeling costs will be expanded. To achieve this:

① Mixed residential, commercial, and retail buildings, small complexes with less than 300 households, and housings constructed under urban redevelopment projects will be also managed in this system,

② Long-term loans with low interest rates will be provided for a large-scale repairing/refurbishment of apartments, and

③ Management services such as home delivery service, mini post office, fax transmissions, and laundry services will be provided.

The government also will nurture and support remodeling businesses. To be eligible for the support, the business should fulfill the condition as follows;

① The company requires technology for remodeling and fostering professionals,

② The company should promote various materials and facilities for major repairs, remodeling, and additional work, and

③ The company facilitates standardization of facilities that make it easy for remodeling.

12.4. Improvement in Housing Finance and Taxation

A mortgage-backed security system will be promoted to link the housing market with the capital market. The activation of Asset-Backed Securities (ABS), Mortgage-Backed Securities (MBS), and Real Estate Investment Trusts (REITs) will also be promoted.[4] To provide residential stability, various approaches to utilize the national housing and urban fund will be promoted, for example utilizing funding in a long-term residential environment improvement project.

The homeownership tax (asset tax) and transaction tax will also be rationalized. Measures will be taken to prevent dwelling over-consumption by imposing heavy taxes on luxurious housing and adjusting charging standards.

4 In particular, for the purpose of inducing private investors in the rental housing field, REITs will be utilized as an investment vehicle with the leading role of LH and the Housing and Urban Guarantee.

12.5. Vitalization of Communities and Provision of Various Spaces

1) Establishment of Community-oriented Residential Culture

Over the years, the direction of housing policy in Korea has changed from increasing the affordability and security of homeownership policy to a policy to make a sustainable and pleasant neighborhood. To expand community-oriented public facilities and residential complexes, it is required to:

① Provide complex-oriented dwellings with different scale, density, and types,

② Prepare authentic housing construction standards taking into consideration the regional characteristics of each local government,

③ Set up building standards, landscape standards, and street environmental standards depending on the regional characteristics.

The development of community-oriented and Korean-conscious design methods is being emphasized by the government. Residential complexes will be made pedestrian-friendly, equipped with public transportation. The modern style of design will be adopted in the Korean traditional village design method in developing new communities. To expand open spaces and public spaces for residents in the complex:

④ Areas such as public laundry and children's playground will be built to accommodate resident activities,

⑤ Social networks among residents will be encouraged to form community spirit (a sense of belonging to the community) and community awareness.

Resident participation programs will be developed to build connected and resilient communities through resident's activities (e.g. group purchases of daily necessities).

2) Establishment of Eco-friendly Residential Community

To form resource-efficient and eco-friendly housing:

① Green energy facilities, such as greenhouses, solar energy air conditioning, and solar heat collectors will be utilized to accumulate and absorb heat,

② A water recycling system will be applied to collect and utilize rain water in reservoirs,

③ A self-treatment facility for waste will be introduced and diverse ways to recycle waste will be suggested.

To avoid the use of construction materials which are harmful to the human being, indoor space will be created in such a way that humidity level can be controlled by natural materials, securing ecological space and installing waterfront within the residential complex.

3) Promotion of Residential Environment Improvement Programs

The central government plans to promote community-oriented residential environment improvement and to consolidate the existing redevelopment, reconstruction, and residential environment improvement projects. The local government will be responsible for preparing the mandatory residential environment improvement programs. To achieve this:

① A community will prepare and establish a residential preservation plan and the local government will evaluate the plans together and support necessities based on housing and environmental conditions,

② The central government will efficiently provide financial support and encourage competition among communities and local governments to build healthy communities and

③ Each entity will work towards sustaining housing stability, using existing housing resources efficiently, and cultivating community consciousness.

4) Diversification of Residential Types to meet Various Housing Demands

To diversify residential types and residential complexes:

① Various types of housings will be promoted for different needs such as housing for people with family and housings with extra facilities for the disabled and the elderly,

② Models of housing with various materials and shapes will be promoted and built-in facilities for high-speed telecommunications service will be provided.

The level regulations will be decreased to allow people to utilize indoor space of housings to a great extent based on family's different needs. To achieve this, various types of housing will be constructed with different types of materials, interiors, variables, frameworks and internal isolations, amalgamation housing, and so on.

References

1 Boelhouwer, P. (2011) "Neo-classical economic theory on housing markets and behavioral sciences: Alley or opponent?" *Housing, Theory and Society*, Vol.28 Issue.3.

2 Cheshire, P. & Sheppard, S. (1998) "Estimating the demand for housing, land and neighborhood characteristics". *Oxford Bulletin of Economics and Statistics* 60(3).

3 Cho, Man, ed. (2012) *Midterm plan of housing policy into the structure change of population society*, Seoul: KDI (Korean).

4 Cho, Man & Lee, Chang-Moo (2014) "Policy perspectives and the effect on housing market in elderly society and small family". *KDI FOCUS*, Vol. 39 (Korean).

5 Cooper, G. (2008) *The Origin of Financial Crisis: Central Banks, Credit Bubbles and the Efficient Market Fallacy*, New York: First Vintage Books Edition.

6 Follain, G., Lim, G.C. and Renault, B. (1980) "The Demand for Housing in Developing Countries: The case of Korea". *Journal of Urban Economic* Vol.7 Issue 3.

7 Forrest, Ray and Lee, James, ed. (2003) *Housing and Social Change: East-West Perspectives*. London: Routledge.

8 Green, R. K. & Malpezzi S. (2003) *A Primer on U.S. Housing Markets and Housing Policy*. Washington, D.C.: The Urban Institute Press (Areuea Monograph Series No. 3).

9 Gyourko, J. (2003) "Access to Home Ownership in the U.S.: The Impact of Changing Perspectives on Constraints to Tenure Choice". *Housing Economics and Public Policy*, Presentation material, The Wharton School, University of Pennsylvania.

10 Ha, Sung-Gyu (2010) *Housing Policy*. Seoul: Bakyoungsa (Korean).

11 Han, Man-Hee. & Cho, Man (2008) *Real Estate Investment and Financing*. Seoul: Bosunggak (Korean).

12 Husock, Howard (2003) *America's Trillion-Dollar Housing Mistake*. Chicago: Ivan R. Dee.

13 Jones, C. & White, M. (2012) *Challenges of the Housing Economy: An International Perspective*. Oxford: Wiley-Blackwell.

14 Korea Housing Finance Corporation (2010) *Housing Finance Monthly*, each month (Korean).

15 Korea Research Institute for Human Settlement (2013) *The Housing Policy in Korea with the focus on Affordable Housing*, Presentation Material.

16 ____________________ (1990) *The study of the Effect of Metropolitan housing construction* (Korean).

17 La Grange, A. and Jung, H. (2013) "Liberalization, Democratization and Korea's Housing Welfare Regime". *International Journal of Housing Policy V0l.13 No.1*

18 Lund, B. (2006) *Understanding Housing Policy*. Bristol: The Policy Press.

19 Ministry of Land, Infrastructure and Transport. *Directions of Korea Housing Policy*, each year (Korean).

20 ____________________ *Business handbook of National Housing Fund*, each year (Korean).

21 ____________________ Housing Business Handbook, each year (Korean).

22 ____________________ Housing Construction Records, each year (Korean).

23 ____________________ Housing Survey, each year (Korean).

24 ____________________ (2018) Housing Welfare Road Map (Korean).

25 ____________________ (2013 & 2018) Long-term Comprehension Housing Plan (Korean).

26 Ministry of Land, Infrastructure and Transport and Korea Research Institute for Human Settlement (2012) *Modularization of Korea's Development Experience: Policy for the Construction and Supply of Affordable Housing in Korea*, Ministry of Strategy and Finance, Republic of Korea.

27 Ministry of Land, Transport and Maritime Affairs (2002) *Housing white book* (Korean).

28 National Statistical Office. Population and Household Census, each year (Korean).

29 O'Sullivan, Tony and Gibb, Kenneth ed. (2003) *Housing Economics and Public Policy*. Oxford: Blackwell Science Ltd.

30 Seoul Metropolitan Government (2012 & 2014) *Urban Policy Indices Survey* (Korean).

31 Schwartz, Alex (2010) *Housing Policy*. New York: Routledge.

32 Turkington, R and Watson, C. ed. (2014). *Renewing Europe's Housing*. Bristol: Policy Press.

33 UN-HABITAT (2009) *Housing Finance Mechanisms in Republic of Korea*. The Human Settlements Finance Systems Series.

34 Weicher, John C. (2012) *Housing Policy at a Crossroads: The Why, How, and Who of Assistance Programs*. Washington, D.C.: The AEI Press.

35 Yoon, Ju-Hyun and Shin, Seok-ha (1994) *The Study of Market Effect on control of House Parcel Price*. KRIHS (Korean).

* The Ministry of Legislation website http://www.moleg.go.kr.

Index

About Authors

Woo-Hyun Cho

- Bachelor degree in sociology at Korea University
- Completed Science of Public Administration, Graduate School of Public Administration, Seoul National University,
- Master degree in Public Administration, Graduate School of Public Administration Han-yang University
- Ministry of Construction and Transportation:
  - Vice-minister
  - Assistant Secretary to Minister
  - Head of the Planning and Administration Department
  - Director General, Housing and Urban Bureau/ Land Bureau
  - Director, Housing Policy Div. National Land Planning Div.
- Deputy Head, Korean National Railroad Authority
- President and CEO, Incheon International Airport Corporation:
- President, Research Institute for Construction Policy of Korea.
- (Currently) Member, Steering Committee of Korea Housing Finance Corporation
- (Currently) Executive Advisor to Boo-young Co., Ltd.

Man-Hee Han

- Ph.D. in Urban and Regional Studies, Center for Urban and Regional Studies, University of Birmingham, U.K., 1992
- M.Phil. in Urban and Regional Studies, Center for Urban and Regional Studies, University of Birmingham, U.K., 1988
- M.A. in Public Administration, Yonsei University, 1980
- B.A. in Business Administration, Yonsei University, 1978
- Ministry of Land, Infrastructure and Transport(MOLIT) (1983 – 2013)
  - Vice Minister, MOLIT (2011 – 2013)
  - Chairman, Multi-functional Administrative City Construction Commission (Sejong City) (2010 – 2011)
  - Deputy Minister, Housing and Land Policy (2009 – 2010)
  - Assistant minister, Territorial Policy (2008 – 2009)
- Professor and Dean, International School of Urban Sciences, University of Seoul (2013.8~2018.8)
- Professor, International School of Urban Sciences, University of Seoul (2018.9~2022.2)
- Vice-President, University of Seoul (2021.9~2022.2)
- (Currently) Emeritus Professor, University of Seoul (2022.3~)

Housing Policy in Korea

2018년 03월 09일 초　판 제1쇄 발행
2022년 03월 14일 개정판 제1쇄 발행

저자　조우현, 한만희
발행인　서순탁
발행처　서울시립대학교출판부
출판신고　2001년 03월 05일 제2001-000012호
주소　02504 서울특별시 동대문구 서울시립대로 163(전농동90)
전자우편　kimbomi10@uos.ac.kr
전화번호　02-6490-6109
팩스　02-6490-6149

ISBN　978-89-85831-97-0　93320

값 30,000원